ID0886701

OUTRAGE
AT SEA

OUTRAGE AT SEA

Naval Atrocities of the First World War

by

TONY BRIDGLAND

LEO COOPER

First published in Great Britain 2002 by
LEO COOPER
an imprint of Pen & Sword Books,
47 Church Street, Barnsley
South Yorkshire, S70 2AS

ISBN 0 85052 877 1

A CIP catalogue record for this book is
available from the British Library.

Typeset in 11/13pt Sabon by
Phoenix Typesetting, Ilkley, West Yorkshire.

Printed and bound by
CPI UK

CONTENTS

ACKNOWLEDGMENTS

It would be impossible to write a book such as this without calling on many people for help. The author may pore endlessly over dusty records in museums and archives, but that alone will never produce the desired result. Many people have helped me in a host of different ways, from giving access to ancient news cuttings, private family papers or collections, to the translating of some Danish or German nautical text, to lending photographs or imparting some technical knowledge in one field or another. Together, they comprise a sizeable group and it is not surprising that, owing to the nature of the book itself, they are widely scattered. I hope they will forgive me for naming them all *ad hoc*, in one list.

My sincere thanks to each of the following, in no particular order: Jim Allaway, Editor of *Navy News*, Portsmouth; June Brogger; Jill Burchell; Marjorie Schindler; Gordon Wise of Dover Coastguard; Patrick Frost of Argyll Etkin Ltd, London; Peter More of the *Grimsby Evening Telegraph*; Louise Higgs of the *Halifax Herald*, Nova Scotia; Marvan Moore of the Museum of the Atlantic, Nova Scotia; Andy Rutter and Philip Cone of The Harwich Society; Stephen Rabson of P & O archives; Lord Montagu of Beaulieu; David Corbett of the Montagu Museum; Ed Bartholomew of the National Railway Museum, York; Andrew Kirk of the Theatre Museum, London; Camilla Boesen, Michaela Rosendal and Karin Høgh all of the *Politiken*, Copenhagen; Garry Shutlak of Nova Scotia Archives; Gunnar Brøgger; Anne Brittain of the *Hull Daily Mail*; Kevin Matthews, Jak Showell and Horst Bredow all of U-Boot Archiv, Cuxhaven, Germany and Tim Mann and Lori Douglas, both of Manitoba, Canada.

As always, the staffs of the Public Record Office, the British Library Newspaper Library, the Imperial War Museum, the Ministry of Defence Historical Branch, the National Maritime Museum, Greenwich, the Guildhall Library, the Admiralty

Library, Lloyd's Register of Shipping, the Royal Naval Submarine Museum, Gosport and the Public Libraries at Hastings and Rye rendered invaluable and patient assistance. Tom Hartman provided his usual sterling service with the editing and Gina-Marie Bridgland applied her customary painstaking diligence to the preparation of the index. My thanks to all of them.

It is thought that most, if not all, of the photographs which appear in this book are free of copyright. Where any uncertainty exists, I have made every effort to obtain the necessary permission from the copyright holders whenever they could be identified, or have obtained permission from owners of copyright-free negative images as appropriate. Invariably, this has been granted which is acknowledged with due gratitude. In the one or two instances where it was not possible to trace a copyright holder, I hope that inclusion of such photographs will not be met with any objections. If that should not be the case, however, I shall be only too pleased to acknowledge the matter in future editions.

Tony Bridgland
Rye, East Sussex. October 2001.

PROLOGUE

The brotherhood of the sea acknowledges the overwhelmingly obvious fact that all seafarers face a common peril – the very depths of the element on which they sail. That assistance be given to those who are endangered by the relentless waves is a rule, unwritten for centuries, which transcends all others. Even in time of war, once a battle is over, this ancient maritime of chivalry has been humanely observed through the ages. Whether friend or foe is of no primary consideration. First, the rescue.

At dawn on 6 October 1779 the 32-gun British frigate HMS *Quebec*, commanded by Captain Farmer, was cruising off Ushant in company with the cutter HMS *Rambler* when they encountered two French warships, the 40-gun frigate *Surveillante*, which also had a cutter in attendance. A hot fight ensued at point-blank range, during which both frigates were dismasted and *Quebec*'s gunners were handicapped by having to fire blind, through their own sails, as her masts were lying over the side. The flames which belched from the muzzles of the British guns set fire to these sails and soon the whole ship was ablaze. About seventy of *Quebec*'s crew died in the inferno, while dozens more jumped into the sea. Farmer, with his arm shot through, bound his handkerchief round the shattered bone and cried, "My lads, this is warm work, therefore keep your fire with double spirit. We will conquer or die!" He was last seen sitting on the fluke of the sheet anchor, still shouting words of encouragement to his crew. Towards six o'clock in the evening, her timbers having been burning all day, *Quebec* blew up with a "dreadful roar" as at last the flames reached her powder magazine. Of the British sailors in the water, seventeen were picked up by the *Rambler*, including the mate, Mr Moore. A passing Russian vessel rescued thirteen more, while the lives of Mr Roberts, the First Lieutenant, the Lieutenant of Marines, the surgeon and thirty-six seamen "were all preserved by their late antagonists".

On 21 October 1805, even in the midst of the bloody inferno that was the Battle of Trafalgar, there were many examples of this humanity between sailors. Nelson is said to have told his crews, "You must hate a Frenchman as you hate the Devil". Nevertheless, men, who moments before had been fighting each other with fury while the decks of their ships ran slippery with gore, ceased firing to rescue their enemies who were struggling in the water. The French ship-of-the-line *Achille* was afire and had lost most of her crew. The senior officer still alive was the young Ensign de Vaisseau Couchard, who kept her few remaining guns firing. Then a broadside from HMS *Prince* brought down one of the French ship's masts, its sails in flames. This sent more fire racing the length of the ship and her sailors dived over the side for their lives. With that, the crew of the *Prince* ceased firing and manned their boats to rescue them. By late afternoon they had saved more than 200 Frenchmen, plus a swimming pig which later provided Jack Tar with a hearty supper, and a naked girl named Jeannette who said she was the wife of a French gunner. She was taken aboard HMS *Revenge* and given some clothing in the interests of propriety.

The giant Spanish man o'war *Santissima Trinidad*, with 130 guns on four decks and a crew of 1,115, had all her masts shot away during the Battle of Trafalgar. Once the pride of Spain, but now little more than a charred jumble of broken masts and shattered timbers, she heaved and wallowed while storm-force winds roared across the Bay of Cadiz for a solid week after the fighting had ceased, creating mountainous seas which tossed her around like a cork, but slowly sinking, inch by inch, nonetheless. At great risk to themselves, British sailors from HMS *Revenge* and HMS *Ajax* came across to her in boats, to give help to the hundreds of wounded who lay strewn on her splintered decks and to toss the dead overboard from the sinking ship. They managed to save less than half the wounded, lowering them over the side into the lurching boats as carefully as the terrible conditions would allow, before she finally disappeared beneath the waves.

This code of honour has prevailed over the years up to more modern times. In late April 1915 Captain Meland, of the neutral Norwegian vessel *Varild*, observed a skirmish between some British minesweepers and German torpedo boats near the North Hinder lightship. After the fighting had ceased, Meland's crew pulled a semi-conscious German out of the water and one of the Grimsby-based minesweepers rescued another.

Nor were the Germans, particularly their submariners, devoted entirely to the heartless tactics for which several of their number became famous. Hans Rose, who was Germany's second most successful U-boat commander of the First World War, was known on at least one occasion to take in tow the lifeboat of the ship which he had just sunk and not cast it off until they had reached easy rowing distance of a friendly coast.

On the other hand, any treachery in contravention of the time-honoured code received very short shrift. On 7 May 1808 the 16-gun sloop HMS *Redwing*, Commander Ussher, fell in with seven armed Spanish vessels which were escorting a convoy of twelve merchantmen. Although heavily outgunned, outnumbered and out-manned, Ussher took his ship to leeward of the Spaniards and closed the range. He loaded his guns with round shot and canister, each bag containing 500 musket balls, and concentrated his aim on the *Diligente*, the flagship of the Spanish Commodore. With three lusty cheers the *Redwing*'s crew opened fire. The broadside struck the *Diligente* all along her waterline, cutting her wide open from fore to aft. With a couple of mighty rolls as the sea rushed into her, she turned turtle and sank. The same fate awaited another Spanish ship, the *Boreas*, and several others, including four merchantmen. Only three of the enemy ships escaped. When the *Boreas* sank, Ussher despatched his only available boat to rescue as many of the Spaniards as possible, but the other enemy ships disregarded the flag of truce which he had raised and continued firing, which "compelled him to recall the gallant men he had sent to the rescue of their antagonists".

All these anecdotes should be considered in the light of several of the incidents we will deal with later in this book.

The nineteenth and first half of the twentieth century was an era which saw a crescendo in the scale of wars fought around the globe. The Napoleonic Wars, which at their time seemed to give rise to some of the greatest battles in history, were mere scuffles compared to those which ensued only a hundred years or so later. And the volume of bloodshed and brutality increased in geometric propor-tion. The suffering of soldiers wounded at the Battle of Solferino in northern Italy in June 1859 prompted a campaign for humanitarian laws to protect the wounded during times of war. Even Napoleon III himself was said to have been shocked by the scenes he witnessed at Solferino. The carnage of the Crimea was fresh in the memory, and indeed the American Civil War was still raging, when, in response to the campaign, the First Geneva Convention took place in 1864. The convention, which was to be the seedbed in which the International Red Cross germinated, sought to ensure humanitarian behaviour towards prisoners, the wounded and field hospitals in time of war. These objectives were extended to include sailors wounded in sea battles by a Second Convention four years later.

For forty years before the outbreak of the First World War the major European powers had been engaged in an arms race with an accompanying advance in the technology of destruction. By the end of the nineteenth century the age of the cannonball was long dead. Modern battleships had grown to mammoth size and possessed huge guns that could throw an enormous explosive shell well over the horizon. Great Britain, France, Germany, Russia and Japan watched each other warily, forming alliances and *ententes* between themselves in a dizzying number of permutations, to the alarm of those excluded. But by 1898 the Russian Tsar Nicholas II, with commendable perception as the Russo-Japanese War was to prove a few years later, had realized that his gigantic, largely ice-bound country, occupied, paradoxically, a somewhat precarious position, with its navy fragmented and separated between east and west by thousands of miles. Russia was never likely to emerge as the victor from any major war fought outside her own confines, or at sea, regardless of which opponent Fate selected for her. Moreover, the British had adopted their Two Power Standard policy in 1889. Thenceforth the Royal Navy was to be equal in power to the next two biggest navies in Europe. And as each of her rivals built bigger and more powerful ships, so did Great Britain, adhering religiously to her Standard. Nicholas foresaw Armageddon. He called for an international convention to limit "the progressive development of existing armaments" as "the most effective means of assuring to all peoples the blessings of real and lasting peace".

Twenty-two nations responded to the Tsar's initiative and assembled at The Hague in 1899, but they could not agree on any general limit of armaments. In fact, the British Admiral 'Jacky' Fisher, sent to the Convention by Prime Minister Lord Salisbury in the knowledge that he, Fisher, would defend his corner with his usual fiery vigour, declared, "The humanizing of War? You may as well talk of humanizing Hell. I am not for War. I am for Peace. That is why I call for a supreme Royal Navy. If you rub it in that you are ready for instant War . . . and intend to be first in and hit your enemy in the belly and kick him when he is down and boil your prisoners in oil (if you take any), and torture his women and children, then people will keep clear of you." However, despite Fisher's attitude, the delegates were able to hammer out agreements to outlaw certain weapons of war, (the dum-dum bullet for example), and to codify various areas of international law.

A second peace convention was held, again at The Hague, in 1907, this time at the instigation of US President Theodore Roosevelt. Forty-four nations were represented. Again it proved impossible to reach any accord on the matter of general dis-armament, but the Convention was very fruitful in other areas. Regulations were adopted which outlawed or limited such practices as the laying of mines. The rights of neutrals within war zones were clearly defined, an international Prize Court was created and agree-ment was adopted which called for a formal Declaration of War before any hostilities commenced. Furthermore, the Final Acts of the Second Peace Convention at The Hague concerned themselves with "the Adaptation of the Principles of the Geneva Convention to Maritime War". These Principles are central to the context of this book. The special considerations to be afforded to Hospital Ships and the people aboard them formed a major part of the Articles of the Convention. They are dealt with later, in the appro-priate chapter of this book. Notably, the many countries which signed and ratified these Acts included all of the following – France, Germany, Great Britain, Italy, Japan, Russia and the United States.

Chapter III of the Final Act dealt with the status of merchant seamen from a sunken or captured merchant vessel. Article 6 thereof laid down that "the captain, officers and crew, if subjects or citizens of an enemy state, are not made Prisoners of War, provided that they undertake, on the faith of a written promise, not to engage while hostilities last in any service connected with the operation of the war".

Seven years later, in 1914, an armed struggle erupted in Europe which was to see a hundred times more bloodshed, maiming, death and destruction as it spread around the globe than any of its pre-decessors throughout history. Total Warfare had arrived. For aeons, wars had been fought between armies and/or fleets. In Total Warfare, nation fights nation. It brings into play all the efforts and resources of a belligerent nation and requires all the active support and public approval of its people. High morale and a sense of being 'in the right' are essential ingredients. Investments in war loans, longer and harder work in the factories churning out munitions and other vital war material, economies of food and fuel are all needed to swell the general surge towards the desired victory. One of the easiest ways to ensure the co-operation of the people in working to all these ends is to stir up their hatred of the enemy. In turn, one of the easiest ways to do this is by recounting atrocities committed by the enemy, regardless of whether or not such stories may be strictly true. Even the Romans, as ever far ahead of their time, had employed such tactics during their wars against the Carthaginians. In 1914 illiteracy in Europe had shrunk to less than 5% of the population, compared to about 40% in 1840. It was commercially logical, then, that the number of European newspapers should double between 1880 and 1900. It followed that, with the means of communication now so dramatically expanded within a couple of decades, let alone since Roman times, a powerful new weapon of war should appear – written propaganda.

As early as 25 August 1914, with the First World War barely three weeks old, the Belgian Minister of Justice issued an official report on atrocities committed by German troops as they advanced through his country. An old man had been hung upside down and buried alive, the report asserted. Young girls had been raped and other inhabitants mutilated at Orsmael. A Belgian soldier-cyclist, having stopped to aid a wounded comrade, had been tied to a telegraph pole and shot. A German soldier had cut off a young woman's breasts with his bayonet. Another had lifted a two-year-old child on his bayonet and tossed it into the air like a sheaf of corn. And on 2 May 1915 the *Sunday Chronicle* ran a story of how a child with her hands buried in a muff in a Paris refugee centre had been heard to ask her mother to blow her nose for her. It turned out that she was unable to do so herself because the Germans had cut off her hands.

Not surprisingly, the German press was quick to retaliate. According to the *Kölnische Volkszeitung* of 15 September 1914 a company of German soldiers had been enticed into a church by a Belgian priest, only to be mown down by a machine gun hidden behind the altar. And in Charleroi a wounded German dragoon had had his eyes gouged out with daggers by a gang of civilians, while sleeping German soldiers had had their throats cut by Belgian women in the quarters that they themselves had offered to the invaders. Germany was, in fact, to make quite a meal of its objections to this *franc-tireur* style of warfare. Indeed, their judicial murder of Captain Fryatt, of whom more later, was based purely on those objections.

As regards any allegations of British brutalities, however, the Germans had difficulty in dredging up any examples, largely because the war was not being fought on British soil. Instead, they were reduced to raking back through the past and resurrecting cases from the Indian Mutiny and the Boer War. There were to be, however, in the course of the world's first global conflict, several notable incidents at sea which caused outrage on both sides, adding fuel to the already seething cauldron of hate.

THE *LUSITANIA* AND THE *ARABIC*

When Kapitänleutnant Walther Schwieger sent a torpedo streaking from the submarine *U-20* towards the massive 32,000-ton four-funnelled profile of the Liverpool-bound Cunard liner *Lusitania* on 7 May 1915 off the Old Head of Kinsale, at the tip of southern Ireland, he sparked an outrage that was to fester for years. Indeed, it was to become one of the most remembered single incidents of the First World War.

Only two months before, the lanky German Chancellor, Theobald von Bethmann-Hollweg, a fifty-nine-year-old academic and, ironically, if the truth be told, a pacifist, had finally relented under pressure from his belligerent Admirals (with the exception of the canny old von Tirpitz), and issued the following grim statement:

> Germany hereby declares all waters surrounding Great Britain and Ireland, including the entire English Channel, to be an area of war, and will therein act against the shipping of the enemy. For this purpose, beginning 18th February 1915, she will endeavour to destroy every enemy merchant ship that is found in this area of war, even if it is not always possible to avert the peril which threatens persons and cargoes. Neutrals are therefore warned against further entrusting crews and passengers and wares to such ships. Their attention is also called to the fact that it is advisable for their ships to avoid entering this area, for, although the German naval forces have instructions to avoid violence to neutral ships, in so far as they are recognisable, in view of the misuse of neutral flags ordered by the British Government, and the contingencies of naval warfare, their

becoming victims of attack directed against enemy ships cannot be always avoided.

Solid reminders of the German announcement had appeared in the New York papers, some even directly alongside the sailing time-tables of the great liners which plied between the USA and Europe.

> Travellers intending to embark on the Atlantic voyage are reminded that a state of war exists between Germany and her allies and Great Britain and her allies; that the zone of war includes the waters adjacent to the British Isles; that, in accordance with formal notice given by the Imperial German Government, vessels flying the flag of Great Britain or of any of her allies, are liable to destruction in those waters and that travellers sailing in the war zone on ships of Great Britain or her allies do so at their own risk.
>
> *Imperial German Embassy, Washington DC April 22, 1915.*

Little serious heed seems. to have been given to this ominous warning by the 1,257 souls who took passage in the *Lusitania* from Pier 54 on New York's Lower West Side at 12.30 pm on 7 May 1915, as was witnessed by the fact that first-class passengers had still been happy to pay the reduced price of $4,000 one-way that Cunard had placed on offer. A light springtime drizzle did little to dampen the spirits of the usual crowd of straw-boatered men and long-skirted ladies which had gathered to see 'Lucy' depart for the Old World as they sang along to the strains of 'Tipperary' and 'The Star Spangled Banner' from the band and a forest of paper streamers cascaded from the liner's sides to the quay below. Slowly, she backed away from the dockside and the harbour tugs fussed around, nudging her huge bows to point down river to the Narrows and the ocean beyond.

Surely, a passenger liner was of little value as a prize of war compared to one carrying troops or vital material as cargo. *Lusitania* had been a regular crosser of the Atlantic for years – this would be her 202nd crossing – and nothing untoward had befallen her in this war up to now. And on this particular voyage she would be carrying a considerable number of neutral Americans. Why would Germany risk bringing a hesitant America closer to entering the war for the sake of such a comparatively worthless scalp?

2

The crossing was uneventful until the ship neared the coast of Southern Ireland and entered what had become known to British sailors as 'U-boat Alley'. At about eleven o'clock *Lusitania*'s fifty-nine-year-old master, Captain William Turner, received a wireless message from Admiral Coke at Queenstown. It was in high-grade cryptic form and Turner needed to retire from the bridge to his cabin to decypher it in private. It ordered him to divert to Queenstown rather than steam direct to Liverpool and warned him of the presence of U-boats in the vicinity. What the Admiralty did not tell Turner was that they had recalled the old cruiser HMS *Juno* to Queenstown. She was to have escorted the liner through U-boat Alley, but had been considered unfit for such work at the last minute. Although it was perhaps strange that such a decision was not made earlier, it was an understandable one. After all, *Juno* was already well obsolete, having been built in 1897, and her maximum 19 knots could not have kept pace with Lucy, not if Turner had been steaming at his own best speed. But, tragically, the top-brass had overlooked to send another ship in her place, although there was a pack of destroyers available at Milford Haven which had been purpose-built for such work. Such an oversight was to lead to several serious allegations against First Lord of the Admiralty Winston Churchill many years later.

At 12.40 pm another Admiralty signal was received in *Lusitania*'s Marconi room. This time it was not in code. "Submarine 5 miles west Cape Clear, proceeding West when sighted 10 am." Turner breathed more easily when he read this. It looked as if any immediate danger was past. All the same, he posted extra lookouts, swung out his lifeboats on their davits and ordered all portholes and bulkhead doors to be shut. But he did not heed the other advice from the Admiralty, which was to go at maximum speed through the area and to zig-zag. Although only nineteen of the big ship's twenty-five boilers were fired, owing to a breakdown in No. 4 boiler-room, she should have still been capable of twenty-one knots, considerably faster than the surface speed of any U-boat at that time. When Turner had encountered banks of fog off Cape Clear he had reduced his speed, but he had not picked it up again through U-boat Alley, even though the visibility had improved with some pale sunshine. Nor did he zig-zag. He steered a dead-straight course at eighteen knots. The *Lusitania* was an easy target.

Fregattenkapitän Herman Bauer had ordered three of his submarines, *U-30*, *U-20* and *U-27*, out on patrol from Wilhelmshaven on 25 April. *U-30* was to operate off Dartmouth and the other two were to enter the Irish Sea and Bristol Channel to "await English troop transports coming out from ports on the west coast of England".

Kapitänleutnant Walther Schwieger in *U-20* had sunk a small schooner, the *Earl of Latham*, and two Harrison Line cargo ships, the *Candidate* and the *Centurion* on 5 and 6 May, all in U-boat Alley. The morning of 7 May dawned revealing dense banks of springtime fog which had built up overnight. Schwieger had run submerged at sixty feet, to avoid the risk of being run down in this busy sea lane. Notwithstanding his caution, *U-20* had had a close brush with such disaster already, just after daybreak. Hearing the sound of powerful propellers churning the water nearby, he had risen to thirty feet to take a look through his 'asparagus stick', as a periscope was known in the German Navy. The propellers were those of a Royal Navy armoured cruiser steaming at speed and it had passed directly above the submarine! Schwieger had surfaced just in time to see the stern of the big ship moving away. If he had come up just a minute or so sooner *U-20* would almost certainly have been sliced in two!

By late morning the sun had gathered enough strength to burn off the heavy fog banks. It was set to be a fine and sunny spring day. Schwieger brought *U-20* to the surface and went into his conning-tower to enjoy the bracing Atlantic air after being dived for several hours in the muggy stuffiness of the submarine. Suddenly the lookouts drew his attention to a group of ships approaching over the horizon from the westward. He swung his binoculars in their direction, trying to establish how many vessels were represented by the cluster of large funnels and masts. It took only a few seconds for him to decide that he was not looking at a group of ships at all. There was only one ship there, and she was big, very big.

"Dive! Dive! Dive!" he yelled and instantly *U-20*'s crew snapped into action, rushing to Diving Stations. Amid the urgent clanging of the dive alert bells, switches were thrown, levers were pulled and strong hands spun the big control wheels which opened the vents to flood the ballast tanks and send the boat beneath the surface. Schwieger slammed shut the conning-tower hatch and slid down the steel ladder with practised ease. He nodded to his First Lieutenant, who disconnected the oil engines and switched to electric. Suddenly all was quiet, but for the steady murmur of the electric motors.

Now the tall thirty-two-year-old Berliner leaned on his periscope handles, peering at the big ship in the mirrors and quietly passing on what he saw to his pilot, Lanz. "Four red funnels, black hull, white upperworks. Looks 20,000 tons at least." Lanz, at his little table, checked with *Janes' Fighting Ships* and *Brassey's Naval Annual*. "She's either the *Lusitania* or the *Mauretania*", he said excitedly, "and both are listed as Armed Merchant Cruisers!"

That was enough for Schwieger. He would never have an easier shot. In fact, it was his only chance, because he had only three torpedoes left and was under orders to reserve two for the trip home to Wilhelmshaven. "*Feuer Ein!*" he rapped and *U-20* gave a slight jerk as a G type torpedo hissed from its tube at thirty-eight knots, set at a depth of three metres, with 300 lb of high explosive in its warhead.

It struck the liner on the starboard side, slightly for'ard of mid-ships, just as the first-class passengers were finishing lunch. It detonated inside the hull, blowing a yawning hole in her side through which hundreds of tons of sea-water immediately poured. One passenger said that it sounded like "a million-ton hammer hitting a steel boiler 100 feet high and 100 feet long". The ship took on a sharp list and quickly settled by the head. Third Officer Bestic hurried to his Boat Station on the portside, No. 4 Boat. The boat was still under its davits but already full, with fifty people in it. Captain Turner had already given orders for the launching of the boats to be delayed until the ship lost headway. But as Bestic arrived he heard the loud metallic clang of a sledgehammer hitting an iron pin. The lifeboat, suspended in its davits, was made fast to the deck by means of a short stubbing chain. This had to be released by knocking out its securing pin before the boat could be launched. This had been the sound that Bestic heard. Somebody, no doubt in panic, had knocked out the pin. The word "No!" stuck in the young Officer's throat as he tried to shout out, but it was too late. The five-ton boat, now left to swing free, swung inboard owing to the ship's list and crashed into the crowd of people cramming themselves onto the boat deck, crushing them against the super-structure. Then it slid down the deck, ploughing its way through

5

more passengers, some already injured, until it came to rest jammed under the wing of the bridge. And Boat No. 2, also full of horrified people, then glided down the sloping deck and crashed into the wreckage. Electric power failed, leaving screaming passengers in pitch darkness in the saloons and cabins. Some became trapped in pitch darkness, stuck between decks in the lifts which were to become their tombs. Others, hurrying up or down companionways, drowned as water rushed into the stairwells. Only the starboard-side lifeboats could be lowered, owing to the heavy list. Of these, several came down 'end up', ejecting their occupants into the cold calm sea. In eighteen short minutes the giant ship was resting on the bottom of the Atlantic.

Only 761 people were saved. Some of them described the awful scenes. One passenger, a Boston bookseller and author called Charles Lauriot, was a veteran transatlantic voyager. He hurried to his cabin, tied on his life-jacket, collected his business papers and ran back on deck to do all he could to help those around him put on their own life-jackets correctly. Some were wearing them upside down. One man had his head through an armhole. Lauriot came up the companionway and found the well-known writer Elbert Hubbard standing on the portside with his wife, apparently unsure of what to do. He urged them to return to their state-room to collect their life-jackets, but both seemed unable to do so, as if they were rooted to the spot. When Lauriot returned, however, they had gone, never to be seen again. He managed to get into a lifeboat which, owing to the list, was already almost touching the surface of the sea, but it had become snagged on its ropes and stubbornly refused to float free. A crew member – Lauriot thought he recognized the man as one of the stewards – was frantically sawing away at the thick ropes with his pocket-knife. It was a job which really required an axe and the man was making little progress. Thinking quickly, Lauriot leapt over the side and swam as hard as he could away from the ship to avoid being sucked down as she plunged, spurred on by the terrifying sight of a giant red funnel looming over his head as the *Lusitania* leaned further and further to starboard. Strangely, there was little of the expected suction, probably because, at 762 feet long, her bows would have already been touching the 315-feet-deep seabed well before her stern disappeared. Lauriot was fortunate in being rescued later.

Passenger Isaac Lehmann, of New York, said,

I was in the smoking-room with a friend when the first torpedo struck. I ran out to the lifeboats. While an attempt was being made to launch one of the boats, one of the ropes snapped and about thirty people were thrown into the water. I ran to my cabin and got my revolver and lifebelt, and came back to a second boat that had been loaded. I shouted, 'For God's sake launch that boat!' A man replied, 'The Captain's orders are not to launch the boats yet.' I promptly drew my revolver and said, 'I'll shoot the first man to refuse to help to launch that boat.' The boat was launched with about sixty people in it. They got away all right, but the *Lusitania* lurched and the boat came back and struck her side, about twenty people being killed or injured. At the same moment I heard an explosion in the forepart of the ship, and two minutes later she went down. I was thrown clear of the wreckage, but went under twice. Then my lifebelt brought me up and, by placing oars under my arms, I kept myself afloat for about four and a half hours until I was rescued.

Another survivor, Isaac Jackson, of Paterson, New Jersey, recalled, "Those who were standing on deck tried to hold together, but when we were in the water I had to break away from a man who was dragging me down by the wrist. I was picked up by a lifeboat that was so crowded that the oars could not be used. The passengers were wonderfully calm. There was very little screaming until the last cry as she sank. All the survivors with watches tell me their watches stopped at half past two."

Mr W. G. Ellason Myers of Ontario and his friends had been about to start a game of deck quoits when the ship was hit. He climbed down a rope into a half-swamped boat and helped to bale it out. It was still attached to the davits by its ropes, but somebody produced a hatchet and the ropes were cut to set it free.

Captain Turner had first thought to try to save the huge liner by beaching her – she was well in sight of the Irish coast, with its scattered cottages quite clearly visible – but the intercom system had been damaged by the explosion and his orders had not been heard. Now she was too far awash for there to be any hope of saving her. Hurrying onto the bridge, Turner turned to the man at the wheel and said, "You can go now and try to save yourself. You have no further business here. Goodbye."

Those who were unable to find a lifeboat were grabbing planks, bits of furniture, kegs, oars or anything that would keep them afloat. A floating grand piano, with its three legs sticking up like stumpy masts, rocked incongruously on the gentle ocean swell, surrounded by a dozen bedraggled and gasping people, hanging onto its polished sides for all they were worth. Captain Turner himself was clinging to a chair, which he rode for three hours until being picked up by the steamer *Bluebell*. A new bride, Mrs Gwyer, was sucked into one of the liner's gigantic funnels as she finally sank, only to be shot out again immediately to land in the sea next to the lifeboat in which sat her astonished husband. Perhaps the most heart-rending sight of all was that of another young woman actually giving birth, all alone in the green and chilly water.

One of the liner's several celebrity passengers, Alfred G. Vanderbilt, of that fabulously wealthy family, had been on his way to England to look at some thoroughbred horses. But he could not swim a stroke, and was last seen standing calmly on deck, sartorially immaculate, clutching a blue leather jewel case. He did not survive, although his body was recovered and later taken home to the USA. His family had offered a £1,000 reward to whoever found it. Later, there was a story, probably apocryphal, that before sailing Vanderbilt had received a telegram from a friend who was 'in the know' warning him that the *Lusitania* was a marked target and that he should cancel his reservation.

Warships raced to the scene, together with an assortment of fishing vessels from the small harbours dotted along the coast in response to *Lusitania*'s wireless calls. With Queenstown Harbour only thirty miles distant, the first of them reached the spot a couple of hours after she had sunk. The destroyer HMS *Stormcock*, with the tugs *Warrior* and *Julia*, a couple of trawlers, the local lifeboat and three torpedo-boats plucked about 500 survivors from the water, and an assortment of fishing-boats rescued several more. The cruiser HMS *Juno*, although she had been ordered back to Queenstown, and many merchant ships in the area now all pounded furiously towards the Old Head of Kinsale. A chain of crowded lifeboats, their occupants shivering with shock and cold, was towed to Kinsale Harbour by a Greek steamer. According to some of the merchant skippers, however, the German submarine had not departed from the scene and did all it could to thwart the rescue operation. One captain was even of the opinion that there was a *second* U-boat.

Reuter cabled from Boston, Massachusetts, dateline May 18,

Captain Wood of the steamer *Etonia* has arrived here from Liverpool, and reports that his and other steamships in the area were prevented from going to the assistance of the *Lusitania* by the attempts of two submarines to attack them. The *Etonia* was about forty miles from Kinsale when she got the *Lusitania*'s call for assistance. The steamers *City of Exeter* and *Narragansett* also picked up the call and were proceeding ahead of the *Etonia* in the direction of the stricken liner, when suddenly Captain Wood saw the periscope of a submarine directly ahead. He rang down for Full Speed but the submarine dived and re-appeared moments later directly astern of the *Etonia* and pursued her for about twenty minutes, but the steamer was able to escape owing to her superior speed.

Later, Captain Wood saw another periscope on his starboard bow, whereupon he turned sharply to starboard, the submarine swinging round as well, but the *Etonia* again got away. Later, the *Narragansett* informed the *Etonia* by wireless that one of the submarines had fired a torpedo which missed the *Narragansett* by eight feet only. The *Narragansett* advised the *Etonia* not to go to the assistance of the *Lusitania*.

And the following day Captain Wood's story was confirmed from New York. "The Standard Oil Company's steamer *Narragansett* arrived at Bayonne, New Jersey, last night. The captain confirms the story of the crew of the *Etonia* that a torpedo passed between the *Narragansett* and her log-line, which was hanging astern. The submarine pursued the vessel for several miles before it gave up the chase. The officers of the *Narragansett* thought that possibly the *Lusitania*'s distress call was a German ruse to bring about the ship's destruction and so did not alter course – *Reuter*."

In Ireland the Easter Rising was less than a year away and the Sinn Fein movement had been making its voice heard of late. Given that situation, Captain Wood's story seemed to fit in with rumours that the Germans had, in fact, been operating from secret submarine bases around the southern Irish coast, although these were never substantiated.

Whether or not there had been a second submarine, there had certainly been a second explosion as the *Lusitania* finally sank. Exactly what caused it has been a matter of debate for students of such things ever since. Schwieger had used his last available torpedo to sink her; therefore, if the second explosion was created by another torpedo, (and a study of the wreck does show that this was possible) then there must have been a second U-boat. Or it could have been her boilers exploding, which is common within a sinking ship. Or, as the Germans strongly suggested, it could have been the explosion of the ammunition that she was carrying.

Meanwhile, in Queenstown there were mournful scenes. *The Times* Special Correspondent wrote,

> Queenstown today is a town of the dead and the dying, the maimed, the sick and the sorrowing. The hotels are hospitals and the town hall and other buildings are mortuaries. The arrival of survivors has ceased, and most of the passengers and crew of the *Lusitania* who escaped with little or no injury have departed, but everywhere evidence of the disaster is to be seen, and the brilliant sunshine has only served to heighten the feeling of gloom. Every now and then has passed through the main street a mournful little procession of men bearing stretchers on which, covered by a flag – I saw several on which the flag was the Stars and Stripes – were the bodies of the latest victims of submarine attack. As they passed along the street all hats were reverently raised and soldiers and sailors who were among the crowds standing stiffly erect gave the salute.
>
> A visit to the mortuaries has brought home more thoroughly than anything before the frightful reality of war as it is waged by the Germans. The chief of the resting-places of the dead is the market-hall, a small bare chamber emptied of its everyday furniture and filled with as many of the victims of the nameless submarine as it can hold. Men and women have been passing down the files of dead all day long, seeking relatives and friends who, they feared, were among the missing. Men broke down when they looked upon a young mother lying there with her dead baby, perhaps eighteen months old. I am told, too, of a sailor who was found with the body of a little child strapped on his shoulders.
>
> And with all the solemn panoply of death, there is nothing to

suggest to the mind of the reverent observer that this spectacle had even a remote connexion with civilised warfare. So it is that Queenstown is seething with the fury of men who ask themselves what they can do to make the Germans answerable for this appalling crime.

In Liverpool, *Lusitania*'s home port, the air was heavy with sorrow. One of the treats that young Liverpudlians had grown accustomed to had been being taken to watch "Lucy" as she was entering or leaving the Mersey. And a large proportion of her crew were Scousers. Indeed, Captain William Turner himself was one of them, having been born in Everton on 23 October 1856. Now, anxious crowds gathered outside the Cunard offices to scan the lists of survivors in the window, many of them turning away in tearful disappointment. The scenes at Lime Street Station were no less laden with emotion when a train came in carrying some of the surviving crew – petty officers, stewards, firemen, trimmers, some with bandaged heads or arms in slings; some even on stretchers. A throng of nervously distressed women had assembled at the barrier. They peered at the faces of the arrivals as they passed from the train, praying to spot the one which would bring them relief from their anxiety. One grey-haired elderly woman, her nerves clearly in tatters, clutched the arm of each crewman as he passed and asked if he knew the fate of Dan Daly the Fireman. Most of them answered her with a sad and negative shake of the head, but eventually one was able to give her the news she dreaded. Dan Daly was lost, and she sank onto a packing-case, wringing her hands, in floods of tears.

Days later, two Admiralty tugs were still cruising up and down the Irish coast searching for bodies. They found over 100 floating in the water off Glandore Harbour. And the crew of a fishing yawl found an upturned lifeboat seven miles off Schull. It was marked – 22A – Lusitania – Liverpool. As they righted it, to prepare to tow it to Long Island, they made a grisly discovery. Trapped beneath it were the bodies of four women and two boys. It was not possible to identify them all. One of the women was a Miss Taylor of Dorchester, Massachusetts, and another was believed to be a Miss Lilian Clay, of Bushey Heath, England, whose pockets bore postcards she had written to her friends Miss Duck and Miss Highfield-Jones. The body of a third woman was encircled by a lifebelt in which was wedged the body of her baby boy.

The College of Arms announced on 13 May that "The King, as Sovereign of the Order of the Garter, has given directions that the following names should forthwith be struck off the Roll of Knights of the Order:-

The Emperor of Austria, The German Emperor, The King of Würtemburg, The German Crown Prince, The Grand Duke of Hesse and the Rhine, Prince Henry of Prussia, The Duke of Saxe-Coburg and Gotha, The Duke of Cumberland."

Thus had King George V been sufficiently incensed to expel several of his close relatives from one of the most prestigious Orders of the realm.

In fact, all over England people with German-sounding names were hounded by the populace, so much so that, as a means of self-defence, many of them took to publishing their names in the national press under a statement that they deplored and condemned the German war tactics. In Gravesend, Kent, a riot erupted when a mob of 500 crossed the Thames on the ferry from Tilbury to smash the premises of a printing firm owned by a Mr Schultz.

An appalled indignation reigned in America. Anti-German demonstrations spread all over the country, even across the border into Canada. Even on the day following the sinking, the Victoria *Daily Colonist* published a rumour that German U-boats were operating off Vancouver Island, and that evening a drunken crowd spilled from the bar of Blanshard's Hotel (its name had been recently changed to something less Germanic than "Kaiserhof") and started to destroy all property in the vicinity with Teutonic-sounding names. By the following week many German-born citizens had been sacked from their jobs and fled across the border to make new lives for themselves in Seattle. One US newspaper, *The Nation*, snorted disgustedly that the sinking of the liner was a "deed for which a Hun would blush, a Turk be ashamed and a Barbary pirate apologise". The *Richmond Times-Dispatch* made a brief but aloof diagnosis, stating that "Germany surely must have gone mad". From Washington, President Woodrow Wilson dispatched an "excessively firm and outspoken" note of protest to the Berlin Government via the cable office at Gibraltar, to be re-transmitted through Rome and Vienna. The Associated Press Agency reported that the note contained nine points, viz:

1. The United States Government calls attention to various incidents, such as the sinking of the British liner *Falaba* with the loss of Mr Thrasher, the attack by German airmen on the American steamship *Cushing*, the torpedoing without warning of the American steamship *Gullflight*, flying the Stars and Stripes, and finally the torpedoing without warning of the *Lusitania*, with the loss of more than 1,000 lives of non-combatants, among them more than 100 Americans.

2. These acts are declared to be indefensible under international law. The United States points out that it never admitted the right of Germany to do them, and warned the Imperial Government that it would be held to strict accountability for attacks on American vessels or lives. A strict accounting, therefore, is now asked for from Germany.

3. The usual financial reparation will be sought, although Germany is reminded that no reparation can restore the lives of those sacrificed in the sinking of the *Lusitania* and others.

4. Expressions of regret may comply with legal precedents but they are worthless unless accompanied by a cessation of practices endangering the lives of non-combatants.

5. The right of neutrals to travel over any portion of the high seas in neutral or belligerent merchantmen is asserted.

6. In the name of humanity and international law, the United States demands a guarantee that these rights will be respected and that there will be no repetition of attacks on merchantmen carrying non-combatants.

7. The giving of warnings to the American public without first communicating them to the United States Government is commented on in connexion with the German Embassy's printed advertisement before the sailing of the *Lusitania*, but irrespective of the failure to advise the American Government of the German purpose, the point is made that notice of the intention to do an unlawful act neither justified nor legalised it.

8. A suggestion is conveyed that the German Government, of course, may not have intended to destroy innocent lives, and that consequently the German submarine commanders must have misunderstood their instructions. The American Government indicates its hope that this will be found to be true, and that a cessation of these unlawful practices will result.

9. The attention of Germany is called to the earnestness of the

Government and people of the United States in this situation. It is made plain that the United States will leave nothing undone either in diplomatic representations or other actions to obtain compliance by Germany to the requests made.

Berlin's response was bereft both of remorse and of any of the guarantees demanded by the US President. The German Government merely "regretted" the loss of life. The Germans contended that the *Lusitania* had been armed (which was firmly denied by the British Admiralty) and was carrying war material, which was also denied, but which later transpired to be true. The German Government claimed that the warnings it had put on prominent display in and around New York and in major US newspapers, prior to the liner's sailing, placed passengers on firm notice of the risk they were taking and served further to absolve Germany of guilt. And the *Frankfurter Zeitung* trumpeted, "For the German Navy, the sinking of the *Lusitania* means an extraordinary success."

Woodrow Wilson, impatient now, fired off a second note. This time he showed no willingness to compromise. The United States, he said, was contending for nothing less high and sacred than the rights of humanity, and Germany must cease unrestricted attacks on merchant vessels. The President had, for the moment, marginalized his own political unease with the vociferous anti-British faction within the immigrant, i.e. German–American and Irish–American, population of the USA, and allowed it to be overridden by his natural concern for Christian ethics. He made a speech on 10 May berating those naturalized Americans who still clung to their old nationalistic prejudices. "A man who thinks of himself as belonging to a particular national group in America has not yet become an American," he lectured, "and the man who goes among you to trade upon your nationality is no worthy son to live under the Stars and Stripes."

The US Secretary of State, William Jennings Bryan, a devoted pacifist and appeaser, took the view that war between Germany and the USA was now inevitable. He wanted nothing to do with it and promptly resigned, to be replaced by his deputy, Robert Lansing, a New York lawyer with strongly contrasting views. America seemed to be another step nearer entry into the war.

A Board of Trade Inquiry into the loss of the *Lusitania*, chaired by Lord Mersey, was re-opened on 1 July at the Westminster Palace Hotel. Fresh evidence had come to light, submitted by a Frenchman, Joseph Marichal, who had been a passenger on his way to England for a holiday. He said that the nature of the explosion when the ship was struck was "similar to the rattling of a Maxim gun for a short period". In the context of the German allegations that the *Lusitania* had been armed and was carrying ammunition, this was a statement which deserved further investigation.

Lord Mersey: "Do you suggest that a Maxim gun was discharged?"

Marichal: "I suggest that the explosion of the torpedo exposed the secret existence of some ammunition. I have experience of explosives. I have served as an officer in the French Army."

The Solicitor-General: "Where did the sound of the explosion which you attribute to ammunition come from?"

Marichal: "From underneath the whole floor." He went on to make a long rambling statement about how they had landed at Queenstown practically without any clothing, after being four hours in a leaking boat, and then had to wait another two hours before being directed to an hotel. In the morning he had gone to the Cunard offices for information, but was told that they did not open for business until 9 o'clock. Eventually he learned that there was to be a special train to Dublin at 3 o'clock and went to the station at 2.30 pm. But he could not get onto the platform and it was not until the evening that he was able to get on a train. And then, he complained, they had been overcharged by an hotel in Dublin.

The President: "Is this a charge against the company or the hotel?"

Marichal: "Against the hotel people in the first place, but mainly against the company."

There was no doubt that Marichal was a petulant witness. His criticisms had not yet all been heard. He went on to claim that the captain and crew of the liner were most incompetent. His lifeboat had oars and a mast, but no rowlocks or a sail. And the boat leaked. In the end, they were rescued by a fishing smack, and when the smack found another lifeboat, which was number 19, there were about twenty crew members in it. "We were so indignant that there were no women in it," he said.

The Inquiry seemed to be drifting away from the main issue, that of the sinking itself. A Mr Cotter, for the Union of Ships' Stewards, refocused matters. He asked where Marichal had been at the moment of the explosion. The Frenchman replied that he had been in the second-class dining-room, which was situated in the after-part of the ship. He did not know whether that would have placed him somewhere above the turbines. Cotter continued to challenge several of the witness's statements.

"The effect of the explosion on a steampipe at high pressure would be a rattling sound?"

To which Marichal replied, "Yes, but not anything of the magnitude of that one."

Then came the turn of a Mr Aspinall, for Cunard, to cross-examine the witness. First of all, he established that Marichal had not been present at an earlier hearing, when evidence had been invited from passengers.

Aspinall: "You kept quiet at first. Am I right in saying that you are making a claim on the company?"

"I am making claims against the company or against Germany, whichever is found guilty. I have lost everything. I have sent in claims to the French Foreign Office and to the company."

Aspinall: "Did you write to Mr Booth, in an envelope marked 'Private and Urgent', as follows? 'The French Foreign Office will formulate a definite claim before long, but I must ask you to make some immediate allowance on account, or else I shall have the unpleasant duty to claim publicly and in doing so to produce evidence that will not be to the credit either of your company or the Admiralty'."

"Yes, I have done so now."

Aspinall: "Did you intend to keep your mouth shut?"

"Oh, no."

The President: "Be careful. What that letter says is 'Pay me some money or I will do this and that'. Am I to understand that if you had got the money you would have done this all the same?"

Marichal: "I should have spoken at the earlier Inquiry."

Lord Mersey: "I am sorry to say, but I do say, that I don't believe you."

Marichal: "This is the first time I have been called a liar in my whole life."

Lord Mersey: "I am sorry, but if you tell me that this letter did not mean that you wanted money to keep your mouth closed, I don't believe you."

Marichal had been seen to be a scheming witness, but regardless of the credibility, or otherwise, of his evidence, information came to light much later which appeared to put a final seal on the question of the legality of the sinking of the liner. It was true that she had not been armed, nor was she being used as a troop transport, but, according to Cunard's records, she had in fact been loaded with 4,200 cases of Remington small arms ammunition and 1,259 cases of empty steel shrapnel shells, plus a large quantity of cheese and butter for the Royal Navy at Shoeburyness. Under International Law, this had been enough in itself to make her a legitimate target.

But, as is common with many of history's controversies, some years later one or two historians suggested that there had been a measure of intrigue associated with the loss of the *Lusitania*. If they were correct in their assertions, they painted a black indelible mark on the character of Winston Churchill. Just two days before the sinking, on 5 May, a top secret Admiralty conference was held. Those present were Churchill himself as First Lord of the Admiralty; the First Sea Lord, Admiral of the Fleet 'Jacky' Fisher; Vice-Admiral Henry Oliver, Chief of War Staff; Captain Reginald 'Blinker' Hall, Director of Naval Intelligence and a Lieutenant-Commander Kenworthy, Hall's assistant. One item on the agenda was the recall of the elderly HMS *Juno* from escort duty for the *Lusitania*. It was Churchill, allegedly, who commented that her absence would leave the liner exposed to the U-boat wolf pack which was known to be in the area, and if she were sunk and American lives were lost, it would trigger a fresh wave of anti-German public opinion in the United States and exert more pressure on President Woodrow Wilson to declare war on the Kaiser. Kenworthy left the room, apparently in disgust at what was being suggested.

Now Kenworthy was a well-known pacifist, as were the historians who later subscribed to and embroidered his insinuations. In fact he became a left-wing Labour MP in the Twenties after having left the Navy. To have such a man with strong anti-war views closely associated with Naval Intelligence in time of war seems to have been patently absurd. Nevertheless, there he was. He became the author of several books and pamphlets, and, although he never actually accused Churchill of planning such a cold-blooded double-cross, he left no doubt as to his opinions. Indeed, it was quite

17

possible that Churchill may have commented on the likely effect of a sinking. Fisher was present, too, and his ruthless streak was well known. As for Hall, his job, almost by definition, involved deviousness of the highest calibre. But to state all that is a far cry from saying that these men wanted the *Lusitania* to be sunk. It is even more far-fetched to suggest that they had actually planned it.

What would the likely outcome have been if *Juno* had *not* been recalled? (It is not clear who was the ultimate authority for the order for her to be recalled. Admiral Coke had certainly ordered the movement, but was this on his own initiative, or had he been ordered to do so by his superiors at the Admiralty? Kenworthy's case must surely have turned on the answer to that question.) *Juno* was old and slow, slower, in fact, than a U-boat's surface speed, and much slower than Lucy's. Her presence would probably not have added very greatly to the safety of the liner. Indeed, given enough torpedoes, Schwieger would have been perfectly capable of sinking both her and the *Lusitania*. And even Churchill could hardly have engineered a situation where a German U-boat would be at a certain spot at a certain time. As regards replacement escorts, it was Admiral Coke's responsibility to order out the destroyers from Milford Haven or elsewhere if an escort was considered essential. In any event, although the *Lusitania* was sunk and American lives lost, it did not bring the USA into the war, or even slide her closer to it. That event was still nearly two years away. In fact, things were to happen in the meantime which would persuade her to step even further back from the brink.

Following the sinking of the *Lusitania*, an official Inquiry cleared Captain William Turner of any blame for the loss of the liner. He stated that he had not even known that there was going to be an escort provided for his ship, let alone known that it had been withdrawn. He was later to survive another torpedo attack, on 1 January 1917, when in command of the troop transport *Ivernia*. After the War he went to live in Devon with his common-law wife Mabel Every (having left his legal wife many years before), but they were unable to settle down there and soon moved back to Liverpool, where they bought a house in a quiet leafy suburb – 50 De Villiers Avenue, Great Crosby. He died in 1933.

As for Walther Schwieger, he met his fate two-and-a-half years after he had dispatched the *Lusitania* to the deep. But the exact nature of his end is still swathed in mystery. One version has it that on 17 September 1917, cruising in the big *U-88* off south-west Ireland, he fell in with a harmless British coaster, only a couple of hours steaming, in fact, from where the corpse of the *Lusitania* lay in its watery tomb. There were two men in cloth caps busily chipping away the rust on the rails of the scruffy little 1,680-tonner. They gave no indication that they had even seen the submarine. At 4.43 pm the German opened fire. He had made a fatal mistake. The salt-caked tub was, in reality, Commander Maurice Blackwood's Q-ship HMS *Stonecrop*. Having lured the U-boat to point-blank range by means of all manner of well-practised theatrical 'acts' of innocence, Blackwood dropped the screens hiding his guns. Within a minute, or maybe two, Petty Officer George Lee, "the best gun-layer in the Navy" according to Blackwood, had blasted *U-88* along the waterline with at least eight 4-inch shells. Amid clouds of acrid brown smoke, and with her crew unable to open her damaged conning-tower hatch to escape, she sank by the stern. Another (German) version of the story denies Blackwood the killing of Schwieger. It says that *U-88* was in fact sunk ten days earlier, on 7 September, in the Heligoland Bight, either by a British mine or by an explosion of one of its own torpedoes in its tube. This was witnessed by the captain of "another U-boat", which was proceeding submerged in company with *U-88*. He heard the explosion, he said, and immediately surfaced to render assistance to any survivors, but none appeared. There was no trace of anybody or anything from *U-88* except a large lake of oil and flotsam. If that was the case, which submarine was it which tangled with HMS *Stonecrop*? It seems most unlikely that any U-boat could have survived the terrible damage inflicted on it by Petty Officer Lee. And a cynic might muse that it gave less of a morale boost to the British if the killer of the *Lusitania* was seen to have died by way of an accident rather than at the hands of the brave crew of a Q-ship. The British authorities obviously believed Blackwood's account, because prize bounty was awarded to *Stonecrop* in December 1921 for sinking *U-88*.

The sheer size of the *Lusitania* is the obvious reason why her sinking is the best remembered of a series of controversial submarine attacks that took place throughout that long painful summer of 1915, but as Woodrow Wilson's very first point had been at pains to state, it was not the first incident of the war in which neutral

Americans had been attacked. On 27 March von Forstner in *U-28* had sunk three ships off the Scillies and was alleged to have fired on passengers from the *Aguila* as they took to their boats, and he continued to display this ominous brutality the next day when he stopped the 4,800-ton Elder Dempster liner *Falaba* in the Irish Sea. He gave the passengers and crew just five minutes to abandon ship before sinking her, but it was impossible for them all to get into and launch their boats in that time, whereupon the German fired a torpedo into the ship at point-blank range. 104 lives were lost out of 242, including that of an American passenger, Leon C. Thrasher, who was drowned. And a peeved America was none the less so when it turned out later that the ship herself had been a legitimate target as she was carrying thirteen tons of explosives to West Africa.

The other incident to which President Wilson had referred had taken place on Saturday 1 May when the American oil tanker *Gullflight*, from Port Arthur, Texas, with £80,000 worth of oil for Rouen, was torpedoed off Bishop's Lighthouse. Owned by the Gulf Refining Company, she grossed 5,189 tons and was of the very latest design, using oil to fuel her own engines. After landing in Penzance, the ship's Second Officer, Paul W. Bowers of Chicago, recalled that they had been shadowed right across the Atlantic by a warship of some description. The mysterious vessel had remained out of sight, but had stayed in contact with them by wireless, issuing various instructions, in particular that they should maintain wireless silence. At noon on Saturday 1 May, when they were about twenty-five miles off the Scillies, their lookout saw a submarine a couple of miles dead ahead. Bowers immediately informed Captain Gunther and the Chief Officer, but three minutes later the submarine dived and disappeared. Nearly half an hour later, without any warning, the *Gullflight* was struck by a torpedo on the starboard side. Two of the crew, Short, the wireless operator, and a Spanish sailor, had promptly dived overboard and were never seen again. It was fortunate that the tanker had already been met by two escort patrol boats, who were steaming, unseen in the fog, on either side of her. Such was the impact of the explosion that the crew of one of the patrol boats first thought that it was their own boat which had been attacked. They took Captain Gunther and the remaining thirty-three American sailors on board from their lifeboat and made them comfortable for the night. By now the fog had become so dense that the patrol boat captain decided, wisely in these treacherous waters which had been the graveyard of so many ships over the centuries, not to attempt to make land until the morning but to ride out the night on a sea-anchor.

At about midnight Captain Gunther sent for Bowers. The Second Officer went to the cabin which had kindly been made available and found the fifty-year-old Gunther in bed. He said he wanted someone to roll him a cigarette, but while Bowers was doing this for him, he suddenly threw up his arms and fainted under a heart attack. By 3.30 am he was dead. The official response from Berlin to the sinking of the *Gullflight* was an apology, saying that the U-boat captain had not seen the Stars and Stripes flying at the stern of the tanker.

But these two incidents were merely isolated clashes of cymbals against the repetitive grind of the theme music of everyday sinkings that were taking place at that juncture of the War. In the short space of seventy-two hours, the list was astonishing. The U-boats were running amok. Almost certainly it was the same submarine that sunk the *Gullflight* which had sunk the 3,110-ton Middlesbrough steamer *Edale* a few hours earlier off the Scillies as she headed for Manchester from the River Plate with a cargo of cereals, and that same afternoon the French collier *Europe*. The steamer *Fulgent* was attacked and sunk forty-five miles north-west of the Skelligs, and when a trawler picked up nine survivors in a lifeboat to take them to Kilrush, they had the body of their captain with them. He had been shot.

On the previous day (Friday) the Russian vessel *Svorono* of Marinpol, lugging coal from Port Talbot to Archangel was shelled and sunk without warning by a German submarine off the Kerry coast. The U-boat continued firing as the merchant crew took to their boats, although none of them was hurt. Again on the Saturday, the neutral Norwegian mail-steamer *America* was torpedoed and sunk 200 miles out of Bergen. The North Shields fishing trawler *Sunny* was sunk on the Sunday off the Tyne, as were the smacks *Mercury* and *Martaban* off Aberdeen.

The *Lusitania* had rested on the bottom for barely two and a half months when she was joined nearby by another big liner which was also sunk in controversial circumstances. She was the 15,801-ton White Star liner *Arabic*. It was about 9.30 am on 19 August 1915, on her second day out from Liverpool, bound for New York with

181 passengers. She was about fifty miles off the southern coast of Ireland, in 50°50'N 8°32'W to be precise, and making a steady sixteen knots through the calm water.

Passenger Wells Ingram finished his breakfast and went out onto the promenade deck to take the bracing Atlantic air. There he found two fellow-passenger friends and they strolled together, chatting, towards the *Arabic*'s towering prow. Suddenly, away on the starboard bow, there hove into view what appeared to be a derelict ship, lying with her bows buried deep in the water. There were no signs of life on board, nor was she flying any flags. In the distance Ingram could see two small sailing boats picking up the light breeze, heading for the Irish coast. The *Arabic* slowed perceptibly and altered course to take her across the bows of the sinking ship. Ingram's lady friend remarked intuitively, "Surely we are not going to stop? This ship is a decoy."

Decoy she was not, but she might as well have been, because that was what she was to serve as, unwittingly, in the space of the next few minutes. She was the 4930-ton freighter *Dunsley*, bound from Liverpool to Boston with general cargo and she had just been torpedoed by *U-24*, commanded by Kapitänleutnant Rudolf Schneider, which but two days before had been shelling the oil-tanks at Whitehaven on the Cumberland coast. The *Dunsley*'s plight had already been observed by Captain William Finch from the *Arabic*'s bridge, high in the superstructure of the liner. Finch had sailed under the White Star colours for twenty-seven years. There was not much that he did not know about ship-handling and he was well accustomed to taking rapid action to deal with emergency at sea. Only seven years before, he had received a presentation at Liverpool Town Hall, having played the major part in the rescue of the crew of the oil-carrying tramp steamer *St. Cuthbert* in the Atlantic. The *Arabic* had received no distress calls, which probably meant that the sinking ship had no wireless. Finch rang his own wireless room. In fact, 21-year-old wireless-operator Leonard Batchelor had already sent out an SOS on the *Dunsley*'s behalf when she was spotted by Ingram and his friends. Two of her crew had been killed and the thirty-five survivors were in the lifeboats seen making for the Irish coast.

No sooner had Ingram's lady friend expressed her concern about decoys than the submarine surfaced "like a porpoise" from behind the sinking ship's bows and Ingram saw the grey streak of a torpedo flying through the water towards them. "I knew the sight well," he said, "as I once spent a day at Whitehead's torpedo works at Fiume, and I shouted that it would miss us." But he was wrong. It struck the *Arabic* about ninety feet from her stern. There was a mighty roar and the whole ship trembled. A column of water and somer-saulting debris rose fully fifty feet above the level of the bridge. Leonard Batchelor's Marconi apparatus was shattered into pieces, which prevented any further SOS calls being made. Fortunately, the *Arabic*'s call for help for the *Dunsley* had already been heard and rescue ships had been alerted. As it turned out, therefore, the tor-pedoed freighter had not only been the cause of *Arabic*'s misfortune but also the means of salvation for her survivors. Gathering his wits, Ingram looked over the side to see what damage had been done to the hull, but the Atlantic had already filled the hole and the liner was settling aft. Schneider said later that he had mistaken the *Arabic* for a troop transport.

Immediately the crew sprang into action, calmly urging passen-gers to put on lifebelts and busying themselves with lowering the boats from their davits. There was no sign of panic. Ingram helped some of the women and children into several of the boats and then set about finding one for himself. There was an empty one being lowered, further aft on the starboard side, where it was easier owing to the list of the ship. In fact, the *Arabic* had now taken on such a list that the keel of the boat was touching the water whilst it was still attached to its davit and Ingram needed hardly to jump at all. He had only to step into it. But as soon as he had done so the big ship rolled back on the ocean swell, lifting the lifeboat, which tightened its pulley ropes. Other people had now joined him in the boat. Desperately, they tried to free it from its ropes, but they were far too taut to allow it. Their language, said Ingram, was not for publication. The *Arabic* was about to sink with the lifeboat still roped to her side. It seemed that they were doomed to be sucked down with the liner. Then, at the last moment she gracefully heaved herself upright, which slackened off the ropes enough for them to cast off. But it was too late. Already the suction was strong enough to prevent them from rowing away from her side. All that they could do was to push the boat along her plates with their oars and out from under her bows, which were now standing skywards, looming high above them like a cliff. For some little time confusion reigned in the lifeboat. Everybody was trying to give orders to everybody else and many people, including some of the ship's crew, were violently sick. They watched the *Arabic* sink. Ingram thought that it had taken about eight minutes after the torpedo had struck. For about an hour and a half they drifted among the floating wreckage, picking up survivors. Ingram's boat picked up a woman and eight men, one of whom was all in and lay in the bottom of the boat groaning. Another lifeboat drew near. This one had a sail. They hitched themselves to it with a painter and together they set off for the Irish coast. After about three hours they sighted 'a vessel' (it was probably a Royal Navy ship out of Queenstown, but war-time censorship prohibited her from being identified in Ingram's account), which was approaching them rapidly. She came along-side, took everybody on board and made for Queenstown at full speed.

The *Arabic* had been carrying several members of the show business fraternity. A well-known actor of the day, Kenneth Douglas, was on his way to New York to join the impressario W.A. Brady. Douglas was in his cabin, dressed in pyjamas, when he felt a terrible thud which shook the whole vessel. He grabbed a couple of top-coats and rushed on deck, barefooted, and jumped into the last boat but one to leave the stricken liner. What impressed him most, he said, was the calm courage of the women in the boats as they faced their ordeal. The scene on the water struck him as being more akin to a sailing match at Margate than a shipwreck, with each boatload cheerfully trying to outpace the others.

The famous singer, Stella Carol, had been travelling to New York with her husband. From her lifeboat she reported seeing two submarines which "hung about" until they were picked up. In the meantime, she led the singing of "It's a long way to Tipperary" to cheer everybody up while they awaited rescue. It seems that her professional career did not suffer much more than the slightest of dents from her adventures in the *Arabic* sinking. A mere four days later, on 23 August, *The Times* was reporting that she was safely back in London and "is due to sing today at the Palladium".

As the rescue work continued throughout the afternoon and evening, White Star Line issued a series of official statements, re-assuring those anxiously awaiting news of friends and families that there had been more than enough lifeboats to carry everybody and that thus far it could be hoped that there had been no loss of life.

Frequent news from Queenstown was passed on with regard to the numbers of people saved and missing. Shortly after eight o'clock, they said that 375 had been saved, leaving only forty-eight unaccounted for. At 9.30 pm it was announced that "with the exception of five or six, all the passengers were known to have survived". At 11.30 pm, "saved 175 passengers and 216 crew. Regret third engineer Lurgan missing". Finally, a revised, more detailed list was posted, stating that there were still thirty-three people missing. In fact, the final number of lives lost was to be forty-four.

Two of the rescue ships arrived at the deep water quay in Queenstown at about 6.30 pm, having picked up survivors from eleven lifeboats. All of them were in a pitiable and bedraggled state, shivering from cold and shock. Several ladies had not yet risen from their berths when the torpedo struck and were still clad in their nightdresses, which clung to their bodies, soaked as they were with salt water. Some of the people had injuries, mainly to the head and face, where they had been struck by anything that would float being flung into the sea by others still on deck. Motor cars stood by to take them to a hotel nearby where doctors and Red Cross nurses waited to attend to them.

Four Americans were landed safely and hurried to send telegrams to friends in London. They were Doctor James Rowley from Chicago and a troupe of variety artists known as "The Flying Martens", Charles McTamney, Claude McRoodie from Schenectady, New York, and John Olschewski of Trenton, New Jersey, who had recently completed a London engagement. A Mr Tattersall from Ashton-under-Lyne tried to comfort his two little daughters who were weeping in despair for their mother, who had not been rescued. One of them, nine-year-old Gladys, had a deep cut over her left eye, where she had been hit by a piece of wreckage. She said that she had fallen into the sea and floated for a short while before sinking, but then she came up again and hit her face on a floating oar, which she grabbed and held onto until she was pulled into the lifeboat. The following day, five miles away from the spot where the liner had gone down, the patrol steamer *Adventuress* came across three *Arabic* lifeboats. In one was the body of a woman. She was wearing a gold ring on her right hand and was thought to be Mrs Tattersall. In another was the body of a man, one of the deck stewards. He was wearing an Ingersoll watch, which had stopped at 9.45.

White Star Line made another official statement, saying that the following should be deleted from the list of survivors: Mrs M. Eaton, W.J. Randall, Mrs Florence Davey, George Lyons and John Dighton. But two more passengers had been saved, Miss Ellen Melia and Monsieur Le Leilleur. Subject to confirmation, it seemed that this left only three people still missing. However, this was proved to have been inaccurate over a month later. On 24 September *The Times* reported, "A Clonakilty message says that the bodies of three men were washed ashore at Rosscarbery, the body of a woman at Long Strand, near Castle Freke, and another woman's body at Galley Head. The body of one man had been identified from papers as that of Doctor Edmond F. Woods of Janesville, Wisconsin, USA. A lifebelt round the body bore the name 'Arabic'. The bodies were in a much decomposed condition".

The American press was scathing in its criticism of what it considered to be the empty talk in which the President had dealt with the *Lusitania* affair and hoped that the *Arabic* sinking would result in America showing its teeth more fiercely. The *Chicago Herald* recalled that Wilson's last note to the Germans had warned that any repetition of the *Lusitania* horror would be regarded as "an unfriendly act". The *Herald* headline was limited to one word, "Well?" The *Cincinnati Commercial Tribune* told the President that "the situation can no longer be met with strong and virile phrases", but the highly critical *Worcester Telegram* was not hopeful that Wilson would translate his words into resolute action. "More beautiful phrases will flow from Washington – that's all. The American government, for some time past, has been chiefly a talking machine", it scoffed, "with a fondness for spending billions, getting little therefrom". From America's Deep South, the *Charleston News and Chronicle* pointed an accusing finger straight at the Kaiser. "The torpedoing of the *Arabic* proves that Germany either is convinced that this country will not defend its honour and its rights, or that she does not care whether we break with her or not". Even the normally placid and non-belligerent *St. Louis Globe Democrat* hoped that Wilson would "prove equal to the emergency".

In New York it fell to the *Tribune* to be the only morning daily to demand a diplomatic break with Germany. "Without delay", it fumed, "without further protest or any diplomatic exchange whatsoever, the German Ambassador at Washington should receive his passport and the American Ambassador in Berlin should be recalled. The time has come to act. To talk further is to encourage, not avoid, murder".

And ex-President Theodore Roosevelt thundered: "Germany will care nothing for the severance of diplomatic relations. The time for words on the part of this nation has long passed and it is inconceivable to Americans who claim to be the inheritors of the traditions of Washington and Lincoln that our Government's representatives shall not see that the time for deeds has come". *Reuter*, New York, 22 August 1915.

Predictably, the German-American newspapers, which had been ranting at Wilson for trying to deprive Germany of her "most valuable weapon", did not follow the same line of clamour, although the *Staatszeitung* admitted that "the atmosphere is charged with electric sparks which may be expected at any moment to ignite powder magazines".

For the moment, however, Wilson received all this comment in silence, waiting to assess public opinion after the immediate furore had settled and for Germany to be given the chance to state her justification for the attack on the *Arabic*. Schneider's apologia was that he had mistaken the alteration of course by the liner, which was zig-zagging, for an intention to ram his boat, and he had loosed off a torpedo in self-defence. Few on the Allied side believed this flimsy excuse.

From Copenhagen, the Berlin correspondent of the *New York World*, Karl von Wiegand, cabled to say that the U-boat campaign would be continued ruthlessly and that the German attitude was that Americans should travel under their own flag for protection. And in London US Ambassador Walter Page found himself acutely embarrassed to walk past news-vendors crying, "We are too proud to fight – Woodrow Wilson".

On balance it was plain that, notwithstanding all the media rhetoric, and despite Wilson's apparently lukewarm attitude, another tooth in the cog that was grinding the USA inexorably towards war had been engaged. However, there were still several more teeth to grind before she finally reached the brink.

THE MULE SHIPS

Humans were not the only species to lose their lives in the carnage of the First World War. Horses and mules died too, in their thousands, and both sides could never get enough of them. For the British one major source of supply of mule-muscle was the USA and a constant stream of ships carrying animals destined to haul guns and limbers through the muddy moonscape of shell-blasted Flanders ploughed across the Atlantic from New Orleans and Newport News. On the voyage they were in the care of men known as muleteers. Most of these men were of the hobo type, for whom a trip across the ocean, at $15 wages all found, even with their eyes and nostrils stinging on the dung and urine-drenched deck of a giant floating stable, made a welcome change from riding as half-starved vagrants in railroad box-cars to nowhere in particular around the wide expanses of America. That said, some muleteers were from well-to-do families, even the bored sons of millionaires, who were actually prepared to pay for the excitement of such an adventure. One or two were simply men who, being temporarily short of funds, signed on to raise a few dollars to tide them over until they could find something better.

At 7 o'clock on the morning of Tuesday 29 June 1915 the Belgian steam trawler *President Stevens* sighted some men in lifeboats off Trevose Head on the Cornish coast. She stopped, took the men on board and later transferred them to a British destroyer for landing at Avonmouth, from where ten of them were taken to the Bristol Infirmary for treatment. They had been drifting all night after their ship, the mule carrier *Armenian* of the Leyland Line, had been torpedoed and sunk by the German submarine *U-38*. Twenty-nine of their shipmates, nearly all coloured American citizens, had been either killed by shell-fire or drowned. *The Times* of Saturday 3 July listed the names of seven foremen muleteers who were missing. All were Americans.

J.M. Munroe, of New Orleans,
E. Williamson, address unknown,
S.R. Sutton, of Catersville, Virginia,
B.N. Cranberry of 4115, Washington Street, Montgomery, Alabama,
Harry Stone, of New York State,
Carpenter Brown, of Harrisburg, Pennsylvania,
and the Chief Foreman, R.H. Brooks, a naturalized American from London, England.

The 8,900-ton *Armenian* had been bound for Avonmouth from Newport News, Virginia, with a cargo of 1,414 mules. At the time of her sinking she had been the largest ship to go down at the hands of the Germans, with the exception of the *Lusitania*. It was 6.40 pm by the chartroom clock when *Armenian*'s lookout sang out that there was a submarine about four miles away and was signalling them to stop. But the mule ship's master, Captain Trickery, had no such intention and continued on course. At this two shells burst in the sea across his bows. Trickery still did not stop. He had decided that he would run for it and rang down for Full Speed Ahead. The *Armenian*'s boats had already been swung out, which was standard practice for ships passing through U-boat Alley and he ordered his crew to get into them, or to stand by in case of emergency.

But the mule-ship did not possess the turn of speed necessary to carry her to safety and soon shells began to crash into her. Flying shrapnel from the submarine's first few shells killed several of the crew and cut the falls of some of the lifeboats as they swung from their davits, hurling their occupants into the sea. The *Armenian* pounded on, with its mules braying and stamping in panic at the noise of the shell-fire. It was a desperate chase, but the submarine was gaining on them every minute, and then the steering gear was knocked out by a shell, the Marconi room was wrecked by another and two more exploded in the stokehold and engine-room. Rapidly, the *Armenian* lost steam and almost came to a stop. By that time she was on fire in three places and there were a dozen men lying on her deck. The chase had lasted for an hour, but now Trickery had no option but to surrender. It was 7.40 pm.

Trickery said later that the German commander showed them every civility. He ordered him to clear his ship before putting two torpedoes into her, even taking on board the submarine the *Armenian*'s Puerto Rican doctor and three seamen. It was seven minutes past eight when her stove-pipe apricot funnel with its black boot-top disappeared beneath the waves and 1,414 terror-stricken animals went with her to the bottom.

There followed the usual protests in the American press in general, but the Government and one newspaper in particular, the *New York World*, quickly realized that in this case it was clear that the Germans had "some sort of ethical excuse".

The consignment of mules had been for the benefit of the British Army. Their presence was enough to make the *Armenian* as much of a legitimate target as if they had been British soldiers. And Trickery had tried to escape when summoned to stop, which gave the Germans even more reason to claim justification for the sinking, as Berlin was quick to announce. This time the Germans had acted perfectly legally. They had cleared the ship and done all they could to put the crew in a place of safety before sinking her. America had no alternative but to accept the position with good grace. A few days later the incident was officially classified as a closed file.

HMS *Baralong* was a Q-ship, an ex-Ellerman Line 4,000 ton tramp freighter, built on Tyneside by Armstrong & Whitworth in 1901. She had been taken into war service by the Royal Navy, armed with three cleverly concealed 12-pounder guns and assigned to decoy work under Admiral Lewis Bayly based on Queenstown. Her captain was thirty-one-year-old Lieutenant-Commander Godfrey Herbert, a maverick character with a pugnacious streak.

In April 1915 the harmless-looking *Baralong* sailed from Portsmouth to roam the Channel and Western Approaches in search of U-boats to lure within point-blank range of her hidden guns. Herbert soon found that some of his crew (which was composed of a mixture of merchant seamen, Royal Navy officers and ratings and Royal Marines) were not responding to his free and easy style of discipline in the way that he desired. Some, in fact, had swum ashore against orders and caused drunken mahem in Queenstown. In Dartmouth, where Herbert had granted some shore leave, there was more drunken brawling resulting in one of the normally sedate town's public houses being completely wrecked. Three stokers had deserted altogether, while another was languishing in Falmouth prison.

All that summer they trudged around the south-western waters of the British Isles, where the U-boats were gorging themselves on a veritable feast of merchant shipping. They heard the explosions, saw the blazing wrecks of the submarines' victims, the towering plumes of smoke on the horizon that indicated yet another sinking and the assorted debris of the massacre floating by their sides, but they were never in time to do much to help. And they saw not a single U-boat. Thousands of miles steamed, all for nothing. Their one brief taste of excitement had been when they had pounded flat out to help the *Lusitania* as fast as their sweating stokers could make them go. But that had been three months before. They were bored, frustrated and itching for a fight.

At last, at 9.15 am on 19 August, as *Baralong* patrolled off the Scillies, her wireless hummed and pipped into life. An SOS call! From a 16,000-ton passenger liner – the *Arabic*. Off the coast of southern Ireland she had encountered a torpedoed British ship, the *Dunsley*, in a sinking condition. A few minutes later the *Baralong*'s wireless chattered again. *Arabic* herself had now caught a torpedo! They were only twenty-fives miles, or two hours, away. Again the sweat poured from the Q-ship's stokers as they worked her up to her full twelve knots and she ploughed her way across the calm water towards the stricken ships. Herbert had his gun crews closed up, ready for action, behind their dummy screens (one gun was disguised as a sheep-pen and the other two were behind false lifebelt lockers) and a hidden squad of a dozen Royal Marine Light Infantrymen under 7762 Corporal Frederick Collins clutched .303 rifles. But when they reached the fateful spot they found nothing. No wreckage, no lifeboats, no bodies. Nothing.

Herbert was beside himself with rage. "We're bloody well too late again!" he stormed. What he did not know was that Batchelor, the *Arabic*'s wireless operator, no doubt in panic, had transmitted the wrong position with the result that the would-be rescuers were searching thirty miles away from the Old Head of Kinsale. Dejected, Herbert turned about and headed for the Bristol Channel. Halfway through the afternoon the wireless crackled into life yet again. Another SOS! That made three that day. This time it came from a ship less than twenty miles away: "Am being chased by enemy submarine!"

At that moment *Baralong*'s forward lookout yelled that he could see smoke ahead. Herbert swung his binoculars. He could see the ship himself. He rang down for Full Speed Ahead and sent his gun crews and Marines back to Action Stations. She was the *Nicosian*, a work-worn 6,250-ton black-painted Leyland Line freighter, with a tall skinny funnel, on her regular run from New Orleans to Liverpool with a cargo of mules for the British Army.

Meanwhile, the *Baralong*'s gun crews prepared for action. After the long summer's idle cruising in fruitless search of U-boats, all the boredom and all the frustration, they were seething. Angry tight-lipped mutters rumbled among the tensed-up men. They had seen the corpses from the *Lusitania* laid out in lines on the jetty at Queenstown and they were bent on revenge. And for the *Arabic*. And all the rest.

Now only a couple of miles away, Herbert could see a low grey shape in the water astern of the *Nicosian*, like a crocodile stalking a drinking wildebeest. It was *U-27*, commanded by Korvettenkapitän Bernard Wegener. The submarine fired a shot at the mule-ship's wireless aeriels to silence it and hoisted a string of signal flags ordering her to stop. It was a perfect aim and the wires came looping down to drape themselves over the starboard rail. The German fired again, to prove that he meant business. This time the shell exploded harmlessly among the freighter's upperworks. At this the *Nicosian*'s master, Captain Charles Manning, obedi-ently rang down to Stop Engines and ordered his lifeboats to be swung out. The mules, 750 of them, wide-eyed and stricken with terror at the sound of gunfire, brayed and stamped their hooves frantically.

Herbert hoisted the Stars and Stripes and lowered boards over the sides of the Q-ship which bore the words, in large letters, ULYSSES S. GRANT. Herbert had seen Wegener in his conning-tower, inspecting the *Baralong* through his binoculars, obviously checking his identity. The US flag and name boards seemed to have reassured the German and the U-boat slid slowly out of sight down the portside of the *Nicosian*, still firing spasmodically at her help-less target.

Herbert now brought the *Baralong* on a parallel course, but on the other side of the freighter, so that all three vessels were now abreast, facing in the same direction. "Clear away guns!" he bellowed, and down went the Stars and Stripes, up jerked the White Ensign, in came the portside name board (the other one stayed down, because the galley boy who had been assigned to haul it in had run below in fright, but it was now out of sight of the U-boat), down clanged the dummy lifebelt lockers to expose the 12-pounders and Collins' Royal Marines levelled their rifles. The harmless tramp had become a spiteful man o'war.

Herbert picked up his megaphone. "Marines concentrate fire on forward gun. Guns' crews aim at conning-tower and hull. Range 600 yards." It can only have been a minute or so, but it seemed like an age to the tensed-up gunners before the submarine's bows peeped out from behind the mule-ship. Then her forward gun came into view. At that there erupted a sudden rattling volley as the Marines opened fire and a vicious torrent of .303 bullets splattered from the U-boat's casing. The German gun-layer jerked backwards like a marionette on its strings, dead, into the sea. The others around the gun ran to huddle for shelter behind the conning-tower, but that too came under fire almost immediately from the British 12-pounders. A barrage of shells plastered the U-boat. One hit the conning-tower, blowing two men high into the air, and another struck the perfect blow with which to kill a submarine – midships, just below the waterline. The doomed U-27 heeled over and there was an internal explosion which seemed to lift her fully clear of the water. "Cease firing!" Herbert yelled, but his crew were in no mood to obey such an order, even though the German sailors were appearing on the upper casing, stripping themselves naked and jumping in the water to swim for their lives. The 12-pounder shells continued to pummel the submarine until she emitted an enormous hiss of compressed air from her tanks and vanished beneath the surface in a boiling mass of bubbles, leaving only a few plumes of smoke hanging over the spot where she had been.

The *Nicosian*'s crew, who sat in their lifeboats watching the onslaught with open mouths, now broke into raucous cheering as they rowed toward the *Baralong*, where tots of Navy rum awaited them. A beaming Herbert took Captain Manning into the saloon for a drink, but emerged shortly to give urgent orders for the Marines to open fire again. The wallowing *Nicosian*, although damaged by a couple of shell-holes near the waterline, was not sinking, being kept afloat by the baulks of Canadian spruce timber packed tight in her holds. Several of the Germans had swum towards her, in understandable preference to the *Baralong*, and were clambering up her ladders and dangling lifeboat ropes. It was on these men that Herbert directed the Marines to fire. He explained to the Admiralty later that he had been told by Manning that there were some rifles in the mule-ship's chartroom and he was concerned in case they should find them. Fearing this, and also the possibility that the Germans might try to scuttle her, together with her valuable cargo, he had ordered them to be shot. Nevertheless, six of the U-boat's crew did manage to dodge the hail of bullets and reached the *Nicosian*'s deck.

Herbert placed the *Baralong* alongside the freighter and ordered a party of Marines, under Corporal Collins, on board to flush these men out. This was done with prompt efficiency, with the result that there was then not a single survivor from the doomed *U-27*. Little more may have ever been heard of the incident but for the outpourings of the American contingent in the mule-ship's crew.

As the *Baralong* towed them laboriously towards Avonmouth, the muleteers were forced to spend a nauseating night with shovels and brooms and buckets of disinfectant cleaning up the stinking mess. Arriving back on board their own ship, they had found that twenty-four mules were dead, lying in a pungent swamp of urine, blood, guts and dung. Driven frantic by the gunfire, the frenzied animals had reared and kicked up in their stalls so violently that some had battered themselves to death against the bulkheads. Several more were so badly injured that the mule-ship's vet, William Banks, ordered them to be shot.

Temporarily repaired in Avonmouth, the *Nicosian* eventually arrived in Liverpool, where three American crew-members, New Yorker Henry Christie, Kentuckian steward Herbert Young and Louisianan Bill Roberts, all hurried ashore to give signed statements to the US Consul, alleging that they had seen the German submariners killed in cold blood. The vet Banks was due to sail back to the States aboard the White Star liner *Lapland*. While awaiting her sailing date, he wrote to a relative in Massachusetts describing the U-boat's sinking by a ship wearing the US flag and the shooting of the unarmed Germans. When the *Lapland* arrived in America, the story had already been scooped by the *New York Times* and Banks found himself surrounded by excited reporters on the dockside.

In the USA President Woodrow Wilson had blown hot and cold on the question of entry into the War. US trade with Germany had been reduced to practically nil owing to the solid blockade imposed by the Royal Navy, which was hindering American industry. On the other hand, the Germans had refused to moderate their unrestricted U-boat warfare policy, which had cost American ships and American lives. To complicate matters further, 25% of all the immigrants who had poured into his country in recent years were of German extraction, plus a substantial proportion of vehemently anti-British Irish and anti-Tsarist Jewish-Americans. Wilson had been hobbled to this knife-edged dilemma by his political coat-tails, but, with the sinking of the *Lusitania*, it had looked as if at last America was edging towards joining the conflict on the side of Great Britain and her Allies. Now the *Baralong* affair looked set to put a stifling damper on such a move, particularly when the *Nicosian* berthed again at New Orleans' Ninth Street Docks for another load of mules and some of the American muleteers in her crew came ashore to spin colourful versions of what had happened in the dockside bars and honky-tonks, thus fanning into fresh life what had been the dying flames of anti-British sentiment.

One of these men was a university-educated Irish-American named Jim Curran, a travelling salesman who had found himself financially embarrassed in Fort Worth, Texas. He had used his persuasive skills to land a job taking a consignment of mules down to New Orleans for shipment to Britain. Having conducted them all to the docks safely, he managed to get himself signed on as a muleteer foreman for a voyage to Liverpool, onboard a stinking bucket of a ship called the *Nicosian*.

Now back in New Orleans after the brush with Wegener and the *U-27*, Curran and five of his fellow muleteers from the *Nicosian* were urged by the German Assistant Consul in New Orleans, Dr. Paul Roh, to swear affidavits describing their experiences. Here, Roh quickly realized, was a source of highly valuable propaganda. He passed the stories to the *New York World* and then reported back to Berlin. In double-quick time they had been sent to no fewer than 1,000 newspapers around the world. Meantime, the British people knew nothing at all about the *Baralong* controversy until reports of the affidavits were received in London via the US Ambassador. The British Government issued a White Paper on 4 January 1916. A full report appeared the following day in *The Times*:

The memorandum from the German Government sets forth that six citizens of the United States had been examined on October 5 and 8 1915 before the public notaries Mr E. Ansley of Hancock, Mississippi, and Mr Charles Denechaud of Orleans, Louisiana, and made sworn depositions concerning the murder of the crew of a German submarine by the commander of the British auxiliary cruiser *Baralong*. The names of these witnesses are:

J.M. Garrett, 22, of Kiln, Hancock, Mississippi.
Charles D. Hightower, 22, of Crystal City, Texas.
Bud Emerson Palen, 27, of Detroit, Michigan.
Edward Clark, 21, of Detroit, Michigan.
R.H. Cosby, 21, of Crystal City, Texas.
James J. Curran, 32, of Chicago, Illinois.

In August 1915 the British steamer *Nicosian* was on her way from New Orleans to Avonmouth, carrying mules for war purposes, thus being laden with contraband. The witnesses were shipped as muleteers and superintendents. On 19 August, about 70 nautical mile south of Queenstown (Ireland), the steamer was stopped by a German submarine and fired on after the whole crew, including the witnesses, had first left the ship in the lifeboats. When the witnesses were outside the line of fire from the submarine, a steamer which had already been noticed by witnesses Garret, Hightower, Clark and Curran when still on board the *Nicosian*, approached the spot. It afterwards transpired to be the British steamer *Baralong*. All the witnesses noticed clearly that she was flying the American flag at her stern and was showing signal flags which to the sea-faring members of the crew of the *Nicosian* meant that she was willing to assist in saving life if necessary.

While the submarine was firing on the port side of the *Nicosian*, the steamer came up behind the latter and steamed past her. When she was a short distance ahead of the *Nicosian*'s bow she opened fire on the submarine, at first with small arms and immediately afterwards with cannon, which up to that time had been hidden by screens. The witness Curran also deposed that the American flag flown by the unknown ship was only lowered after the rifle fire.

As the submarine began to sink, the commander and crew sprang overboard. Some of them, (the number given by the witnesses Garrett and Curran as five) succeeded in getting on board the *Nicosian* while the remainder seized the lifeboat ropes. The men clinging to the ropes were killed partly by gunfire from the *Baralong* and partly by rifle fire from the crew while the witnesses were boarding the *Baralong* from the lifeboats or were already on board her. The witness Curran also testifies that the commander of the unknown ship ordered his men to line up against the rail and to shoot at the helpless German seamen in the water. Next, the commander of the *Baralong* steamed alongside the *Nicosian* and made fast to her, and then ordered some of his men to board her to search for the German sailors who had taken refuge there. The witnesses Palen and Curran testify regarding this incident that the commander gave the definite order to 'take no prisoners'. Four German sailors were found in the *Nicosian*'s engine-room and screw tunnel and were killed.

The submarine's commander jumped into the sea from the bows of the *Nicosian*. The English seamen immediately fired on him, although he raised his hands in a manner of surrender. Eventually, he was killed by a shot in the neck. Later that afternoon Curran saw the bodies of the four thrown overboard.

The memorandum went on to name the British captain as 'William McBride', an alias that Herbert had taken to using, and the full wordings of the witnesses' affidavits were annexed, together with that of another American, one Larrimore Holland, who claimed (falsely as records prove*) to have actually been serving in the Royal Navy as a stoker on board the *Baralong*. It closed by stating that the German Government expected the British to bring to trial

---

* Holland had run away from home in Chattanooga, Tennessee, and signed on a New Orleans mule-ship sailing for Liverpool. There he enlisted in the Royal Navy as a stoker under the false name of Tom Hicks and was sent to Portsmouth for training. When his real name was discovered, and that he was American rather than Canadian, he was discharged. He served for four months and never went to sea in any Royal Navy ship.

and punish those responsible for the murders, and was signed: Berlin, Nov. 28, 1915.

British Foreign Secretary Sir Edward Grey penned a scornful reply, dated 14 December and sent via the American Ambassador in London, Walter Hines. It appeared in *The Times* alongside the German protest. His Majesty's Government took great satisfaction, Grey stated sarcastically, in noting that the German Government now expressed anxiety that the principles of civilized warfare should be vindicated and that due punishment be meted out to those who deliberately disregarded them.

The case against the *Baralong*, he went on, was negligible compared to those many which stand against Germany. By way of example, he proceeded to outline three naval incidents which all took place within the same forty-eight hours in which the *Baralong* sank the *U-27*, namely the sinking of the *Arabic*, an attack on a stranded and helpless British submarine on the coast of neutral Denmark and the shooting in the water of the survivors from the crew of the British merchant steamer *Ruel*.

It was suggested that an impartial Court of Investigation be set up, composed of US Navy officers, to administer justice in such cases. Great Britain would willingly comply with the findings of such a Court.

. He closed by recording that the number of German sailors rescued from drowning by British seamen during the war amounted to 1,150, often in difficult and risky circumstances. "The German Navy," he concluded acidly, "can show no such record, perhaps through want of opportunity."

Grey's reference to the other incidents was incisive. 19, 20 and 21 August 1915 had seen disastrous losses of British shipping to the U-boat menace. On the 19th alone, no fewer than nine ships had been sunk, ranging from the tiny 182-ton coaster *Martha Edmonds**, bound for Seville from Rouen with an innocent cargo of silver-sand, up to the *Arabic* herself. Fifty-two thousand tons had been lost to Great Britain in a single day. And on that same day a nearly-new Royal Navy submarine, the 791-ton *E-13*, had become stranded on a sand bar at Saltholm, on the coast of Denmark. Helpless and well within the territorial waters, indeed on the beach, of a neutral country, she was then shelled by German destroyers. Two days later had occurred the *Ruel** incident. The 4,000-ton freighter had been heading for Barry with a light general cargo from

Malta when, forty-five miles south-west of Bishop Rock, she had been stopped by a U-boat, then sunk by shell-fire. At the same time, it was alleged, her crew had been fired on while struggling in the water and one of them was killed.

In all, it was a good reply from the Foreign Secretary, but the suggestion that the US Navy should be the arbiter of such disputes fell on stony ground. *Reuters* reported from Washington, dateline 5 January 1916: "The US Government, adhering to the policy of non-intervention in the controversies of belligerents, will not permit American naval officers to investigate the *Baralong* case under Sir Edward Grey's suggestion".

The USA was back on the fence.

* Research reveals that both these ships, besides at least four others all on the same day, had been victims of Kapitänleutnant Max Valentiner in *U-38*, of whom much more later.

3

E-13

When Danes sailed up the Humber,
Nigh a thousand years ago,
Their prows in British hearts struck terror keen,
And now, their good ship Vidar
Brings her freight of glorious dead,
Our heroes of the fated E-13.

In neutral waters stranded!
Watched by harmless fisher-folk
She helpless lay: our hapless submarine.
And then the pirates flocked around
And worked their wicked will
Upon the fenceless crew of E-13.

Our heroes faced unflinchingly –
As Britons ever shall –
As Britons' way has through the ages been,
Those German guns: they crossed their arms;
They smiled – like statues stood
Our gallant dead of Glorious E-13.

Extract from a poem by 'Wandering Tyke' –
courtesy of the *Hull Daily Mail*.

In the early days of the First World War the Royal Navy's operations in the Baltic were based on two points of strategy. First, the mere presence of British submarines in the vicinity of Kiel, hitherto thought by the Germans to be as safe as a backyard, was highly damaging to the confidence of enemy top brass, and effectively it tied down a disproportionate number of units of the German Navy in a relative backwater. In fact it worried the *Admiralstab* sufficiently to withdraw two complete squadrons of heavy ships to Swinemünde [now Swinoujscie in Poland], which offered better protection from a sea-borne attack and at the same time effectively enabled them to reinforce their presence on the Eastern Front. Second, the ships carrying vital imports of high-grade Swedish iron ore to Germany were placed under threat. The main advantage to the British was that there was a friendly Russian base at Libau [now Liepaja, in Lithuania], although to counter that there was the difficult passage into the Baltic via the Kattegat, with its minefields, heavy surveillance by German patrol craft, and its perilous shallow water. Sweden, anxious to protect her neutrality, had offered an international fairway through her territorial waters, skirting Falsterbro, to serve as a better entrance to and exit from the Baltic. The British Admiralty remained sceptical about the usefulness of such a facility and the ability of the Swedes to guarantee safe conduct to international shipping. The official view was that "it is building on slender chances to expect Germany to respect territorial waters". It proved to be a very accurate prognosis of events.

As early as October 1914 two British submarines, *E-1* and *E-9*, sailed from Gorleston for Libau. They arrived to find the Russians in the process of demolishing the base facilities in expectation that the place would soon be overrun by the advancing Germans. This called for a hasty revision of plan. Fortunately for them, the Russians had established a new submarine base further east at Lapvik on the Gulf of Finland, and it was there that the two boats were able to rest up and carry out repairs. The captain of *E-9*, Lieutenant-Commander Max Horton, a future Admiral who was to find fame in the Second World War, caused considerable consternation by taking his boat to sea under the winter ice which bound Lapvik. Then he made for the Kieler Bucht where he severely shook up the German destroyer *S-120*, much to the alarm of the port's defenders. But the main success of the two British boats came after the spring thaw, when they were better able to set about the ore-carrying ships.

In the light of such success, four more E-class boats, *E-8, E-13, E-18* and *E-19*, ran the gauntlet of the Kattegat to reinforce the operations in the Baltic, while some old C-class boats, *C-26*, *C-27*, *C-32* and *C-35*, sailed to Archangel, where they were to be stripped down and transported by rail and canal barge to Lapvik. The Russians had done well to dismantle their Libau base, because the German had now leapfrogged the place in their advance and their ships had even begun shelling Windau (now Ventspils) at the entrance to the Gulf of Riga at the beginning of July. *E-8* was the first to arrive on 8 August 1915, with *E-13*, commanded by the thirty-one-year-old son of a Liverpool solicitor, Lieutenant-Commander Geoffrey Layton, due to follow a few days later.

E-13 had been built and launched at Chatham Dockyard on 22 September 1914, literally only a cable's length from the very spot where Nelson's *Victory* herself had first felt the water under her keel 149 years before. Thus her birth, and those of her many sisters, was nicely timed to coincide with the onset of the first major War in which their species was used as an instrument of conflict. Fifty-six E-class boats were built and became the British standard First World War design. Many were to distinguish themselves by their service, mainly in the Dardanelles and the Baltic itself. But *E-13* met with disaster as she was making her stealthy way through the treacherous narrows between Malmö and Copenhagen in the early hours of the morning of Thursday 19 August on her way to join *E-8* at Lapvik. It was one of the last places on the planet where a submarine commander would choose to have his compass fail. But that is what happened to Layton. In such a closely watched stretch of water, he had no alternative but to stay dived. Underwater navigation became impossible and *E-13* stumbled blindly among the sand-banks. Eventually she grounded on the notorious mud-flats on the south-eastern edge of Saltholm, a low, flat, featureless one-mile-long sandy island which lay in the narrow Øre Sund between Danish Copenhagen and Swedish Malmö. Saltholm was within the territory of neutral Denmark. Large parts of it were frequently submerged by high tides, and it was almost uninhabited, except for a couple of small farms on its northern side and a prolific population of birdlife and hares. In summer it was a favourite haunt for Copenhagen's picnickers and sun-worshippers, who nicknamed it the Sahara Desert. *E-13* had floundered on a neutral shore. Layton tried everything he knew to get her to float off, but to no avail. Some Danish fishermen were the first to discover her presence just after dawn. She was lying in about ten

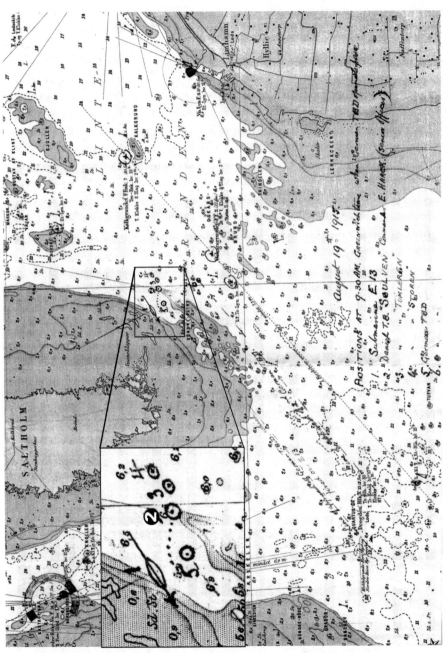

Chart of the incident off Saltholm. The dotted line from 2 shows the course of *Søulven* when she placed herself between *E-13* and the German destroyers.

feet of water, slightly listing, with her deck just visible. At 5 am the Danish torpedo-boat *Narhvalen* arrived on the scene and reminded Layton that under International Law he had twenty-four hours to refloat his boat or be interned. At about 5.20 am the German torpedo-boat destroyer *G-132*, of the German Sound Patrol, appeared and took up station very close to the beached submarine. Her captain, Oberleutnant zur See Graf von Montgelas, appeared on his bridge and called cheerfully to Layton, "Look pleasant and smile please! I'm going to take your photograph!" It was only when two more Danish torpedo boats arrived that the German ship withdrew from Danish territorial waters and steamed away in the direction of the Drogden Light, where she joined another German destroyer whose name is not recorded.

The two Danish torpedo boats, *Søulven* and *Støren*, were now joined by a third, the *Tumleren*, and all three anchored near to *E-13* on her port quarter. It was clearly their intention to ensure that proper protection was given to the helpless boat, and to effect the consequential internment if she did not float free within the twenty-four hours of grace allowed. Meantime, von Montgelas had reported the situation by wireless to his base and had been ordered by Rear Admiral Mischke, commanding the Baltic Coast Defence Division, to destroy it.

At about eleven o'clock the two German destroyers approached from the direction of Kiel. One of them hoisted a string of flags and came to a stop 400 yards away on the beam. Layton ordered a signalman to produce the signal-book so that the message could be understood, but before the sailor had time to do this the German fired a torpedo which exploded in the sandy bottom close to the keel of the submarine. Then she opened up with her deck guns and fired about twenty-five shells in the course of a couple of minutes. Soon the submarine was on fire fore and aft, and quite unable to defend herself owing to the fact that she was keeled over and aground.

Layton ordered his crew to abandon ship and they tumbled out of the hatch to leap into the shallow water and begin to swim and wade ashore. As they did so the air was filled with the crackle of small arms fire and the bursting of shrapnel. A deluge of bullets and shells splattered into the water around them. Several of them fell. The commander of the Danish flotilla, Kommander Haack, quickly placed *Søulven* into a position between *E-13* and the Germans to block their fire and at the same time lowered his boats to come to the rescue of the British sailors in the water. The Germans steamed away, having been obliged to cease fire.

Several British submariners had fallen under the German fire and *Overmatros* [Petty Officer] A.F. Olsen, No. 146, Danish Navy, saw that one of them, Petty Officer Lincoln, was unconscious on the shallow bottom and dived repeatedly to rescue him. Lincoln and another sailor named Watson, who was severely wounded, were detained in the naval hospital, but recovered fully in the course of time. Later, both Haack and Olsen were to be decorated with the Conspicuous Gallantry Medal and the Albert Medal respectively for the parts they played in the rescue. Olsen's award came after a letter of commendation arrived at the Foreign Office from none other than Graham Greene, later the famous author.

The early edition Danish evening papers reported that two British sailors had been wounded, but during the night it became known that, in fact, fourteen men had been killed and one was missing. The bodies of the dead men were taken by torpedo boat to the Danish Naval Hospital and thence to a temporary mortuary in the dockyard gymnasium later that evening. They were Chief Stoker B. Pink, Petty Officer W. Warren, Engine Room Artificer H. Staples, Leading Stoker W. Thomas, Telegraphist E. Holt, Signalman H. Goulden, Able Seamen H. Joynor, R. Smart and A. Payne, and Stokers A. Long, Yearsley, W. Wilcox, F. Wilson, and T. Greenwood. The missing man was Leading Seaman H. Pedder.

The Danes were furious that their neutrality had been violated. Next day the Copenhagen daily newspaper *Politiken*, which normally reflected the views of the Danish Government, accused the Germans of carrying out the attack in such circumstances that they could not have been in the slightest doubt as to the facts. It had not been in any kind of pursuit that *E-13* had been destroyed but while she was lying damaged on neutral territory. Reporters interviewing an old fisherman from Dragør who had witnessed the attack quoted him as saying that he had never seen bravery to equal that shown by the crew of the *E-13*. Passing close to the submarine early that morning, on their way to the fishing grounds nearby, he and his companions had offered to take the British sailors on board their boats. There was ample room for this and they could easily have brought them all ashore. But the invitation was politely declined. Some hours later the Danes observed the submariners assembled on the upper deck of the stranded vessel. Some of them were actually playing cards and chess, while the rest were relaxing, chatting and smoking in the warm sunshine. Then the German destroyers returned and began firing on the helpless submarine. The old man said, "Suddenly we saw a torpedo rush through the water, miss, and explode in the sand bottom. We heard a short sharp word of command and the sound of a whistle. Some of the submariners had launched a small boat, but they immediately scrambled back onto the *E-13* and with their shipmates formed into line on deck, with folded arms, facing the enemy's guns, immovable as statues and looking death in the face without moving a muscle. They were brave men those English." The Germans had twice signalled the crew to get clear of the submarine, but to those signals no reply was given.

Sir Henry Lowther, British Minister in Copenhagen, arrived there on 21 August and went straightaway to the Danish Admiralty to obtain updated information with regard to what had become a delicate diplomatic situation. The Danish Government were on good terms with the British, but were naturally anxious not to provoke their powerful and belligerent neighbours, who, if the whim took them, could have easily overrun their small country. In that case, of course, the geography of the coastline would have made any passage at all by the British into the Baltic next to impossible. Kommander Jøhnke, a senior officer on the Danish Navy's eastern station, explained to Lowther that after careful consideration it had been decided to intern the British sailors, although he himself disagreed with that decision, and he hoped that the British did not think that the Danish torpedo boats had betrayed them by not answering the German fire. In fact, they had already been reprimanded by Admiral Ole Kofoed-Hansen in that regard.

Lowther hastened to explain that Layton, far from being critical of the Danish captain, was only too grateful for the protection that he had given his men by his quick reaction to the German attack. Jøhnke then informed the Minister that the question of whether or not to blow up the *E-13* where she lay had been considered very carefully. Preliminary reports had suggested that she could be raised, and this was preferable to blowing her up as the fragments of her carcass would pose a danger to shipping. Finally, despite the Danish Government's sensible desire to maintain a fragile neutrality, there was a strong and vociferous anti-German feeling

46

within the population itself. Therefore, rather than run the risk of any pro-British demonstrations in Copenhagen at the funeral of the dead sailors, which there would almost certainly be, the Danish Admiralty had offered to carry their bodies back to England for burial. Quite understandably, the incident had made the Danes nervous.

On the Sunday, at St Alban's, the British church in Copenhagen, the Reverend Kennedy addressed the congregation, many of whom were Danes. He made a "sympathetic reference" to the dead men while the organ played the Dead March. On the jetty sailors of both nationalities gathered solemnly, joined by the recovered Petty Officer Lincoln, for another service to give thanks for the lives of the survivors, who were at that time temporarily housed aboard the Danish warship *Peder Skram*.

Before the week was out they had been transferred to more permanent accommodation. The *Exchange Telegraph* cabled, "Lieutenant-Commander Layton and the survivors of the *E-13* are interned on a pretty little island adjoining the Royal Naval Dock. All round is a most magnificent panoramic view of the sea stretching towards Langelinje and Oersunds. The British sailors are quickly beginning to make the most of their forced stay in Denmark. They are allowed full liberty to do what they like and go where they please. They have already made friends with all the officers and men at the docks. The football ground is at their disposal and the first Anglo-Danish match has been arranged. The question as to their future internment has yet to be decided. It is the subject of the friendliest exchange of views between the British and Danish authorities".

One of the survivors, Petty Officer Charlie Bowden, wrote a long letter home to his wife:

Sø vaernets Kaserne,
Orlogsvarftet,
Kobenhavn.
Denmark.

Dearest Susie,

I hope you are not worrying yourself about me, as I am quite all right now. I wasn't injured at all, except for a couple of small burns from the shells and the shock from the shells bursting and the fumes. I wasn't troubled much. We left Harwich on 15 Aug. at 6 p.m. to make an attempt to get into the Baltic. We got through the Skagerrack and Cattegat alright and got into the Sound between Denmark and Sweden, diving when we saw any traffic and we only had about another seven miles to go to get to the open sea when we got stuck on a mud-bank. It was through no fault of our Captain, but on account of our compass going wrong. We grounded at 11.45 p.m. on the 18th. We lightened the boat as much as we could and went full speed astern for about four hours, but found it impossible to get afloat, so waited for daylight to find out where we were, as we didn't know whether we were in Danish or Swedish territory. At about 6 am a Danish torpedo-boat came to our assistance and took one of our officers to Copenhagen, and then a German destroyer came up and hailed us and told us to smile while they took a photo of us. We were expecting that they would attack us then in spite of us being in Neutral Waters. We could have shoved a torpedo into her easily as she made a splendid target, but our Captain wouldn't as it was against International Law. Then the German steamed away again to Kiel for orders about us. So we started our engine and began to charge our batteries, so that we could have another try to get afloat again. There were three ERAs [engine-room artificers] and three stokers on the engines and I was right aft on the Main Motor Starters. When all of a sudden shells started to explode all over the boat. We thought it was a Zeppelin dropping bombs on us until someone shouted down to us that it was the German destroyer and to stop the engine and get out of it. I broke the charge and the ERA stopped the engine in quick time. They all made for the hatch but we never expected to get clear as shells were bursting all round the boat. I went forward to try to get to the midship Torpedo Tube but all the lights had gone out as some shells hit the switchboard and all the battery connections were on fire and fusing up and all I could see was flames smoke and explosions. I expected our torpedo-heads to explode. If they had there would be nothing left of the boat and it would have shook things up ashore – luckily they didn't. Some of the shells went completely through the boat without exploding and water began to come in. She was gradually filling

48

up when something exploded and blew me along the battery boards in the engine-room and I managed to climb up through the after-hatchway.

It was wonderful that I wasn't hit. Anyhow I dived into the water fully rigged and with big sea-boots on and swam for shore. It was about 600–700 yards. It was simply raining metal and our fellows were being hit and stunned with the concussion. I was gradually losing consciousness but I didn't swallow a drop of water. I thought I was gone but one of our fellows shoved an oar at me and I got it under one arm, to float more easily. I was expecting to get hit by a piece of shrapnel or Maxim shot, but I seemed to bear a charmed life. I was losing consciousness when a boat came up and told me to stick it for a minute and they would pick me up. I thought they were Germans, but they were Danish. My mate P.O. Lincoln had just sunk and was lying on the bottom, but one of the Danish sailors dived down and brought him to the surface. They took him and another man who was wounded to hospital. Lincoln recovered but the other fellow, Able Seaman Watson, has an awful arm. They took 36 pieces of iron out of it. Somehow they all missed the bone but lumps of flesh were torn off his arm.

Our Captain, Navigator and I were taken aboard the Danish torpedo-boat *Tumleren* and they gave us neat brandy, about a pint each, stripped our clothes off and put dry ones on as we were all exhausted and couldn't stand. Then they took us on board the Danish battleship *Peder Skram* where they dosed us again and we needed it. I had about the best headache and earache it is possible to have as being down below I got full up with the fumes and gases. The Danish sailors were very kind and made much of us. Their ships' boats searched the water and found fourteen bodies. Some were wounded and the remainder stunned before they sank, as we could all swim more or less and the water wasn't cold. One body was missing so that all told there were 15 drowned and 15 saved. We slept on board the *Peder Skram* on Thursday night. On Friday afternoon they gave us a Musical Entertainment and played "Eileen Alannah", "The Passing of Ragtime", "Home Sweet Home", "Tipperary" and "In the Shade of the Old Apple Tree". We went below to their mess and they opened a few bottles of whisky and they toasted us. Then we had "Auld Lang Syne" and sang both National

Anthems. When we shoved off in a boat to go ashore, they all manned the ship and gave us three cheers and we replied the best we could. We got to the barracks at about 7.30 p.m. where we received the same treatment on a larger scale. We Petty Officers live with the Danish Petty Officers and have a sleeping-room with beds for ourselves and a bathroom. The Government have given us Danish uniforms but with no badges so we look like yachtsmen.

The English Consul and English clergyman and his wife have visited us and yesterday the English Ambassador came to see us and shook hands and congratulated us and all the Petty Officers wives and families came and remained with us all the afternoon and were singing songs and amusing us generally. They are such nice people and have invited us to their homes if we are allowed ashore which we haven't been yet. Of course, there are armed sentries but they don't interfere with us at all, but there is always one who unobtrusively comes and pals on to us if we move far from our quarters. Of course, the Danish Government have to be very careful not to run foul of the Germans for their country adjoins Germany and the Germans would have an easy thing with them. I expect we will be shifted to new quarters further inland shortly. I expect they will ask for our parole but we shall not give it as we all want to get back and get another boat if possible, for we have a nice little score to wipe out with the Germans. I only wish Keir Hardie and Ramsay Macdonald and a few of the peace cranks had been in our boat on Thursday morning. It would have done them good.

Well Suse, please give my best love to all and don't worry as I am quite alright again now and mind you write and let me know how you are all getting on. I'm always thinking of you and hope to be home again shortly. Give my love to Mother and now with all my love and kisses to you and Violet and Charlie, I'll conclude from,

Your ever affectionate husband and sweetheart,

Charlie Bowden, P.O.

Ps. Please write soon. I should be glad of some postcards, views of Milton Abbot. Twelve would do if you can manage it. Please let Lottie and Fred know I'm all right. The Germans fired two torpedoes at us but missed.

The following Wednesday, shortly after 9 am, a party of solemn Danish sailors carried out the coffins of the fourteen dead men along the jetty to place them on board the luxury steamer *Vidar*, chartered for the occasion by the Danish Admiralty from the United Steamship Company of Copenhagen. The *Vidar* was the very latest addition to the Company's fleet of passenger/cargo boats built specially for service to the English and east coast ports. She was beautifully equipped with comfortable saloons and cabins, and her holds were fitted with a modern refrigeratory plant, ensuring perfect delivery of her cargoes of butter, bacon and eggs. For this special voyage across to Hull, her main saloon had been transformed into a chapel of rest. At 10 o'clock her pale grey shape, splendid with its shiny red trimmings, and its cargo of coffins laid out in two rows under an array of flowers in the black draped saloon, slid away from the wharfside. Once into the Øre Sund, she left the island of Saltholm astern and picked up to twelve knots as she steamed up the sparkling Kattegat with her two Danish flags and a white Ensign all fluttering at half-mast in the sunshine.

On the Friday afternoon two British destroyers met the *Vidar* off Flamborough Head and escorted her to the mouth of the Humber, where she took on a pilot, Mr Moore. As they slid slowly up river to Berth 50 on Hull's Riverside Quay other vessels dipped their flags in salute. Hundreds of people were gathered on the pathway to the Quay to watch the arrival. There was a brief exchange of semaphore in the gathering dusk between the steamer and one of the destroyers, its jagged profile dark and menacing in contrast to the *Vidar*'s graceful lines. The warship then swung round in the river and dropped anchor where she was to stand guard overnight.

Lavish arrangements had been made for the arrival of the dead sailors. Next day, in bright sunshine, the coffins were brought ashore down a black-draped gangway, to be greeted by a naval guard with fixed bayonets. The cortege of thirteen flower-laden hearses, each one bearing a wreath from the much-loved Queen Mother, the Danish-born Queen Alexandra, passed from the Quay through the crowd-lined streets of Hull to the Paragon Station. So numerous were the crowds that they had to be kept from spilling into the road by lines of stern-faced soldiers. Two special coaches were waiting at the station, courtesy of the North-Eastern Railway Company, to carry the coffins to naval bases on the south coast and thence into the care of the families of the dead submariners. The fourteenth body, that of Grimsby fish merchant's son 27-year-old Engine Room Artificer Herbert Staples, had been transferred to the tug *Marple* and taken to his home across the river.

But that was not quite the end of the sad scenes in Hull. The body of the missing Leading Seaman Henry Pedder, P/227585, had been recovered. The Danish steamer *J.C.Le Cour*, carrying his coffin in a flower-filled No. 6 hold, arrived in Hull at midday on the following Monday, 30 August. It was greeted by a corps of dignitaries and escorted to the station by a guard of seventy sailors who had been brought up-river from Immingham. As the train pulled out of the station for Pedder's home in Bosham, near Chichester, his coffin was topped by a special tribute which had been arranged in the shape of a large anchor wreath, paid for by a collection among the local sailors' wives and mothers in Havelock Street, Hull, organized by Mrs Walker, Mrs Crozier and eighty-seven-year-old Grandma Holmes. Henry Pedder's grave is in the cemetery at the Royal Naval Hospital, Haslar.

No time was wasted in assessing the possibility of salving the *E-13*. She had lain helpless for little more than twenty-four hours when two engineers from Switzer's Salvage Company arrived on the scene with instructions from the Danish Admiralty to investigate and report. Their expert opinion was that she could be saved and taken into Copenhagen. The Germans, too, were not slow in expressing an interest. A Zeppelin glided overhead, presumably making observations in anticipation of the inevitable exchange of Notes with the Danes over the breach of their neutrality. And the little seaside fishing village of Dragør, home of the fishermen who had witnessed the attack, was enjoying a rare late-season bonanza. In summertime it was usually to be seen crowded with holiday-makers, but by late August its shops were getting ready to close for the season and soon it would become almost deserted except for the few people who lived there, including, of course, the fishermen. Now, people on bicycles and on foot, in motor-cars and even some in taxis, swarmed out of Copenhagen to gawp across the water at the now-famous wreck of the *E-13*. Shutters, so recently put up, were hurriedly taken down again to serve the needs of the crowds. In the tavern glasses were topped up and the weatherbeaten fishermen lit their pipes and told the tale of what they had seen to yet more visitors from the city to the background music of a merrily tinkling till.

Meanwhile, the British internees, now on parole, were given enough liberty to come and go as they pleased. But Layton's instincts were that this was no time to be taking holidays. There was a war to fight. His duty was to fight in it and as a submarine captain his services were invaluable to his country. No fewer than five of his previous commanding officers had used the word "zealous" in their periodic written comments on his Service History sheet. It was an accurate description. Only a few days after his internment he went to the Commandant of the barracks and said that he wished to withdraw his parole. There can have been no clearer intimation of his intention to escape. The Commandant informed him that, in view of that fact, he would have to be closely guarded in future. From then on there was a double guard outside the peep-holed door of his room at night. During the day, he was followed by three or four sentries wherever he went. The prospects of a successful escape seemed slight. But Layton was patient and bided his time. That the opportunity came while he was in the grip of a violent bout of influenza was but a minor hindrance. One night the guards relaxed their vigilance for a few moments and Layton slipped out of the door, carefully leaving his bed appearing as if it still contained a sleeping man. He made his way to another room, where he found a thick serge civilian suit and put it on. Luckily, there also happened to be a piece of rope handy with which he lowered himself from a window into the road. Security in the docks was tight. He managed to avoid detection and arrest, although not without a couple of breath-taking encounters with naval sentries, one of which necessitated jumping into a large pigswill bin. Luckily it was empty. As the barracks were on an island in the dockyard area, the only way to freedom was by swimming. It was a typical Danish late October night, with several degrees of frost in the air. Layton was shivering, sweating and giddy with influenza, but it was no time to be faint-hearted. Choosing a dark corner of the island, he quietly slipped into the icy black water, fully clothed. On the other side he took off his wet clothes, wrung them out as best he could, hastily dressed and made his way to the ferry for Kristiania (now Oslo) in Norway. On the ferry he posed as a porter and brazenly got himself hired to carry a passenger's heavy luggage to the station. From there he caught a train to Bergen. It was 29 October 1915 and he had been interned for sixty-nine days.

Back in Copenhagen, consternation reigned. It turned out that

Layton had not been alone in making a break for freedom. Lieutenants Eddies and Garnock had also tried, but had been apprehended by guards as they were climbing over a wall. An immediate Court of Enquiry was set up, at which no fewer than 100 witnesses appeared, but other than question all the dockyard personnel, including the guards, about the escape there was little else the Court could do but listen to a variety of theories put forward as to how Layton had done it. From Norway had already come an official denial of any knowledge that the Englishman had passed through Kristiania, or that the Norwegians were hiding him. But an interesting wire had been received from Sweden. It claimed that a reliable source had revealed that Layton had crossed on the Malmö ferry on the previous Saturday and had probably taken a steamer to Stockholm along with a large number of passengers on their way to a football match in Sweden. As it was a 'football' boat, the police searches had not been carried out as thoroughly as usual and the fugitive could have simply merged with the crowd. It was assumed that Layton was planning to try to make it to his original destination, Lapvik, so as to rejoin the Baltic submarine flotilla.

The Chairman of the Enquiry, M.V. Moltke, announced that, having examined all the witnesses, the Court was satisfied [1] that it was not likely to have been an 'inside job' and [2] that Layton could not have proceeded direct to Kristiania because of heavy police vigilance. However, it had been suggested that a suspicious character who was posing as an executive with a rubber company had something to do with the escape. He was staying at the Langelinej Pavilion, a luxury hotel in Copenhagen. It was suspected that this man had concealed the British officer in a flat in the Old Town, where he had spent the first night and had boarded the ferry to Sweden the following evening. This suggestion prompted an indignant Mr E. Hudson to visit the offices of the *Politiken* newspaper the next day to announce that he was visiting Denmark on behalf of his company, Messrs Dunlop, and that he had had absolutely nothing to do with Layton's escape.

Moltke felt that the most likely answer was that Layton had managed to conceal himself on board the 'export steamer' which had sailed for England from Copenhagen on the Saturday morning, and at that very moment "may be already treading the soil of his Fatherland". How right he was.

From Bergen, Layton had sailed for Newcastle on the steamer SS

Venus posing as an American. In the course of the two day crossing, he found himself in conversation with a fellow passenger. The man asked Layton if he really was an American, to which he replied, "Yes". "If you were not so darned sure about it," rejoined his companion, "I should say that you were a British naval officer." The *Venus* berthed in the Tyne on 1 November and the well-spoken unkempt Englishman, without a penny in his pockets, presented himself to the Port Officer. Although the Admiralty had already intercepted a Press message stating that Layton had escaped, wartime security meant that stringent questioning was necessary to verify the identify of the young man, who in all truth must have had more the appearance of a tramp. His appearance certainly did not suggest that he was a future Knight of the Bath, Vice-Admiral and Commander-in-Chief of the British Pacific Fleet in the Second World War, but it was not long before officialdom was satisfied. He had made it home, anxious to rejoin the War, although the details of his escape from Denmark may lead us to suspect that he did it with a certain amount of collusion if not outright assistance on the part of the Danes. He had, after all, been a frequent dinner guest in their junior officers' wardroom, where he was popular and entertained lavishly.

The Danish Government took immediate steps to protest to Berlin about the violation of their territory. This immediately produced the expected apology. The German Secretary of State for Foreign Affairs summoned the Danish Ambassador to express regrets for the incident and added that instructions had been issued to commanders of German vessels that neutrality should be respected. But German Wireless could not leave it at that. "If reports about the stranded submarine were true", it blustered, "the German Government will doubtless apologize to Copenhagen for a British practice as indicated by the destruction of the cruiser *Dresden* in Chilean waters, the sinking of the auxiliary cruiser *Kaiser Wilhelm der Grosse* in Portuguese waters and the sinking of the mining vessel *Albatross* by the Russians in Swedish territorial waters". It was a standard riposte, a defensive stroke straight out of the textbook for propagandists and politicians of all hues, an everyday Verbal War tactic. Whenever you find yourself on the back foot, make no attempt to defend the charges against you, simply find examples of your opponent's transgressions and hurl them at him for all your worth. It was exactly what Sir Edward

Grey was to do, of course, using the *E-13* case as ammunition, when replying to the *Baralong* accusations.

No revisionist historian is able, by definition, to let sleeping dogs lie. In 1976 the Danish historian Tage Kaarsted wrote a paper entitled *Flåden under Første Verdenskrig* (Fleet in the First World War). In it he examines the memoirs and records of Admirals Kofoed-Hansen and Jøhnke. It seems that there were vehement disagreements in high circles within the Danish Navy about the rights and wrongs of their reactions in the *E-13* incident. Admiral Kofoed-Hansen had issued orders, via Jøhnke, that the grounded submarine be protected, if necessary even by placing their boats between it and the attacking Germans. But Haack had stood by and done nothing, according to Kaarsted, until the British sailors were all in the water. Then he took up his megaphone and ordered von Montgelas to stop firing. It was not until the firing ceased that he had placed his boats in a protective manner. His defence was that he was anxious not to precipitate a war situation between Denmark and Germany, which may well have been the result if he had placed himself in a position with no alternative but to return the Germans' fire. Nevertheless, if Kaarsted's version of events is accurate, it does seem that Haack was guilty of serious insubordination. In any event, it appears that his naval career was terminated not long thereafter. And, as we know, Jøhnke had taken pains to apologize to the British Minister in Copenhagen for the shortcomings (as he saw it) of his Navy's performance.

Lowther, the British Minister, it will be remembered, had re-assured the apologetic Danes that, far from being in any way critical of their behaviour, his countrymen were grateful for the protection they had received. It was a case of a first-class diplomat exercising his art. In his confidential reports to London, however, Lowther was singing a different tune. The Foreign Office had telegraphed him instructions to try to persuade the Danes that, because *E-13* had been damaged by the illegal attack of the Germans, an extension of the twenty-four hours' grace should be granted to give the British more opportunity to float her off. Layton's brother Reginald, writing to the Admiralty from the family law firm in Liverpool, gave voice to the same opinion. However, it seems that Lowther was unsuccessful. In fact, Switzer's Salvage Co. had appeared on the scene with almost indecent haste. Major items included in the repair schedule for the wrecked boat were a new periscope, hydroplanes, electrics and navigational equipment. There was also substantial damage to her conning-tower and casing.

Lowther telegrammed the Director of Naval Intelligence on 25 August saying that, while Haack had done everything possible to help *short of opening fire*, the Danish force was insufficient in strength to deal with the more powerful German ships. But they could have positioned their boats better so as to prevent the attack. He reported that it was a standing order that the Danish Navy always had two coastal defence ships with steam up, but at the time both of these had been undergoing a boiler clean. The truth was – and Jøhnke had made little attempt to hide this – that nothing had happened in the Sund since the beginning of the war and quite simply the Danish Navy had grown complacent and gone to sleep. Denmark had definitely not applied due diligence to protect the British sailors.

Therefore it cannot be denied that Kaarsted would seem to have had a point. However, there is one matter in his paper which must be disputed. He says that all of the fourteen dead sailors died by drowning and that was the verdict of the Danish coroner. The implication is that they were not harmed at all by the German fire. While it is not a requirement that members of the Royal Navy must be able to swim (although it is hard to qualify as a submariner if you cannot do so), it is highly unlikely that fourteen perfectly fit young men, who were all swimmers "more or less", according to Bowden, could not save themselves from a mere ten feet of water, especially with their shipmates nearby. It must be likely that at least some of them had been wounded, or maybe concussed or disoriented by smoke and fumes before managing to get out, only to lose consciousness and drown. Indeed Petty Officer Bowden affirms this to have been the case. And it seems probable that this is what almost happened to Petty Officer Lincoln. As for the others, it may well have been that the *final* cause of death was drowning, i.e. after being wounded, but what in legal terms is known as the *proximate* cause of death would have been the German gunfire. It stretches the bounds of likelihood to imagine that the shooting of the Germans was so bad that not a single British sailor was at least wounded by it. Tremendous impact would have been applied to the bodies of those men swimming amid shells bursting in the sea nearby. Quite possibly this could have stunned them sufficiently to render them unconscious, thus causing them to drown. There are many wartime accounts of shipwrecked men swimming in the sea and vomiting blood or involuntarily emptying their bowels when subjected to the huge water pressure created by explosions nearby. Another likelihood is that the 'drowning' verdicts were another tacit attempt not to offend Germany.

On 4 November 1915 Lieutenant Eddies received a telegram from Layton confirming his successful 'home run'. When he read it out to his fellows in the mess, they responded with Three Hearty Cheers. By now they were all in custody in the hulk *Hecla*. The only dry route ashore was by way of a very flimsy gangway. The Danes were not prepared to take any further chances.

4

BARALONG AGAIN!

Kapitänleutnant Klaus Hansen, captain of *U-41*, had had an infuriatingly bad run of luck for well over two months. In early July 1915 he had sailed out of Wilhelmshaven and slipped through the North Sea blockade, intending to make his way round the north of the British Isles and into the Atlantic to hunt for British merchant shipping. But an unfortunate meeting with the minesweeper HMS *Speedwell* off the Shetlands had brought an unplanned termination to his adventures. The little 'sweeper had tried to ram the U-boat, but all that she had achieved was to damage both its periscopes with her keel, which left Hansen blind. It was pointless to try to continue. It also left the German in a precarious situation with the blockading Royal Navy now sitting between himself and home, which was hundreds of miles away. It is a tribute to his remarkable seamanship that he managed to ghost his way back to Germany, unable to see at all whilst dived, which must have been frequently the case. A fortnight later, with *U-41* now repaired, Hansen sailed again. This time he had made it all the way round as far as the southern tip of the Outer Hebrides when he spotted a little 198-ton fishing smack. He should have ignored such an insignificant target and proceeded on his way south towards much richer pickings in the Western Approaches. But, for some reason, he did not do so. Instead, he elected to attack her and fired a shot across her bows to order her to stop. To his surprise, she fired back and the shell splashed uncomfortably close to the submarine. Hansen was scornful. The very thought of a fishing smack armed with little more than a pop-gun crossing swords with a heavily armed U-boat was absurd. He was unaware, at that point, that he had met up with a Q-ship, HMS *Pearl*, alias *Ruby*. In peacetime she was a

Grimsby fishing-boat, GY1121, but had now been requisitioned by the Admiralty, armed with a 6-pounder gun and put to work out of Stornoway under the command of Sub-Lieutenant Allman, RNR.

Hansen, still unaware that he was playing with danger, decided that he had time for a little sport. Calling his gunnery officer, Oberleutnant Iwan Crompton, he ordered him to pepper the impertinent upstart with a few more shells. It was then that things started to go wrong for him in a serious way. Firstly, the helmsman shouted out that the submarine's steering had jammed and, secondly, the trawler was seen to be steaming towards them, spitting fire as she came on at her top speed of seven knots. Two of her shells struck the rudderless U-boat, one wounding the officer-of-the-watch, Schmidt. With barely half a mile separating them, *U-41* appeared to be a sitting duck for *Pearl*'s Navy gunner, being unable to dive or steer. The trawler's sturdy bows were almost on top of the U-boat. She was going to ram them! Hansen must have been cursing his luck and his impetuosity. It was *déjà vu*. It had been only a few weeks before that he had been rammed by HMS *Speedwell*. And now again. With mere seconds to spare, somehow the crew unjammed the steering and *U-41* crash-dived. But *Pearl*'s shells had damaged her plates and she was letting in water. Hansen quickly found that if he dived below periscope depth, the increased pressure forced the water in at a rate with which his pumps could not cope. Maybe if he sat still and silent, the spiteful little ship would go away. He waited awhile before deciding to raise his periscope to take a peep. But *Pearl* was still there, very close by. So close, in fact, that when her gunner saw the U-boat's periscope he managed to shoot it off! Once more Hansen was blind.

To make matters worse, he dare not surface while the trawler was still lurking in wait for him. He turned away, hoping to put a safe distance between them before coming to the surface. Once there, all would be well, because *U-41* could make more than double the speed of the *Pearl* on the surface. A submarine heading away from her would present but a very small target and he would soon be beyond range of her 6-pounder.

But he was leaving a tell-tale trail of oil in the water. Allman dogged the submarine for eight hours. The German would have to surface eventually to recharge his batteries. For once, however, luck was on Hansen's side. *Pearl*'s engineer reported to Allman that a faulty pump needed urgent attention and insisted that they return to Stornoway without delay. Technical details of the fault have been lost to history and we can only assume that it must have been of a highly critical nature to warrant calling off the hunt. And we can only imagine Allman's frustration, and that of his crew, as he turned away. *U-41* had been let off the hook, but there was a general hue and cry for her. She was chased by an armed yacht during the night as she re-entered the North Sea, but managed to escape and eventually made it though the blockade and back to Wilhelmshaven again. This time it was not only the boat that was in need of repairs. The ordeal had left Hansen and his crew in such a state of exhaustion that they were ordered on special leave to recover their nerves.

It was not until 12 September that *U-41* sailed on her third attempt to reach the Western Approaches, where she was to relieve the sinker of the *Lusitania*, Schwieger, in *U-20*. It was third time lucky, but Hansen's men were almost thwarted again. While they were on passage, the *Admiralstab* had wirelessed an order from the Kaiser calling off the current U-boat campaign. As it happened, *U-41* was beyond wireless range and the order was never received. Or it may have been that, with so much frustration behind him, Hansen chose to be deaf. Many others in his position would have done just that, Horatio Nelson for one, almost certainly. But if that is what Klaus Hansen did, it was a fatal decision.

Once in U-boat Alley, where the German submarines were like cats among the pigeons, Hansen made sure that *U-41* cornered a good share of the feast on merchant shipping. On 23 September he scored a hat-trick. In mid-morning he sank the 4,750-ton horse transport *Anglo-Columbian* 75 miles off Fastnet Rock. Then, in the evening, the steamer *Chancellor* and a 3,500-ton freighter, *Hissione*, were both sent to the bottom. Night fell and he ran south. Dawn found him 70 miles south-west of the Scillies, ready for another day's work. Almost immediately along came the 6,500-ton *Urbino*, owned by the Wilson Line, bound for Hull from New York. After all the disappointment he had suffered, it all seemed rather too easy. The whole British merchant fleet seemed to be sailing straight for *U-41*. Hansen ordered the freighter to stop and her crew to abandon ship prior to her being sunk. In this, of course, the German was acting strictly within the terms of the Hague Convention. The *Urbino*'s master, Captain Allanson Hicks, and his men took to their boats and watched while the U-boat's deck-gun opened fire. It took a mere five shells at a range of 200 yards to set the steamer on fire. She started to roll over and sink.

It was at that point that another merchant ship appeared in the distance, travelling westwards down-Channel. Another one! On the submarine's upper casing, her crew gave a final jeer to Hicks and the *Urbino*'s crew of forty-two as they pulled away in their boats and then hastened to scramble down the conning-tower hatch to get ready to deal with the newcomer. The lid slammed down, Hansen crash-dived and steered a course to bring him closer to her. He surfaced a couple of miles off and could now see her plainly. She was a 'three island tramp', a standard work-horse of a ship, typical of a breed to be found anywhere on the oceans of the world, about 4,000 tons, in black and brown livery, and wearing the Stars and Stripes. *U-41* raced towards her, signalling her to stop. Her master complied with the order and started to lower a boat. Hansen, now full of confidence, sat watching patiently in his stumpy conning-tower. It looked as if the merchant skipper was going to send over an officer with his ship's papers for inspection. But for Hansen and his men, the pendulum of luck was about to swing again.

When news of the previous day's sinkings had reached the Admiralty, the telegraph wires began to hum, with the result that Admiral Sir Lewis Bayly ordered one of his Q-ships, none other than HMS *Baralong*, out from Falmouth to seek out the U-boat responsible for the massacre. And *Baralong*, under her new captain Lieutenant-Commander Andrew Wilmot-Smith, had quickly found her quarry.

The U-boat and the black and brown freighter sat riding the easy ocean swell and the submarine swung lazily, so that she was now broadside on to the other vessel. Suddenly all hell broke loose. There was a clatter of noise from the 'American' ship and a cluster of rifle muzzles appeared over the side of her after-well-deck. Instantly a drenching rain of .303 bullets poured onto the submarine from Marine Corporal Fred Collins and his men. "Dive! Dive! It's a trap ship!" bellowed Hansen. Oberleutnant Crompton and his deck gun crew hared along the upper casing towards the protection of the conning tower, scrambling over each other to hurl themselves down through the hatch. But before they could get there *Baralong*'s 12-pounder guns opened up and two shells blasted into the conning tower itself. Hansen and the six men there were blown to pieces. Crompton, who had managed to get halfway in, lay stunned. He had a gaping crimson furrow across his forehead and his left eye had been shot out. As for *U-41* herself, the end was near, hastened by the fact that at that exact moment the valves had been opened to flood her ballast tanks in response to the order to dive. Within seconds she was plunging her way, bows first, to the bottom, carrying the wounded Crompton slumped unconscious in her conning-tower.

For Crompton, what followed was a remarkable escape. Very few men can have been as close to death as he was that day and lived to tell the tale. Deep in the dark water, the doomed submarine's diving tanks suddenly gave vent to an enormous gurgle of compressed air, which created a gigantic bubble in which the mutilated boat was carried back to the surface. Her forepart shot from the water like a cork, throwing the still not quite conscious Crompton clear into the sea. Within a moment she had disappeared again.

The survival instinct has roots that burrow deep into the subconscious, and so it was with Crompton. Only vaguely aware of what he was doing, although with the mist before his eyes clearing slowly, he struck out towards the *Baralong*. But she was already turning away. He was now sufficiently conscious to note that the White Ensign had replaced the Stars and Stripes which had hung at her stern. As she grew smaller in the distance, he looked around. He appeared to be the only survivor, quite alone in the Atlantic Ocean, 70 miles from land. He resigned himself to death.

Kept afloat by his life-jacket, he closed his eyes. After about an hour, or so it seemed, he heard the rhythmic throb of a ship's engines. She was coming back! He raised his arms as far as the life-jacket would permit and waved to attract attention. But she steamed straight past him, so close that her bow-wave and wake tossed him around, leaving him spluttering for breath. Men were leaning over her side, jeering and laughing at him, just as his own men had done to Allanson Hicks and his crew such a short time before. Hopes dashed, his spirits fell once more. Then, out of the corner of his one remaining eye he caught sight of salvation. A boat! It was drifting aimlessly, gently nodding as little waves slapped against its sides. It was one of the *Urbino*'s life-boats, abandoned after the *Baralong* had taken her survivors on board, which had been the reason for her return, although of course Crompton had no means of knowing that. It took every last scrap of his fading energy to haul himself up and painfully drag his battered body over the boat's side. He had lost a lot of blood and was close to fainting as he lay gasping on the boards. Then he heard a cry. Dizzy and wincing with pain, he raised his head to look over the side. There was a man in the water. So there had been another survivor after all! It was Godau, the U-boat's helmsman. Crompton had no strength to pull him inboard. It was all he could do to dangle his arms over the side and let the man climb up.

The two men lay in the boat, their chests heaving with exhaustion, for quite some time. And then there it was again, the steady beat of a ship's engines. *Baralong* was coming back a second time and it sounded as if she was travelling at speed. They stood up with difficulty in the rocking boat and waved their arms. She turned towards them, but showed no signs of slackening pace. There was a sailor in her bows, waving his arms. What was he trying to convey? Was he waving to them or was he guiding his helmsman so as to ram the lifeboat? Her surging bows were almost upon them when Crompton's battered wits suddenly recovered enough power to retake control of his brain. "Jump!" he shouted, and the two Germans hurled themselves from the boat. The ship ploughed past them, it seemed at little more than arms' length, so close that they were sucked down under her wash. Gasping and spitting water, they surfaced to find that the boat, which was still dancing violently on the turbulence, was within reach. Somehow they summoned the strength to hold on to her side until she settled down again and dragged themselves back in. It was not long before the *Baralong* arrived back again, this time more slowly as she drew alongside. Voices called out, ropes were thrown down and the Germans were hauled up the side of the Q-ship to become prisoners of war.

Corporal Fred Collins was ordered to take charge of the prisoners and lock them in the sheep-pen on the upper deck. But a change of heart had come over Collins since he had blazed away with his rifle at *U-27*'s unarmed crew barely five weeks before. It was a different man entirely who now ushered Crompton and Godau along the deck of the *Baralong*. Crompton, especially, was in a dreadful condition. His left eye-socket was a dark hole and the blood still poured in rivulets down his face from the slash across his forehead. The Marine brought them hot Bovril from the galley and smeared thick daubs of Vaseline on the wound. Then he wedged himself into the open-sided sheep-pen alongside them to try to shield them from the chill of the night. Just before midnight, an officer woke Collins to tell him that Wilmot-Smith's orders were that, if Crompton was not dead by midnight, to shoot him. The captain did not intend to take the Germans alive into Falmouth. Now Corporal Fred Collins was a hardened Marine. He had been a Marine for seven years and he was trained to kill men in battle efficiently and without hesitation. But it seems that his conscience had plagued him ever since the affair on board the *Nicosian*. Refusal to carry out an order is a serious offence, and especially so in wartime. Fred Collins knew that perfectly well. It could have put him behind bars, but he took a chance with his future. "I can't do it, sir," he replied calmly, "and what's more I shan't order any of my men to do it either." The officer went away, leaving the Marine wondering what would be his fate. It came as no small relief when the officer came back later and announced that Wilmot-Smith had decided after all to take the prisoners into port.

They arrived in fog-shrouded Falmouth roads in the early hours of the morning to find a trawler awaiting them. Two naval intelligence officers came on board and handed Wilmot-Smith some sealed orders. HMS *Baralong* was to be no more. With immediate effect, she was to sail under the name of HMS *Wyandra*. Such changing of names, without notice, was common practice in the secrecy-veiled world of the Q-ships.

Doctors came on board to attend to the *Urbino*'s wounded sailors as soon as they berthed and then went to look at Crompton at about noon. They patched him up, but he was to be kept on board until he was thought fit to be interrogated. Two days later he appeared before a captain of naval intelligence, but staunchly refused to give more than his name and rank. After nine days in Falmouth he was taken to naval detention quarters in Devonport and was reassured to find Godau already there. Although the Oberleutnant had been in no fit state to be questioned at first, the terrified helmsman had been convinced that he was about to be shot and, under interrogation, had simply gushed with information about *U-41*.

Crompton had received little more than first-aid from the medicos in Falmouth and his wounds continued to trouble him. When he complained that he was in severe pain, he was given a fuller examination and X-rays revealed that his injuries were, in fact, far worse than had been apparent. Not only had he lost his eye and suffered the serious head wound, but his jaw was fractured, there were several splinters of glass in his eye-socket and there was a brass screw embedded in his skull. He spent a month in the Devonport naval hospital, Stonehouse, and was then taken to a prison at York and eventually to Dyffryn on the Welsh coast, which was the main prison camp for captured U-boat men. Crompton was to turn out to be a bitterly vindictive prisoner. It is plain from the material available for research that he must have noted every minute point for later use as ammunition with which to criticize his captors. For example, he was insulted by having been placed in an animal pen, although it had never been used as such, and was simply a metal structure fixed to the *Baralong*'s deck. As an officer, he resented the fact that the *Urbino*'s sailors were all seen by the doctors at Falmouth before himself. And he remarked that the naval escort which took him to the detention quarters in Devonport were drunk, which was highly unlikely to have been true. What was probably the case was that the men had consumed their daily 'tots' of rum, the strong fumes of which did tend to linger on the breath for some hours. Complaining was to play a prominent part in his captivity. For all that one makes a natural allowance for the fact that the man had suffered severe and disfiguring injuries, which can hardly have sweetened his attitude towards the British, his constant bitching was hardly likely to have earned the respect of his captors. On arrival at Dyffryn he sat down to compose the first of several letters to the American Embassy complaining about the bad treatment he had experienced at the hands of the British. He never received a reply and became suspicious that all his letters had been withheld.

He started to press for re-internment under a Red Cross scheme whereby certain German officers could be sent for internment in Switzerland if their medical condition was considered sufficiently grave. A team of Red Cross doctors visited Dyffryn in May 1916 and, after examining him, recommended that his state of health did warrant such a transfer. But his contentment was shortlived. When he went before a further medical board (which was composed mainly of British doctors, he noted bitterly) a fortnight later, they refused to endorse the original findings. For reasons which are not entirely clear, however, the decision was reversed yet again and he was released to Switzerland, where he arrived in early November 1916. His vigilance did not falter, even as he waited to board a steamer at Tilbury Docks. There was a hospital ship at the quay, *Llandovery Castle*, and there were some men in khaki boarding her. Soldiers boarding a hospital ship? That was proof that the British were flouting the Hague Convention! He bore that in mind for the next five years and testified to what he had seen at the Leipzig Trials in 1921, where the officers of *U-86* were facing charges of killing the survivors of the *Llandovery Castle*, which they had just sunk, as they rowed away in their lifeboats.

For over a year the British had managed to keep the sinking of *U-41* under a cloak of silence, but, once in Switzerland, it did not take Crompton long to contact the German Press and the very next day's headlines spat words such as "savage", "brutal" and "atrocious" as the belated news of another *Baralong* outrage hit the streets. The Royal Navy was accused of failing to rescue U-boat crews in distress and the catalogue of Crompton's alleged ill-treatment was listed in full. The British Admiralty felt obliged to make an immediate statement in reply. "The facts are perfectly simple," their Lordships rumbled, "On the morning of 24 September 1915, in the western channel, the *U-41* was engaged in sinking a British merchant steamer. While she was so engaged, a converted merchant vessel, commissioned as one of HM auxiliary ships, approached the submarine and the sinking vessel. Her character was not at once recognised and in order that the submarine would not submerge before she was within range, she hoisted neutral colours – a perfectly legitimate *ruse de guerre*. When within range, she hoisted the White Ensign, as all British ships of war are required to do, fired on and sank the submarine. The immediate pre-occupation of her commander was to rescue the crew of the British vessel sunk by the submarine, who had been compelled to take to their boats fifty miles from the nearest port. When this had been done, HM ship closed one of the boats of the sunken steamer, which had broken adrift, into which two survivors of the submarine's crew had climbed. These were rescued in the same way, but after, their victims. The statement that the Admiralty has ever issued orders that survivors of German submarines need not be rescued is an absolute lie and was explicitly denied in the Note of His Majesty's Government on the *Baralong* case dated 25 February 1916."

Wilmot-Smith made two written reports describing how the Germans had been rescued. "One of the *Urbino*'s boats when cleared got loose and drifted astern. On going to it later we discovered that two Germans had got in. There were no signs of them in the water previously. Unfortunately, having got all of the crew of the *Urbino* on board, and not knowing if they [Crompton and Godau] were to be trusted, we had to pick them up; they could not have been left in the boat in case they should have been picked up by a neutral ship."

The second report parried accusations blazed at him in the German Press that he had intended to ram the lifeboat. "On approaching this boat," he averred, "my attention was temporarily distracted from the work in hand, and I suddenly realised that the ship had too much way on. I immediately reversed engines, at the same time putting the helm hard a port. The boat was not struck by the ship and came past along the port side. The prisoners, however, when the boat in which they were was some twenty yards from my bows, both dived overboard. The boat was in no way damaged." He went on to insist that he had treated the Germans fairly, and explained about the newness of the sheep-pen in which they had been first confined. The doctors who examined the prisoners in Falmouth had made no criticism of the accommodation he had provided for them. They had also been given dry clothing and blankets. Godau had behaved in a compliant fashion, but Crompton, "probably because of the seriousness of his wounds", had displayed a very surly attitude.

HMS *Wyandra* was transferred to Q-ship duties in the Mediterranean where the U-boat menace was increasing, although as far as is known she had no further encounters with the enemy submarines. On 9 November 1916 she was finally 'retired' from service with the Royal Navy and resumed life as a merchant vessel, sailing under yet another new name – *Manica*. The infamous name of *Baralong* had been well and truly consigned to the depths of history.

5

KING STEPHEN AND THE ZEPPELIN

George Denny peered into the grey pre-dawn bleakness of a wintry North Sea. He was sure that he had seen something flashing in the distance. They had had their nets down all night, fishing about 110 miles east of Flamborough Head, and your eyes can play tricks on you when you are tired. He blinked and there it was again, just a tiny speck of light. He called the skipper, William Martin. The two men decided that it looked like there was a vessel, or even some shipwrecked sailors, in distress, although the poor visibility made it difficult to gauge the distance from them. It could have been a mile, it could have been five miles. With the First World War raging, it may have been a dangerous thing to do, but Martin decided nonetheless that they ought to investigate at least. It was just after six o'clock on the morning of Wednesday, 2 February 1916.

The crew tumbled up, yawning and stretching. The gear was hauled in and the little 162-ton Grimsby smack *King Stephen*, GY174, set off towards the light. The sea was as smooth as silk, but it was bitterly cold, with a sheen of frost coating the wheel-house roof. Denny, who was the mate, set his eyes firmly on the spot where the light had flashed and, as the daylight gradually brightened, he could make out a great pale shape looming eerily. It must have stood a good fifty feet tall, much higher than the gently rocking masthead of the fishing smack. An iceberg? Surely not, not this far south. No, it was an airship. A German Zeppelin, or rather the wreck of one – the *L-19*. Perched on the very summit of the giant balloon was a man operating a signalling lamp to attract attention. He was lashed to the rail of a platform which ran along the top of the huge craft, and soon there were about eight men alongside him, shouting and waving to the fishermen. Martin brought the *King Stephen* nearer, to be almost alongside the Zeppelin which, although the water was very calm, was bobbing and swaying to an alarming degree, caused by the buoyancy given by the submerged part of the envelope. A lot more men, about eighteen, then emerged from a scuttle hatch. One, who wore the Iron Cross and had brass buttons on his uniform, appeared to be the commander. They all had lifelines attached to them from the hatchway and were shouting, "Save us! Save us! We give you much gold! Take us on board!" One of the Germans made as if to jump onto the trawler's deck, but thought better of it when he realized how far it was to fall.

Martin and Denny looked at each other uncertainly. What were they to do? It was a tricky problem. George Denny said later, "We had a confab about affairs. We looked at the position like this. There were about twenty or twenty-five of them and only nine of us. They would all have revolvers and we had nothing but sticks. So we thought it was not safe to tackle them on board our trawler which their Kaiser called an 'insignificant little ship'. What do you think would have happened if we had invited them on board? They could have easily overpowered us and taken our ship to Germany with us as prisoners – that is if they didn't pitch us overboard first. So the skipper shouted to them that he could not take them off and then they all started shouting and saying that they would not touch us if only we would save them. They screeched for us to save them but the skipper did right when he said that he could not do it. What would their Kaiser have said if he got to know that nine of us had been able to overpower twenty-five of them and bring them prisoners to Grimsby? Why, he would have taken all their Iron Crosses from them."

The Englishmen decided that the best plan was to head for home immediately, report what they had seen and let the authorities do whatever was needed to deal with the situation. In every practical sense, there was really little else that the trawlermen could do.

Martin had spoken directly to the Zeppelin's commander. "He was all soft soap," said the skipper, "but I simply didn't trust him, and I told him so. He promised that I would be handsomely rewarded and my crew would receive gifts of gold if we took them off. I had all my men safe and sound and I was determined to take no risks. I know what the Germans had done to my class in the

70

North Sea, and, besides, Zeppelin crews dropping bombs on houses and killing women and children didn't appeal to me. Even if the Huns had not proved barbarous there would still have been a big risk because they heavily outnumbered us. Nothing we could have done would have prevented them from taking charge of our trawler. If I had sent a boat across, my men in it could have been instantly secured and used as hostages. If half of what the German captain promised me had been true, I should have been rich for life, but there are times when commonsense is worth more than all the gold in the world and this was one of them."

He rang the telegraph "Slow ahead" and as soon as the Germans saw the trawler beginning to move away from the side of the Zeppelin their earnest pleas quickly turned to angry curses. They all started shaking their fists and shouting, "*Gott strafe England!*" Their commander's rage was such that he actually began to howl like a wolf. The trawlermen could still hear the shouting as it grew fainter and fainter in the distance until eventually the *King Stephen* drew beyond earshot.

George Denny said that the after-part and gondolas of the Zeppelin were submerged. It looked as if part of the envelope had collapsed. But all the forward part was fully inflated and there was a considerable amount of noise coming from below the scuttle hatch. It sounded as if they were trying to do some repairs, or at least some damage limitation. Back in Grimsby, he gave a professional sailor's assessment of the airship's predicament: "The water was as smooth as the dock while we were there and there was no immediate fear of the thing sinking. But you know there has been a strong wind since we left on Wednesday morning and I should not like to say that she would float long in that water. With all that gas in the balloons she would float for any length of time in a smooth sea, for although the cars and the bottom part of the Zeppelin would be full of water and be a heavy drag it would take little or no assistance to keep her floating. But in a swell things would be different. The whole ship would have to rise and fall with the sea and the heavy weight underneath would prevent her from lifting with each wave. It would act like a sea-anchor and the sea would smash up against the framework and wreck it. We had no chance of towing her, either, because with all the dead weight in the water she would not stand the strain of a tow-rope. These airships are not made to stand the strain of a pull and as soon as she were under tow the framework would pull out straight and the whole thing would collapse. It would be a difficult feat in the finest weather but quite impossible with any sea or swell on."

The Germans had been having trouble with the new Maybach HSLu power units in their Zeppelins. Melted crank bearings, broken connecting rods and fractured crankshafts were all part of the long list of defects. Nevertheless, on 31 January 1916 nine airships of the German Navy had set out to attack English industrial cities, particularly "if at all possible, Liverpool". All of them reached England safely, but were hampered by thick cloud and fog in finding the desired targets. Afterwards, two of them believed they had indeed bombed Liverpool. Breithaupt, in *L-15*, reported that he had attacked "a large city complex, divided in two parts by a broad sheet of water running north and south, joined by a lighted bridge, recognised as Liverpool and Birkenhead". A lighted bridge? Wherever Breithaupt had dropped his bombs, it was certainly not on Liverpool. It is thought that he had actually hit Burton-on-Trent. Böcker, in *L-14*, cruised west as far as Shrewsbury before turning back to drop two tons of bombs on Derby. Mathy, in *L-13*, mistook Scunthorpe for Goole, fifteen miles away, while Franz Stabbert, in *L-20*, also bombed Burton-on-Trent instead of, as he thought, Sheffield. Others were convinced they had hit Manchester, Nottingham, Immingham and Yarmouth. But they were all wrong. While considerable property damage had been caused, seventy people had been killed and 113 injured in the nine-ship raid, none of these places had been found. All the same, the fact that enemy airships found themselves able to wander all over the British mainland with impunity screamed a fearful warning to those responsible for its air defences.

Odo Loewe was the commander of *L-19*. By all accounts he was a skilful aviator. On one occasion, according to the Grimsby *Telegraph*, he was said to have brought the Zeppelin down to within a few feet of the water to stop and inspect a Swedish steamship in the North Sea. He lowered a boat, sent an inspection party on board the Swede and, being satisfied with her papers, purchased some provisions from her, rowed back to the airship and let her proceed on her way. It was thought to be the only time that such a thing had been done.

Loewe had been exasperated by the trouble with the new engines. He wanted to get on with the war, but for two months he had twiddled his thumbs in Dresden while one problem after another was sorted out. After this he had been all the more determined to punish Liverpool. But again it had been the unfortunate Burton-on-Trent (where there were scenes of intense indignation the following day at the tardiness displayed by the authorities in darkening the town) on which part of his load had dropped, while the rest of it fell on the Birmingham suburbs of Tipton and Walsall. From there *L-19* wandered slowly eastwards towards the North Sea and home. She had floated all over the fog-shrouded English Midlands for nine hours. Loewe wirelessed his attack report to his base at Tondern (now Tønder in Denmark) at 0537 hours on 1 February. He made no mention of any engine trouble, but his last call, at 1605 hours was ominous. "Radio equipment at times out of order. Three engines out of order. Approximate position – Borkum Island". Nothing more was heard from him.

It was learned, some days later, that *L-19* had appeared over the neutral Dutch island of Ameland, flying very low, just after the time of Loewe's last wireless message. She was fired on by Dutch coastal batteries and floated away helplessly, apparently on fire, before a strong south-easterly wind. Early next morning found her in a distressed condition, wallowing in the icy water 110 miles east of Flamborough Head with her crew anxiously watching the approach of a Grimsby fishing smack in the icy grey light of a still winter's dawn.

Skipper Martin was not an unfeeling man. On the contrary, the decision that he took that day was to play on his mind for the short remainder of his life. "The weather had been steadily worsening," he said, "and as there was no other vessel in sight I knew the Germans were doomed, but I felt I had done the right thing under the circumstances." Eleven months later he was dead. He had received several threats from Germans living in England and was convinced that he had been poisoned by smoking a cigarette that had been sent to him in a packet through the post, although scientific analysis proved that his fears had been wrong. His doctor's opinion was that his fatal collapse had been caused by sheer fright.

But if, as was thought, the Zeppelin's crew had all perished, how was it that the Germans knew what had happened and that Martin was at all involved? It was more than likely that there were German agents with their ears to the ground in Grimsby, as there were in most other busy ports. Even so, their gathering of information in this case was made simple by what appeared in the Grimsby *Telegraph* the very next day under the heading "Zeppelin in North Sea – Seen by Grimsby Trawler – waterlogged and sinking". It said, "The Grimsby trawler *King Stephen* (Consolidated Steam-fishing and Ice Co. Ltd.) Skipper William Martin, came in by today's tide. Reported having sighted in the early hours of yesterday (Wednesday) morning, in the North Sea, a Zeppelin marked *L19* in a distressed and waterlogged condition. The cabins and under-portion of the envelope were submerged and a number of men were seen to be repairing the airship. As the Germans greatly outnumbered the crew of the trawler, the skipper considered that it was inadvisable to attempt to capture them and accordingly continued his voyage."

The *Telegraph* was forbidden by the wartime censors to publish any more about the incident for the time being, but for all practical purposes it was too late. It had already said more than enough to put a price on Martin's head in Germany, where he was branded as a war criminal, and the *King Stephen* herself became a target of hate.

The German press was not slow in claiming that the nine-ship raid had met with glowing success. "German airships over Paris, over Manchester, and over Salonika, and all within three days", crowed a triumphant *Cologne Gazette* in its first edition on Wednesday 2 February, clearly unaware that at that very time the *King Stephen* was heading for home to tell of her meeting with the Zeppelin. "This is a measure of the enormous area which the world war has assumed, and a brilliant picture of the immense military strength which Germany has displayed in this life-and-death struggle. The last attack reported by the *Admiralstab* was aimed at the industrial district in the centre of England – Sheffield, Nottingham, Manchester, Birmingham and Liverpool. It struck at one of the powerful veins of England's economic life, and carried the terrors of war into districts of the British Island Empire which had never yet seen an enemy. These thickly populated districts have countless factories, ship-building yards and mines, a great number of which are devoted to the production of munitions. All the airships returned uninjured. With regard to the damage which they did, our military report is very definite. We must therefore correct the statement of the English Press Bureau."

But as soon as the news broke of the loss of the *L-19*, the morale-boosting stories of the alleged successes of the raiders were replaced by the angry torrent of condemnation which was turned on the Grimsby fishermen. "The crew of an English fishing vessel say that they had not the courage to take on board the crew of a ship-wrecked German Zeppelin," sneered the *Frankfurter Zeitung*, "because the unhappy men, who had nothing but their bare lives, were more numerous by a few heads than these simple fishermen. Were they cowards or criminals? We do not know whether the bold deeds of our German sailors have so affected our enemies, or many of them, that they do not dare to approach our sailors even when they are struggling with death."

The *Hamburger Nachrichten* asked some pointed questions: "When the trawler *King Stephen* and her cowardly crew reached Grimsby and made a report, why were not adequately armed and manned ships sent out immediately to search for the shipwrecked men and perhaps even to bring in the Zeppelin? It seems that a great deal of time was wasted. Was it due to fear of the German heroes? Two vessels went out later to search the North Sea area, and returned with the cheerful news that no traces could be found and it was concluded that the Zeppelin had sunk."

There was a poignant message from the grave from the crew of the *L-19*. On 24 February, three weeks after her encounter with the trawler, *Reuter* wired from Stockholm, "The yacht *Stella* has picked up a bottle near Gothenburg containing messages from the *L-19*. Two letters are from Commander Uhle to his parents and his wife and little son. A third letter states the airship was 300 feet above the water when the motors failed to act, and all were expecting to fall into the sea. A fourth letter states that the crew were then drowning."

Straightaway after she had made headlines, the Admiralty requisitioned the *King Stephen* to serve as a Q-ship, a miniature *Baralong*, as it had done with dozens more of her kind from ports all around the British Isles. The guns that these innocent-looking little decoy craft were given were concealed in all kinds of artful ways. *King Stephen* was mounted with a six-pounder Hotchkiss quick-firing gun, which was hidden in a dummy boat abaft her bridge and a Royal Naval Reserve skipper from Lowestoft, Tom Phillips, was put in command of her. Quite how dangerous it was to operate as a decoy, and how coolly courageous it was necessary to be, can be gathered by describing how Phillips had already made his name as a Q-ship captain in the smack *Inverlyon* by sinking the little German coastal submarine *UB-4* near Smith's Knoll Spar Buoy off Yarmouth on 15 August 1915. The U-boat had hailed the fishing boat, but when it had come to within a mere thirty yards, the Royal Navy gunner (at least one of which all Q-smacks carried) had opened fire and two of his first three shots had exploded in the submarine's conning tower. Four more shells blasted the U-boat, which by then was drifting out of control and it sank by the bows with its hatch open.

The catalogue of subterfuges that were employed by Q-ships to lure the U-boats to their doom is lengthy. Some of the larger ones even put on a convincing theatrical act whereby men would instantly take to the boats in a show of panic when confronted by an enemy submarine leaving the Q-ship apparently deserted. But the naval gunners would still be on board, concealed at their stations, waiting for the submarine captain to bring his boat into point-blank range. Q-ships frequently changed their appearances. Often they would be repainted a different colour at sea, overnight, or a dummy funnel or mast would be added or removed. Canvas screens would be used to alter the deck profile or the outline of the bridge. And very frequently the Admiralty changed their names. For example, one of *Inverlyon*'s Lowestoft sisters, the *G & E*, also sailed under the aliases *Bird*, *Extirpator*, *Foam Crest*, *I'll Try* and *Nelson*. But they omitted to change the name of the *King Stephen*. At first this might appear to have been a careless oversight, but the devious-minded naval authorities (and they were very devious) may well have considered that her very name would act as an extra lure to any U-boat captain who wanted to earn some kudos by capturing the hated 'criminal' skipper of a vessel which was known for sure to be an innocent fishing boat. (Author's note: I tell the story of the British Q-ships, and their German counterparts in my book *Sea Killers in Disguise*.)

On 24 April 1916 the now HMS *King Stephen* (Patrol Boat 1174) sailed from Lowestoft under her new captain. Phillips headed for his favourite U-boat hunting ground – the Smith's Knoll Bank, about twenty-five miles off-shore. He did not have to wait long for some action. Spotting a U-boat about two miles distant, he released a pigeon to inform base that he was going into action and set off to pursue the submarine. The gunner splashed about six shells around their quarry, but it escaped. This was a dreadful

76

mistake on the part of Phillips, of course. In the excitement he had overlooked the fact that the plan was that he should lure the enemy into close quarters and then kill him at point-blank range. Instead, he had rushed at him like a bull at a gate. He should have known that his boat would have no chance of catching a submarine which could make nineteen knots or so on the surface. Now he had revealed the true purpose of his vessel to the Germans and had achieved nothing in return.

Shortly afterwards two large shapes appeared in the sky. Zeppelins. To destroy one of them would have really been an achievement, but the Hotchkiss was not designed for anti-aircraft work and it would not elevate to anything like the required angle. Anxious not to let them escape, Phillips turned south and set off to find an anti-aircraft naval patrol boat. (Many of the East Coast fishing smacks were in the habit of carrying pigeons in the days before wireless was commonplace. Presumably, Phillips had no pigeons left in the loft with which to sound the alarm back in Lowestoft, which would have been much quicker.)

The little Q-smack had not steamed far when her lookout spied some low smoking shapes in the distance. They were travelling at a very high speed, and their course would bring them directly towards the *King Stephen*. Destroyers! These were the boys to shoot down Zeppelins!

The problem, as it turned out, was that they were German destroyers! Not only that, but they were the screen for the battle-cruisers of German High Seas Fleet which were returning to Germany after an abortive raid on Lowestoft and Yarmouth and the 162-ton *King Stephen* had run straight into them!

The Germans had taken to making sporadic raids to bombard seaside towns along the East Coast of England ever since the very early days of the war. Some ports, such as Harwich and West Hartlepool, were light cruiser and destroyer bases, and as such were understandable targets, but even unlikely places such as Scarborough and Southend, of no strategic importance, had felt the effect of enemy naval shells. The rationale of this was to tie down a disproportionate number of Royal Navy vessels in a defensive role and, of course, to dent the morale of the civilian population.

Admiral Reinhard Scheer planned such a raid on 25 April. It was to be on a large scale. The idea was to coincide with the Easter Rising in Dublin, which was naturally supported and encouraged by the Germans. The High Seas Fleet sailed from Wilhelmshaven at noon on 24 April. The British Admiralty were aware that it had done so, having decoded vital signals, but had no idea as to its intended destination. They immediately ordered the Grand Fleet to sea from its Scottish bases, with Commodore Tyrwhitt's Harwich light cruisers to put out in support. At 0700 hours the Harwich ships spotted the German battle-cruisers as they made for Lowestoft. Tyrwhitt turned south in an attempt to draw them away from their target, but they refused to follow him. He turned back to the north, but came face to face with the enemy battle-cruisers, which were escorted by six light cruisers and two complete flotillas of destroyers. With the heavy ships of the Royal Navy still barging their way through rough weather on their way south from Scotland, Tyrwhitt, with but three light cruisers and a few destroyers, had no alternative but to retire. Konteradmiral Bödicker, commanding the German battle-cruisers in the absence of the indisposed Hipper, then made a strange decision. With Admiral Beatty's Rosyth ships still 130 miles away, and Jellicoe's farther still, he would have had ample time and ships to annihilate the Harwich force, and, if he had chosen, to carry out the planned bombardment of Lowestoft and Great Yarmouth more or less at leisure. But he did neither of these things. He turned away to rejoin Scheer, who had brought the remainder of the High Seas Fleet to about 70 miles off Great Yarmouth. Scheer, too, reversed course, and they retired together to their base in the Jade River estuary, shadowed by Tyrwhitt until he was ordered to return home.

It was at the point where Bödicker turned away that his destroyer screen found the midget Q-ship *King Stephen* and her excited crew innocently sailing towards them. Phillips was taken before a destroyer captain, who assured him he would be shot. As for the trawler, she was sunk by shellfire without further ceremony. Three days later Phillips found himself facing a court-martial in Berlin. He was put on oath and asked what he knew about the airship *L-19*. It was then that he realized his predicament. The Germans thought that they had captured the despised war criminal Bill Martin, and that he was using the name Tom Phillips as an alias!

"Nothing," he replied, "except what I have read in the papers."

The Germans were not convinced. Prospects looked very bleak indeed for Phillips. The German officers continued to fire questions at him. If he was not Martin, where was he on 2 February, when the *King Stephen* found the crashed airship? If he was a fisherman, why did he have a gun on board his boat! Was he not ashamed to sail in such an infamous craft?

In the end, it was a photograph of William Martin, taken from the pages of an English illustrated paper, that saved Phillips' life. It was produced from somewhere. Exactly where from Phillips knew not. One of the German officers laid it on the table. Phillips picked it up and asked them to look at it. Surely they could see that there was no resemblance. They said that further enquiries would be made. It seemed that they were satisfied, because he was not called to answer any more questions. He and his crew were imprisoned in the *gefangenlager* at Hameln, of Pied Piper fame, near Hanover.

At home the Admiralty were bombarded with letters from the worried wives and mothers of the *King Stephen*'s crew. Their Lordships could only say that they could see no reason to doubt the German report about the trawler's sinking and capture of its crew. (Actually the Germans had taken *King Stephen* to be part of Tyrwhitt's force and been unaware that she had simply stumbled upon their battle-cruisers by mistake!) Eventually Phillips and his twelve-man crew were reported as prisoners-of-war via the usual wartime channels.

War Office List X18596 – 20 June 1916

Phillips, Thomas	Captain		Gorleston.
Butland, Richard	Able Seaman	P154335	Gosport, Hampshire.
Francis, William,	Deckhand	DA5460	Grimsby.
Gooding, Thomas,	Trimmer	TS5191	Aldeburgh.
Greenwood, John,	Deckhand	SA2395	Scarborough
Grunnill, Walter	Trimmer	TS5026	Skegness.
Kerrison, Ernest,	Engineman	ES1424	Yarmouth.
Leech, George,	Deckhand	DA10836	Wangford, Suffolk,
Priestley, Mark,	Engineman	ES1423	Lincoln.
Samson, Edwin,	Seaman RNR	898X	Newfoundland, Canada.
Smith, Charles,	Deckhand	DA9089	Grimsby.
Smith, Frank,	Deckhand	DA10386	Grimsby.
Taylor, Robert,	Deckhand	DA10404	Hull.

In May 1918 the men were transferred into internment in neutral Holland. Returning to England after the war, it appears that Tom Phillips, DSM, decided that he had seen enough of the North Sea. He settled down to become a market gardener.

1. Walther Schweiger, who sank the *Lusitania*.

2. Schweiger's *U-20 (U-Boot Archiv, Cuxhaven)*.

3. Klaus Hansen, captain of *U-41*, sunk by HMS *Baralong*. (*U-Boot Archiv*)

4. *U-41*, which sank the *Arabic*. (*U-Boot Archiv*)

5. Stella Carol, Queen of Song, who was rescued from the *Arabic* and sang 'Tipperary' to her fellow survivors in the lifeboat.

6. One of the coffins from *E-13* is taken into Hull's Paragon Station via a window. *(British Newspaper Library)*

7. *E-13* stranded on Saltholm, peppered with shell-holes. *(R.N. Submarine Museum)*

8. The cross-channel ferry *Sussex*. *(National Railway Museum)*

9. Captain Charles Algernon Fryatt. *(Imperial War Museum)*

10. HMS *Orpheus* enters Dover Harbour bearing Fryatt's body. *(Imperial War Museum)*

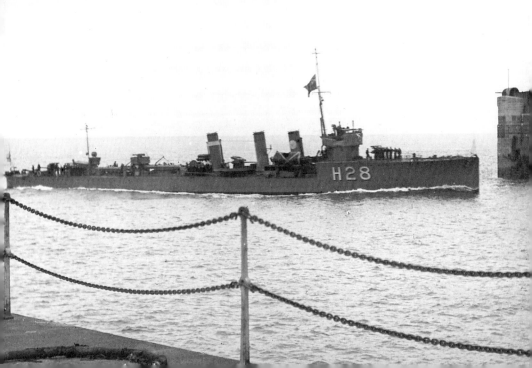

11. The crew of SS *Brussels* in captivity. *(Mrs Jill Burchell)*

12. Some of the *Brussels* officers as POWs, watched over by an attentive guard. *(Mrs Jill Burchell)*

13. Gansser's *U-33*, which Fryatt tried to ram. (*U-Boot Archiv*)

14. Max Valentiner.
(*U-Boot Archiv*)

15. Valentiner's *U-38* crew enjoy some fresh air.

16. The hospital ship *Anglia* sinks off Dover. *(Imperial War Museum)*

17. HMHS *Llandovery Castle*.

18. *U-73* at Cattaro. Was the *Britannic* sunk by one of her mines? (*U-Boot Archiv*)

19. *Dover Castle's* nurses watch a German aeroplane in the sky.
(British Newspaper Library)

20. Siess, captain
of *U-73*.
(U-Boot Archiv)

21. Kapitänleutnant Karl Neumann who sank the *Dover Castle*, but was found not guilty of war crimes.
(*U-Boot Archiv*)

22. Wounded soldiers being hoisted aboard a hospital ship in a box stretcher, possibly in the Dardanelles. *(British Newspaper Library)*

23. Neumann's *UC-67*. *(U-Boot Archiv)*

24. HMHS *Rewa* at Malta. *(Imperial War Museum)*

25. Werner's *U-55* which dived at least twice with British seamen on deck.
(U-Boot Archiv)

26. Rücker's *U-34*. which attacked and sank the Milford Haven fishing boat
Victoria.   (*U-Boot Archiv*)

27. *U-55* officer, possibly
Werner himself.
(*U-Boot Archiv*)

28. Kiesewetter's *UC-56* in internment at Santander. *(R.N. Submarine Museum)*

6

THE *SUSSEX*

It was a bright early spring afternoon on 24 March 1916. The English Channel rippled under a light cool breeze as the French State Railways-owned 1,353-ton twin-screw steam ferry *Sussex* throbbed towards Dieppe with the tricolour flapping at her stern. She was crowded with 380 passengers, far more than her average number, and carried on board mail for the British Armed Forces in France, India and the Colonies. She had sailed from Folkestone at 1.25 pm and carefully threaded her way through the buoyed-off mine barriers that protected the Kentish ports, making for mid-Channel with the famous white cliffs growing smaller and then falling over the horizon behind her. Now it was just before 3.30 pm as her French captain, Mouffet, took her over an area of sea known as The Shallow Water, just over the halfway point on the voyage. The war seemed a million miles away and the fresh sea air had been invigorating for those who had chatted on the open deck, amused by the aerobatics of an aeroplane which had appeared from nowhere, it seemed for their special entertainment.

On the bridge Mouffet started with surprise. That was surely a torpedo streaking towards his ship. He could see its wake quite plainly. There had been absolutely no warning of any kind and it was only about a hundred yards away. He swung to avoid it, but it was too late. The torpedo hit the *Sussex* squarely, for'ard of midships, with a loud explosion. A passenger ferry boat is not constructed to withstand blows of such ferocity and the consequent damage was alarmingly extensive. The forepart of the ship was blown clean away, as far back as the saloon bulkhead. Debris and several people were thrown high into the air to splash into the sea

81

all around and the foremast toppled over, bringing down the wireless aerials.

Mouffet himself suffered injuries to his head and leg. A Belgian passenger was among the twenty or so in the gentlemen's saloon when the explosion erupted, most of whom were either killed outright or severely injured. He said that a flying fragment of steel narrowly missed him but cut off both legs of a man nearby. There was a rush of air so strong that he himself was thrown off his feet. There were agonized cries coming from the injured and he could hear screams from the ladies' cabin. He clambered up on deck to find a general panic, which Mouffet and his officers were trying to calm. The pandemonium subsided after a few minutes, but in that time several tragedies occurred. There was a mad rush for the boats, with young men pushing women and children out of the way to get in. Desperate mothers were literally flinging their children aboard the lifeboats even as they were being lowered. Some women threw themselves into the sea. Two of the lifeboats capsized through overloading, jettisoning the shrieking occupants into the water. Many of them drowned. On board the *Sussex* one man, clearly off his head with shock, ran around screaming. He had just discovered the bodies of his wife and son, horribly crushed under twisted wreckage. Nearby, some sailors struggled to free from the debris another man who was trapped by his legs.

A Mr McHarg, a London-based Australian businessman, was standing at the foot of the saloon companionway when the explosion occurred, throwing him to the deck. McHarg had travelled all over the world and had experienced more than one emergency at sea. He kept calm and let the crowd rush past him to get up on deck. When he got there himself he found that one boat had already been lowered and that people were hurling themselves into the sea. He had just dismissed the idea of jumping himself and was making for one of the boats when he was caught by a violent blow on the shoulder from an excited passenger pushing past him, which threw him off his feet again. This proved fortunate for him, because the boat he had planned to board capsized as it hit the water, caused by the solid mass of people who had jumped into it. Eventually he managed to board another of the boats. One woman who had jumped into the sea managed to swim near to a raft. She was in a state of nervous excitement. For some reason she had taken off most of her clothes, but the water was very chilly and she soon collapsed with the cold. A man swam to her assistance, but as soon as he tried to lift her onto the raft it capsized and the fainting woman fell into the water to drown. Another passenger, Norwich Town Councillor W.O. Snelling, urged a young English nurse to go with the other women into the boats, but she refused, saying that her place should be given to a married man with a family of children. Then she calmly resumed her work tending the wounded and dying. The *Sussex* carried no ship's doctor to attend to the seriously injured, but there was a young Dane, a Mr H. Albeck, among the passengers, who lived in Paris. He had a smattering of surgical knowledge which he had picked up from his medical student friends and was able to give first-aid where required by those around him. His services, such as they were, were to become even more valuable later.

The passenger list of the *Sussex* included a wide assortment of nationalities. Besides British and French people, there were Italians, Spanish, Belgians, Russians, Japanese, Portuguese, Swiss, Danish and Chileans, and twenty-five Americans, at least two of whom were journalists on national newspapers. One of them, Edward Marshall of the *New York Sun*, had been on his way to Paris. His story appeared in *The Times* of 27 March:

The boat which capsized was lowered from the starboard davits, about opposite the smoking-room, where I was standing. The boat seemed to make a great deal of water, which must have been due to its condition, as I saw no sea break into it. It was very low in the water as there were so many people in it, and there seemed to be a good deal of excitement and people constantly changing places. The boat suddenly went over, throwing everybody into the sea. I shall never forget the moan which came from those people as they realised the boat was capsizing. I have been in various disasters, but I have never heard so painful a sound before. I should like to pay tribute to an American lady, Mrs Hilton, the daughter-in-law of a celebrated American judge. Although it was feared that her own daughter had been washed out of one of the boats, as she probably was, Mrs Hilton devoted herself to the injured with a sympathetic energy which was not less than marvellous. I was told that twelve of the crew were killed in the explosion, and I tried to get down into the wrecked parts of the ship, but could not do so, for it was very difficult and I am hampered owing to having lost my leg in the Spanish War.

So far as I could see, the boat which capsized was not in charge of an officer. There were certainly no men in uniform in the boat. Various life rafts the width of a door and longer had been thrown into the sea to the drowning people and some of the people from the capsized boat tried to cling to these, with the result that in most cases I saw the rafts overturned. Fifty per cent of those who jumped into the sea were not wearing lifebelts, although I saw plenty of lifebelts on the ship. I saw plenty of men and more women who appropriated two lifebelts, while others lost their heads and did not get one. A lifeboat was sent off to a sailing ship which did not look far off, but the sailing ship turned away.

It would be difficult to exaggerate the indignation which was expressed on board by the American survivors. The fact that the ship was absolutely unarmed – she did not even carry a signal gun – that she carried no munitions, nor was any part of her cargo designed to give comfort to the fighting forces of the Allies, combined with the fact that she was known to be a boat on which women and children would sail of necessity in making the Channel passage, made the act of those who struck at her particularly inexcusable. To an American who looked about upon the company of white-faced, shivering women during the long hours of gloom and peril before the rescue ships appeared, and who listened to the wail of babies vainly wrapped against the chilling cold, sometimes by strangers' hands because their mothers' hands were still forever, a growing feeling of hot anger was inevitable.

With the wireless aerials wrecked and in a tangle, it was about an hour before some temporary ones could be rigged to enable distress calls to go out. It was unfortunate that the ship's position had been wrongly given, because it delayed by several hours the arrival at the scene of ships of the Dover patrol and many other rescue craft which steamed out from both British and French ports. The *Sussex*'s managers, the London, Brighton & South Coast Railway Company, issued bulletins throughout the evening: "At 7 o'clock tonight the steamer was still afloat and all vessels in Dieppe harbour had gone to her assistance." "Later news states that the *Sussex* was still afloat at 8.30, and in the charge of a tug, and it is assumed that all passengers have been saved." "A message has been received from Dieppe stating that the vessel was still afloat at 9.30." But it was not until 11 pm that the first rescue ship found the stricken ferry and came alongside. She was the Boulogne trawler *Marie Thérèse*, which had been searching since receiving the first distress call at 4.45 pm. The ferry's sailors rigged ropes from the lifeboat davits, whilst an unnamed "English speaking middle-aged French corporal" took charge of the swarming passengers keeping them calm and cheerful and marshalled them into fours to slide down the ropes into the trawler. With survivors crowded on board, the trawler steamed back to Boulogne, while more were taken on board the Dover Patrol destroyer HMS *Afridi*, Lieutenant-Commander P.R.P. Percival, which had raced to the scene on receiving the wireless distress calls.

It had been a long and busy day for *Afridi*. She had slipped from Dover at 10.45 that morning to search for a hostile submarine which was reported in the Channel. All day had been spent on this, fruitlessly, until the late afternoon when she had been ordered to resume her normal station with No. 10 patrol. At 10 pm that evening the call had gone out to give aid to the *Sussex* and it was not until 11.15 that she had found the damaged ferry. It was a nippy early spring night, with temperatures hovering barely above freezing point as she transferred eighty-six people on board and sped towards Dover. As she sliced through the water the Danish amateur doctor, Albeck, showed an astonishing skill in performing two major and essential amputations, and rendered efficient first-aid to a number of other people. Unfortunately, one person died en route. It was 2.40 am before *Afridi* secured alongside the hospital ship at Admiralty Pier, Dover, and disembarked her passengers. Then she hurried to the oiler to take on another 108 tons of fuel and went back on patrol. The following forenoon watch was not without excitement. First, it was reported to the Officer of the Watch that there had been lost overboard, by accident, "1 magazine lamp, 1 electric torch, and 2 iron buckets", and then the log recorded that they had "rescued two Lieutenants from a damaged seaplane which eventually sank". Then, in the afternoon, *Afridi* accompanied HMS *Amazon* to Calais as escort for some "Very Important Persons". There was little time for rest on the Dover Patrol.

Captain Mouffet said later that he knew the *Sussex* well and could see that the saloon bulkhead and all the watertight doors were holding. He took the way off the ship by reversing his engines, which relieved the pressure on that crucial bulkhead. He was sure that the *Sussex* was not going to sink and ordered all the lifeboats to return. And sink she did not. She waited, bowless, until tugs arrived to tow her backwards in the safety of Boulogne harbour. If only the passengers had heeded him, Mouffet lamented, and not stampeded to lower the boats (badly) or jump into the sea, the list of casualties would have been restricted to those killed or maimed by the explosion itself. As it was, many people had drowned unnecessarily, increasing the total of fatalities to an estimated fifty.

Another American passenger was fifty-five-year-old Professor James Mark Baldwin, a world renowned psychologist, who was travelling with his family on their way home to Bryn Mawr, Pennsylvania. Only nine days before he had delivered the Herbert Spencer lecture at Oxford University, taking as his subject 'The Super State and the Eternal Values', which was a sketch of the theory of Pan-Germanism. Many of the survivors, unharmed, had simply continued their onward journey from Boulogne rather than Dieppe as they had originally intended, without reporting their names. This had not helped with the compilation of any reliable list of those missing and press reports varied widely in the confusion. Baldwin's family was not on any list of survivors and at first it was feared that they had been killed in the explosion or drowned. Indeed, another American passenger, a Miss Hale from Tuxedo, stated that she had seen the Baldwins killed, side by side, as she had gone to the assistance of a young Frenchman who was bleeding profusely from a head wound. But Miss Hale had been mistaken. They had been landed safely at Boulogne. On 29 March the Paris *Le Matin* published the Professor's account of the attack. He and his wife had been in the afterpart of the ship but for some reason his daughter had gone forward. "There was a terrible shock, then an explosion," said the Professor. "The two things were quite distinct, a fact which immediately induced me to believe that it was not a question of a mine, but of a torpedo, although I did not see a torpedo. We were both knocked down. I was uninjured but my wife was severely bruised. We thought of nothing for the moment but our daughter. We rushed forward, at least as far as we could get – for the *Sussex* had been cut clean off, just beyond the bridge.

We could learn nothing of our daughter, so great was the panic, in spite of the captain's efforts to restore calm. My wife becoming overwhelmed with fatigue and misery, I decided to put her in a boat, and I seized a rope and jumped in my turn. Imagine our joy at finding our daughter already lying in the boat. She was insensible, and we found that she had been dangerously injured in the head by the explosion. After a time we returned on board the *Sussex*. Our remaining on board accounts for our names not appearing in the list of survivors. The telegraph at Boulogne being reserved for military purposes prevented our informing our friends of our safety. No words are strong enough to denounce this act of barbarism, which is the shame of civilisation and humanity."

Baldwin had arranged to meet up with a friend of his in Paris, Donald Harper, before making the last leg of his journey home. He immediately wrote to him,

Wimereux, Saturday.

Dear Harper,

Knowing you knew we were coming on Friday the 24th, I write to tell you that we are all safe, but Elizabeth is seriously injured. We are here with her in hospital. Will you kindly spread the news there?
Yours etc
Baldwin

While there had been no American loss of life in the *Sussex*, there had been four cases of injury caused by the explosion. Three of them were serious. Apart from Elizabeth Baldwin in France, there were Mr Wilder G. Penfield of Hudson, Wisconsin, and George Crocker of Fitchburg, Massachusetts, who now lay in the Military Hospital in Dover along with ten others of various nationalities. And as with both the *Lusitania* and *Arabic* sinkings, there was much uncertainty at first as to exactly who had survived and how many had not. The London, Brighton & South Coast Railway issued a statement in *The Times* of 27 March, saying that they had so far received but few names of definite survivors, as many had gone forward in the ordinary way after landing, especially on the French side, without leaving any information as to their safety.

87

The Company had a list of the thirty-eight people landed at Dover from the destroyer, but only a few were known of the large number who landed at Boulogne. There were Miss Baldwin (USA), Madame Tinto or Pinto, Madame Rosini, Madame Masquillier (Belgian), Monsieur des Rousseaux and Mr Boheme. The report went on: "The following are known to have arrived in Paris, whither most of the passengers proceeded: Mr E.L. Dane, Mr A.J. Morton, Mrs Moore and Mr C.B. Hopkins, Messrs G.H. Crocker, F.E. Drake, and A.E. Huxley (Americans) and also the Comte de Monseau. Messrs Pankaert (Belgian) and Giuseppe Gaja (Italian) have died in hospital in Dover; also a lady who has not so far been identified. (She was wearing a ring inscribed A. Bastin and L. Vivroux.) Nine dead have been landed at Boulogne. Mr C.H. Julius (Dutch) is safe in Paris and Mr Bogdanoff (Russian) has landed safely in Dover."

On the Monday, business was suspended on the Baltic Exchange in the City of London for half an hour as a mark of respect for the deaths in the *Sussex* of two Exchange members, Manville Fraser Goodbody of Kensington and Walter Alvin Lamarque of Orpington. Only the day before sailing across the Channel Goodbody had been victorious in a £20,000 Court case involving the sale of 40,000 horses to the French Government. The two men had been killed instantaneously by the explosion, and a third member of the party (who had been travelling to Boulogne to visit his wounded soldier son in hospital) was faced with the task of identifying the bodies. "The news of their death has caused a revival of feeling on the Exchange against members of enemy birth," announced *The Times*, "especially among the younger men. The question of admission of such persons to the Exchange has recently been the subject of petitions to the directors, who will be considering the points raised."

The names of survivors and those missing came in by dribs and drabs for a considerable time. *Reuter* cabled from Nice, 29 March: "The death is announced of Prince Bahram of Persia, son of Zill-es-Sultan, who lived in Nice. Prince Bahram was on board the *Sussex* when the ship was torpedoed, and, in spite of all their efforts, the family have had no news since."

On the same day *Exchange Telegraph* sent from Madrid: "King Alfonso has ordered the Spanish Ambassadors in London and Paris to inquire whether the Spanish musical composer Granados, who recently returned from New York, was on board the *Sussex*, and has perished as reported. The catastrophe is causing considerable feeling throughout Spain."

The torpedoing of the *Sussex* constituted another chapter in the series of attacks on innocent Americans at sea. It did little to ease what was already a fragile relationship between USA and Germany and it brought renewed demands from large numbers of Americans for USA to enter the war, or at least to break off diplomatic relations with Germany. But America was as divided as ever. The *Chicago Sunday Tribune* carried a cartoon on its front page caricaturing US vacillation about entry into the War. It showed a milling crowd outside Madison Square Garden, New York, clamouring to see the Willard v. Moran heavyweight boxing match, while outside the US army recruiting centre there were a couple of hesitant men rubbing their chins thoughtfully. The caption read, "Do Americans love a fight? Sometimes they do. And sometimes they don't."

For President Wilson it was another case of a weary and tiresome *déjà vu*. Determined to maintain his precarious policy of 'peace with honour', he remained silent while the press seethed with fury. The *New York Sun* restricted itself to the coldly terse comment that all the sentiments that could be expressed about German atrocities had already been expressed and it was useless to repeat them. The *New York World* intoned: "The question to be considered very seriously by this country and by all other neutrals having self-respect is whether anything is to be gained by maintaining any longer the ghastly pretence of friendly diplomatic correspondence with a Power so notoriously lacking in truth and honor." It went on to call for the public punishment of the submarine's captain, saying that this was the only thing which would satisfy the American people.

The *New York Times* devoted a column and a half of its front page to indignation and anxiety as to how much credibility should now be given to German assurances made the previous week about humane maritime warfare. The German statement had been carefully annotated with the news of the retirement of Tirpitz, it observed, thus making an implicit scapegoat of the wise old Admiral by suggesting that he had somehow been to blame for the present crisis, although in fact he had been strongly against the policy of unrestricted submarine warfare right from its onset in early 1915.

The United States Chamber of Commerce in Paris sent a telegram to the White House: "In contempt of what the Declaration of Independence calls just respect for the opinion of mankind, in violation of the legal and moral principles of humanity, and in spite of repeated remonstrances and solemn warnings on the part of the United States, the German Government, like a murderer in the night, has again traitorously and without the slightest warning sunk merchant and passenger ships, thus causing the death of innocent victims, men, women and children. In the name of humanity we ask that this intolerable situation shall stop. In the name of our fellow citizens who have been killed or maimed on the *Englishman** or the *Sussex*, we protest against the continuance of diplomatic relations with a Government whose lust for blood, savagery and scorn of all laws have earned the execration of the whole civilised world."

Another issue gave rise to severe criticizm of the *Sussex*'s operators and crew at the inquest in Dover on the bodies of two men and a woman who had died in the attack. One witness, American passenger Charles T. Crocker, told the Coroner that he saw some people trying to put lifebelts on, but the tapes broke. They were absolutely rotten. He tried to put a couple on some women, but the same thing happened. When he tried to find a lifebelt for himself, he found that all were similarly defective. After a time the crew brought up some life-preservers, which were better. The rotten belts had been hanging on the rails of the ship and the tapes had become perished by salt-spray. After the explosion, the witness said, he saw one lifeboat hanging from a broken rope and people in the water. One end of the boat was hanging in the air and the other was just touching the water. There was a terrible rush for the boats. They were overloaded. People "just jammed into them" and some had to be got out. He saw many people in the water and to these rafts and ropes were thrown and two or three people were pulled out of the sea. On going to the forepart of the vessel he found many people wounded and some dead. He assisted with the injured.

The Coroner: "Did everybody behave well during the accident?"

---

* Four Americans, M.A. Burke, G. McDonald, F. MacDonald and F. Buckley, *had* been killed aboard the *Englishman*, which was sunk the day after the *Sussex* attack. See below. Why this did not create an even greater stir of opinion in the USA is a mystery.

Crocker: "The crew did not appear very efficient. Some of them got champagne and the officers had to take it away."

The Coroner: "Did they get drunk?"

Crocker: "No, but I imagine they would have."

Chief Constable Fox: "Did you see any other persons trying to fix lifebelts and have misfortunes with the tapes?"

Crocker: "Yes, one or two."

Fox: "Were there enough lifebelts for all?"

Crocker: "Yes."

A juror said that the question of the lifebelts was a serious matter and ought to be brought before the Board of Trade. The Coroner agreed, saying that there would be an inquiry. The jury returned a verdict that the victims had met their deaths through the ship being hit by an enemy torpedo.

The immediate German reaction had been to deny the torpedoing altogether. When the German Ambassador, Count Bernsdorff, arrived in Washington on 29 March he was immediately surrounded by reporters. When told that the tension over the matter had reached a very high pitch in the White House and the State Department, he replied coolly, "I cannot help it. One cannot blame Germany because the *Sussex* was struck by a British mine." And when asked if the German Foreign Office had sent instructions for him to discuss the *Sussex* with the State Department, Bernsdorff maintained, "Why should we discuss it? It doesn't concern us."

The suggestion that the explosion had been caused by a British mine was immediately refuted by witnesses. In Paris American passenger Samuel F. Bemis, a Harvard research student, made a deposition to the US Embassy: "I was on deck at the time. I saw a torpedo coming towards the steamer. Its wake was plainly and unmistakeably visible. The moment it reached us there was a terrible explosion and many persons were blown into the water. Some I saw killed before my eyes. Rafts and boats were lowered and I climbed upon a raft. Men were drowned about me. I was picked up by a lifeboat."

And a French infantry corporal who had been a passenger went to a news agency when he reached Paris and claimed to have been the first person to see the torpedo and raise the alarm. A short time afterwards, he said, a submarine flying a German flag appeared about four miles away and, after a few evolutions, disappeared.

The corporal appears to have been the only person to claim to have actually seen the submarine, which was revealed after the War to have been the *UB-29*, commanded by Oberleutnant-zur-See Herbert Pustkuchen, one of Admiral Andreas Michelsen's *Flandern Flotilla*, operating out of Zeebrugge. (*UB-29* was eventually to meet her end when she was depth-charged and sunk on 6 December 1916, twelve miles south-west of Bishop Rock by the destroyer HMS *Landrail*.)

Meanwhile, the US German-language press (which had a considerable circulation) intensified the controversy by propagating a rumour that British agents were paying American seamen £5 a head to sail in British ships, so that if they were torpedoed it would heighten anti-German feeling in the States. And in Germany itself the Government continued to make protestations of wounded innocence. When Berlin intimated that the German Government was deeply insulted and hurt by the refusal of the American press to believe that the *Sussex* had been struck by a British mine, the *New York World* was bitingly caustic in its retort. "We have," it snarled, "the word of the Foreign Minister von Jagow that no German submarine attacked the *Sussex*. Last May we had the word of the same gentleman that the *Lusitania* when she left New York undoubtedly had guns on board which were mounted under decks and masked, that she was an auxiliary cruiser and that contrary to the American law she carried explosives. The man who swore he saw the *Lusitania*'s guns is now in Atlanta penitentiary, a convicted perjurer*, and the German Foreign Office, when challenged for proof, has not repeated its charge. . . . Practically every month since the submarine warfare began we have been officially informed by von Jagow and Herr von Bethmann-Hollweg [the German Chancellor] that one excuse for the lawless undersea operations was Britain's effort by a blockade to starve the civil population of Germany. The submarine atrocities were ushered in by the proclamation of 4 February 1915. The American ship *William P. Frye*, loaded with grain for England, sailed from Seattle on 6 November 1914 and was sunk at sea by the German raider *Prinz Eitel Friedrich* on 28 January 1915. Britain began to commandeer foodstuffs believed to be consigned to Germany on 11 March 1916.

* A man named Stahl had been convicted of giving false evidence in connection with the *Lusitania* sinking.

"Not to mention other instances, it will be seen, we think, that what the German Foreign Office says is not always so, that it does not always insist that it is so and on some occasions it frankly admits that it is not so."

Still the Germans refused to admit one jot of guilt in response to the accusations piling against them, although, in fact, a junior official at the *Admiralstab* had remarked to the US Ambassador in an unguarded moment that "the *Sussex* was probably regarded as a troopship and if the submarine commander was under the impression that she had soldiers aboard then he was within his rights to torpedo her". *Reuter* cabled from Amsterdam on 12 April that an unsigned telegram had been received by the US Ambassador in Berlin on 12 April in reply to a request by Washington for an explanation of attacks on the *Sussex* and other vessels.

The undersigned [!] informs the Ambassador of the United States in regard to the steamers *Sussex*, *Manchester Engineer*, *Englishman*, *Berwindvale* and *Eagle Point* that these cases have been carefully examined.

A steamer which might possibly have been the *Berwindvale* was encountered in the evening of 16 March in sight of the Bull Rock lighthouse, on the Irish coast, by a German submarine and was ordered to stop by a warning shot. The steamer extinguished all lights and tried to escape. Consequently, she was fired on until she stopped. The crew were given ample time to man the boats and get away before she was sunk. The assertion that the *Berwindvale* was torpedoed without warning, therefore, is not borne out by the facts.

The steamer *Englishman* was ordered to stop on 24 March, 20 sea miles west of the Island of Islay, by a German submarine which fired two warning shots. These, however, were disregarded and the submarine compelled her to stop by gunfire after a long pursuit. When the German commander had ascertained that the crew had taken to the boats and rowed away, he sank the steamer.

As regards the steamer *Manchester Engineer*, investigation so far has not been able to establish whether the attack on the vessel can be attributed to a submarine. Exact details of the time and place would be desirable so that the matter can be concluded.

The steamer *Eagle Point*, on the morning of 28 March, about

100 – not 130 – miles off the south-west coast of Ireland, was requested by signal and shot from a submarine to stop, but she continued her journey, whereupon she was fired upon until she stopped. After the commander was convinced that the boats had been lowered he sank her. At the time of the sinking, the boats had set their sails and were free of the steamer. There was a NNW wind of strength 2, not a 'stormy wind', a slight sea, not a 'heavy sea', and the boats had every prospect of being picked up as the place was on a much frequented steamer route.

The establishment of whether the steamer *Sussex* was damaged by a German submarine or not is rendered extraordinarily difficult by the fact that no exact details of the place, time or circumstances of the incident are known, and no picture of this vessel could be obtained. Therefore, all the operations which took place on 24 March between Folkestone and Dieppe had to be investigated.

On 24 March, in the middle of the English Channel, a long black vessel, flying no flag, with a grey funnel, small grey upper deckhouse and two high masts was met by a German submarine. The German commander was firmly convinced that this was a war vessel, namely a minelayer of the recently built Arabis class. His conviction was supported by the fact that the vessel's build and painting were like that of a warship, by her high speed, and the unusual course she was steering for a merchantman. He therefore attacked her at 3.55 pm. The torpedo caused such a violent explosion in the fore part of the ship that the whole of it up to the bridge was blown off. The great violence of the explosion admits of the certain conclusion that great quantities of ammunition were on board.

A sketch of the vessel made by the commander of the submarine and a picture of the *Sussex* from an English newspaper are appended for comparison which show that the *Sussex* was not identical with the attacked vessel. No other attack was made at the time and place in question, and therefore the German Government supposes that the sinking (sic) of the *Sussex* must be attributable to some other cause.

By way of explanation, it may be added that on 1 and 2 April 26 British mines were destroyed in the Channel by German naval forces. Moreover, all that part of the Channel is rendered dangerous by drifting mines and unsunk torpedoes.

The German Government asks for further material for the investigation, and declares its readiness to have the facts established by a mixed committee of inquiry in accordance with The Hague Convention.

But the world was not at all impressed by Berlin's self-exculpation, least of all the British Foreign Office which issued this statement in response to the unsigned telegram:

1. There is no resemblance whatever, as contended by the Germans, between a vessel of the Arabis class and the *Sussex*, and it is quite impossible to mistake one vessel for the other.
2. The Germans are condemned out of their own mouths by their statement that the commander of the German submarine fired on some vessel at a certain moment. Now that certain moment was precisely the time at which the *Sussex* was attacked.
3. The German commander admitted that he had destroyed the fore part of the vessel he attacked. No other ship but the *Sussex* has suffered in this way.

For these and other considerations based on definite information received by the Admiralty, there is absolutely no room for doubt that the *Sussex* was torpedoed by a German submarine.

The "other considerations based on definite information" constituted two trump cards in the dispute. Firstly, the French had obtained some damning statements from the crew of *UB-26* which they captured on 5 April. The little coastal U-boat, another of Michelsen's *Flandern Flotilla*, commanded by Kapitänleutnant Smiths, having slipped out of the Ems on 19 March and crossed the net barrage between the South Goodwins and Outer Ruytingen, had been stealthily stalking a steamer off Le Havre when she slammed her periscope onto the bottom of a patrolling drifter, which instantly revealed her presence. She had lain doggo on the bottom hoping to avoid being attacked herself, but the French destroyer *Trombe* had peppered her with depth-charges. Other drifters gathered around and, under the orders of Lieutenant J. McLaughlin of HMS *Endurance*, put down their nets, which entangled and jammed the submarine's propellers. This eventually caused her batteries to catch fire and she was forced to surface and submit to capture. Her crew of twenty-one was taken off safely and the French salvaged her, repaired her and re-commissioned her as the *Roland Morillot*. They gathered much valuable information about the *Sussex* incident both from their interrogation of the crew and from incriminating documents that the Germans had failed to destroy thoroughly.

Secondly, two American officers, a Captain Smith of the US Navy and a Major Logan from the US Embassy, had been given an opportunity to examine the wreck of the *Sussex* as it lay in Boulogne. They had discovered two screw-bolts, marked 'K56' and 'K58' respectively. German torpedoes in possession of the naval authorities at Toulon and at Portsmouth contained identical screws, each bearing the letter K and a number. Furthermore, the officers were able to identify positively another thirteen pieces of metal as parts of a German torpedo.

For his apparent kid-glove treatment of the Germans, the Democrat President Woodrow Wilson had been ragged mercilessly in the press and by the Republicans. The pugnacious former President Theodore 'Teddy' Roosevelt had gone as far as to call him "an astute, unprincipled and physically cowardly demagogue". Wilson had borne all this invective stoically and held his tongue. Nevertheless, it was clear that 'peace with honor' was a very narrow path to tread politically. Despite the clarion comments against him, Wilson was not without many supporters. American public opinion was still finely balanced, for and against action, and the next Presidential election was but a few months distant. Closer to home, there was trouble with the Villista revolutionaries in Mexico and rumours abounded that the Germans had approached the Mexicans with a view to making a military alliance against the USA. In return for submarine bases, apparently, Mexico's reward was to be the states of New Mexico, Arizona and Texas! It was also evident that the Germans were far from revising their submarine tactics, although they would continue to throw up their hands in innocence. He decided that it was time for some very firm and final words and composed yet another long 'Note' to the German Government.

In stern tones it referred in particular to the attack on the *Sussex*. It stressed that this was not an isolated case, but was "only one instance of the deliberate method and spirit with which merchantmen of every kind, nationality and designation are indiscriminately destroyed and which has become the more unmistakeable the more the activity of the German submarines has increased in intensity in recent months." The German Government had assured the United States Government that it would apply every precaution to respect the rights of neutrals and protect the lives of non-combatants, but German submarine commanders had practised a procedure of such reckless destruction as made it more and more clear that Berlin was unable to impose on them the promised restrictions. These actions lacked every justification. The United States Government had been very patient and had accepted successive German explanations and assurances in good faith.

"If the Imperial German Government should not now, without delay, proclaim and make effective renunciation of its present methods of submarine warfare against passenger and cargo ships," the Note concluded, "the United States Government can have no other choice than to break off completely diplomatic relations with the German Government. The United States Government views such a step with the greatest reluctance, but feels itself compelled to adopt it in the name of humanity and of the rights of neutral nations. I seize this opportunity to renew to your Excellency the assurance of my most distinguished esteem." Signed Gerard. [The US Ambassador in Berlin]

The statements of the numerous witnesses, the conclusive evidence of the 'K' screw-bolts and the thirteen fragments of torpedo and the President's Note, which effectively constituted an ultimatum, all combined to leave the Germans little option but to try to make a clean breast of things with a minimum loss of face.

Reuter cabled from Amsterdam on 10 May: "A semi-official telegram from Berlin says: 'An investigation into the facts now ascertained about the case of the *Sussex* no longer supports the earlier view that the damage to the *Sussex* was attributable to some other cause than an attack by a German submarine. It can no longer be doubted that the supposed warship torpedoed on 24 March by a German submarine was, in fact, identical with the *Sussex*. The German Government has acquainted the United States Government with this fact, adding that in accordance with the German Note of 4 May the German Government will draw conclusions from it'."

And *The Times* New York correspondent wired the same day: "Germany has handed Mr Gerard a Note acknowledging that the *Sussex* was torpedoed by a German submarine, announcing that the guilty commander has 'been punished' and expressing readiness to indemnify Americans injured by the explosion of the torpedo."

The Germans called off their policy of unrestricted submarine warfare, at least for the time being. There was still the odd instance of attack on innocent shipping, but it was to be another year before the resumption of widespread indiscriminate sinkings, with American ships now being included among the victims, and the USA was at last drawn into the War.

It could be argued that the trigger-happy Pustkuchen had cost Germany the War. Only on 4 March 1916 Kaiser Wilhelm had bowed to pressure from the *Admiralstab* and given orders for unrestricted submarine warfare to be announced again. It was to re-commence on 1 April. But on 24 March came the fateful incident with the *Sussex*, which re-kindled American anti-German sentiment, thus adding a little more weight towards the eventual tipping of the scales.

7

THE KILLING OF A SEA DOG

The news that the Germans had executed fifty-year-old Edith Cavell, a Norfolk rector's daughter who had been working as a nursing teacher in Brussels, on 12 October 1915, for helping over 200 British soldiers to escape from captivity via an organized rat line into neutral Holland, brought roars of outraged disgust from all around a horrified world. Such was the anger generated by it that British Army recruitment doubled in just eight weeks and Edith became a martyr whose name was destined to be inscribed on the rolls of posterity. And nine and a half months later, on 27 July 1916, another event created another martyr and brought fresh waves of red-hot indignation from the Allied side.

Charles Algernon Fryatt was a native of Southampton, born there on 2 December 1871, the son of a merchant navy officer. The Essex port of Harwich-Parkeston Quay was beginning to develop as demand grew for steam ferry terminals to serve the busy North Sea crossings in the early 1880s and Fryatt Senior, who already held a First Mate's ticket, landed a job there as navigating officer with the Great Eastern Railways Steamship Company. With his new promotion secure, he uprooted his family from Southampton and they all moved into a new GER company house in Adelaide Street, Harwich, and the young Charles rounded off his education at the nearby Corporation School.

When he left school he followed in his father's footsteps by embarking on a sea-going career, although it was not until he was twenty-one that he too joined the GER. His first ship was the *Ipswich* and he earned £1.25 per week as an able seaman on the Antwerp run. It was GER company practice to dry-dock their steamers every six months, and they frequently used the facilities at Hull for this purpose. It is almost certain that it was on one of these trips to the dry dock that Charles found romance, because it is recorded that on 2 November 1896 he married nineteen-year-old spinster Ethel Townend at St Peter's Parish Church, Kingston-upon-Hull. The couple set up home in Oakland Road, Dovercourt, Harwich, and were eventually to produce a brood of seven children.

With his new-found marital responsibilities, Charles needed to advance himself. By diligent studying, he managed to obtain the certificate of competency and was promoted to Second Mate in June 1900, on a wage of £1.75 per week. By 1907 he was a First Mate and in June 1913 the Company appointed him Master of their cargo vessel *Newmarket*. At the outbreak of war the Royal Navy requisitioned the *Newmarket* for duties in the Eastern Mediterranean and Captain Charles Fryatt was transferred with most of his crew to the steamer *Wrexham*, which the GER had on charter from the Great Central Railway.

In the very early uncertain days of the war the GER under-standably suspended altogether its passenger services from Harwich to Hamburg, Esbjerg and Gothenburg, although the cargo service was continued to Rotterdam, and somewhat strangely, as it may be thought, passengers could still travel from Tilbury to Antwerp (in enemy-occupied Belgium) if they "made their own arrangements as to getting on board the steamer in the river". Eventually, the *Wrexham* was one of four ships which enabled the Company to maintain a somewhat erratic wartime service between England and the neutral Dutch ports throughout the conflict, sometimes running out of Tilbury when Harwich became congested with naval vessels. It was a dangerous run. Buoys which normally marked the navigation channels through areas of treacherous sandbanks during peacetime had been removed and then there was the U-boat threat as well as the minefields off the coast of the Low Countries.

The early part of 1915 saw the declaration by the Germans of unrestricted submarine warfare in the seas around the British Isles. Chancellor Theobald von Bethmann-Hollweg, against his will it has to be said, finally bowed to pressure by his Admirals. He announced that Germany would endeavour to destroy every enemy merchant ship found within that area, even if it were not always possible to avoid danger to persons and cargoes. He went on to warn neutrals of the dangers of entering the declared zone. The fact that the British were in the habit of using neutral flags to protect their merchant ships meant that Germany could not guarantee to recognize the true identify of neutrals, and thereby ensure their safety. The campaign was to come into effect on 18 February 1915.

On 10 February, in anticipation of the onslaught, the British Admiralty issued clandestine orders to all merchant ships' masters: "No British Merchant Ship would ever tamely surrender to a submarine, but should do its utmost to escape. If a submarine comes up suddenly with obvious hostile intentions, steer straight for it at maximum speed, altering course as necessary to keep it ahead. The submarine will probably dive, in which case you have ensured your ship's safety, as the enemy will be compelled to re-surface astern of you." It was a timely piece of advice, because Fryatt's first brush with the enemy came only three weeks later, on 2 March 1915, when *Wrexham*, with her pistons pounding furiously to produce every one of her maximum twelve knots, just made the safety of Dutch territorial water after being pursued for forty miles by a submarine. In recognition of his skill in saving his ship, the grateful GER presented him with a gold watch and paid 'special compliments' to the *Wrexham*'s engine-room crew, whose sweat had actually saved the day. (As far as is known, it is not recorded what form these 'special compliments' took.)

After this episode the GER decided that the *Wrexham*'s limited speed made her too vulnerable to U-boat attack to continue in service. She was returned to her owners and Fryatt and his crew were transferred to the *Brussels*, one of the other three remaining ships on the Holland service. By now the Germans were getting their submarine campaign into full swing. So much so, in fact, that by the end of April they had sunk no fewer than eighty-eight British merchantmen.

In the face of this intensified U-boat activity, it was not surprising that Fryatt did not have to wait long for his second encounter with the Germans. On 28 March, only twenty-six days after he had run the panting *Wrexham* into Rotterdam, the *Brussels* was approaching the Hook en route to Rotterdam from Parkeston. She was about eight miles off the Maas Buoy when a German submarine was spotted. It was the ocean-going *U-33*, commanded by Gansser, one of the Kaiser's top twenty U-boat aces, who was to sink eighteen Allied ships totalling 140,000 tons in the course of the war.

The German hoisted flags ordering the steamer to stop, but the Admiralty's orders were fresh in Fryatt's mind. He rang down for Full Speed and a game of cat-and-mouse began. It ended when the submarine dived as it was crossing the path of the galloping *Brussels*. The steamer's firemen, in the stokehold, said that they felt a distinct jolt as the submarine passed under their bows. It resurfaced on the port side, very close to the ship, then dived again. By following the Admiralty's recommendations, Fryatt had beaten it off. He reported to his Directors,

> I beg to report that on Sunday afternoon on the 28th inst, when from Parkeston to Rotterdam, I sighted a German submarine. I sighted him about two points on my starboard bow at a distance of four miles steering to the southward. As I got closer to him he turned round very quickly on his port helm and steered towards me, very fast from starboard to port. I at once altered my course E by S to ESE which brought him on my port bow about one point. I could see it was no use trying to get away from him as by steering my course to the southward he could easily have torpedoed me and his speed was far greater than mine. He hoisted two flags for me to stop but I did not like the idea of giving up my ship to him so I decided to ram him.
>
> I starboarded my helm and sent down to the Engineers to give her all speed possible, and sent all the crew aft out of the way in case he fired at me and I got the Chief Officer to fire three of the socket rockets to make him think I had a gun and I steered straight for his conning tower. He was then about 100 yards from me and when he saw me ignore his signal and heard the reports from the rockets he immediately submerged. He was approximately twenty yards ahead of me when he submerged and I steamed straight for the place where he disappeared and when I considered that I was on top of him I then gave the order 'hard a-port' to sweep over his periscope. His periscope came up under our bottom abreast of the fore gangway doors about two feet out of the water and came close along our port side. I could not feel the ship strike her but one of the firemen felt a bumping sensation under the bottom. I think I must have damaged him if I have not sunk him as I consider it was impossible for him to

102

get clear according to the position of his periscope when it came up to the surface.

After it passed our Bridge it came further out of the water showing a decided list after which it disappeared. Although a good lookout was kept, I saw nothing further of him.

I still kept my course, going as fast as the Engineers could drive her, until I reached the Examination Boat inside the three mile limit.

I should think according to my opinion she was quite 300 ft long, very high bow and very large circular conning tower and no distinguishing marks.

I must highly commend my Officers and Engineers and crew for the way my orders were carried out.

Time when first sighted – 1.10 pm
On top of submarine – 1.30 pm
Lat 51°58"N Long 3°41"E
Speed of ship – 15½knots."

After arrival in Rotterdam, the *Brussels* was placed in the Wilton's Yard dry-dock for inspection following the ramming. It was already fairly certain that contact had been made with the U-boat. Firstly, one of the firemen had felt a distinct bump and, secondly, the submarine had surfaced so close on the port side of the *Brussels* that the steamer's crew claimed that they could have hung their hats on its periscope. The lateral scrapings found along her bilge-keel and bottom were enough to provide conclusive evidence when the steamer was taken out of the water.

At home, Fryatt, now known locally as the 'Pirate Dodger', First Mate Charles Stiff and Chief Engineer Robert Smith were presented with commendations for their bravery at a civic ceremony by Harwich Borough Mayor Edward Saunders. And a letter was received at the GER Headquarters at London's Liverpool Street Station from the Admiralty saying that Their Lordships had decided to present Fryatt with another gold watch, while Stiff and Smith were to be regaled with 'Letters on Vellum'.

But that was not the end of the *Brussels*' acquaintance with the German submarine fleet. On 17 June, near the South Inner Gabbards buoy, she came across a U-boat approaching a small fishing smack which it had just torpedoed without warning. Her usual First Mate, William Hartnell, who held a Master's Certificate

103

and who was Sailing Master on that trip, tried to ram it in the Fryatt tradition, but although he managed to get within sixty yards of it, the submarine eluded him and escaped. Almost immediately afterwards the *Brussels* herself was threatened by another U-boat, but Hartnell kept on course at top speed and ran to safety. Similar encounters became commonplace for all three GER ships on the Holland run. But Fryatt continued to run the U-boat gauntlet without meeting with any further major mishap until his ninety-eighth trip in the *Brussels*.

At 2300 hours on 22 June 1916 she sailed from Hook of Holland with 100 Belgian and Russian refugees plus a single fare-paying passenger, 390 tons of cargo, mails, forty-five crew members, a Marconi wireless operator and a Trinity House pilot on board. As she proceeded to sea through the New Waterway, Able Seaman Knights observed a rocket soaring into the night sky from the direction of the shore, which he reported to the First Mate Bill Hartnell. Both Hartnell and Fryatt would normally have been on the bridge at that time, therefore it is strange that Fryatt seems to have remained unaware of what Knights had seen. It was thought later that in all probability it had been a warning signal from a British agent that enemy vessels were in the vicinity. Indeed, Fryatt was heard to say later that he wished that he had known about it. As Master, it is inconceivable that he would not have been privy to the meaning of any coded signals of this type. Twelve miles past the Maas Buoy the blurred shape of a small boat was spotted in the midsummer darkness. It signalled in Morse the repeated letter S. At this Fryatt did become clearly concerned. Was it another warning, issued because it seemed that he had ignored the rocket signal? He rang down for Full Speed while Hartnell continued to sweep the sea with his night-glasses. He thought he could see a ship sailing ahead on the same course as the *Brussels*. It being wartime, of course, both vessels were sailing unlit. To avoid a high-speed collision, Fryatt switched on his navigation lights for one minute. Fifteen minutes later he was surprised to find himself surrounded by a flotilla of no less than nine German destroyers.

This time, there was no escape for the 'Pirate Dodger'. He stopped his ship and hurried to the stokehold to burn his secret Admiralty orders and a diplomatic bag in the furnaces. A crew of German blue-jackets swarmed aboard the *Brussels*, all armed with revolvers and some of them brandishing hand-held bombs. It was quite useless for the unarmed ferry-boatmen even to think of resistance. Quickly, the boarders rounded up the British crew, hoisted the German flag, steamed her into Zeebrugge and thence up the canal to Bruges. In describing the scene, the Dutch *Telegraaf* said that the British sailors "behaved in a very quiet and dignified way when they were brought into Zeebrugge. Captain Fryatt himself stood in the middle of his officers, his face as calm as if he were on the bridge, turning to comfort some weeping Belgian women with a few kind words, thinking of others while conscious of his own terrible position. Captain Fryatt's gold watch alone is believed to be responsible for his detention. It will be remembered that a suspicious character was on board the *Brussels* when she was captured. He was said to be an American but was heard to speak German perfectly." (Presumably this was the mysterious lone passenger. The fact that he was treated with all consideration by the Germans when they captured the vessel and was immediately liberated indicates strongly the likelihood that he was, in some way, acting on their behalf.)

That there were more suspicious characters involved became known when a report concerning the capture of the *Brussels* arrived at the Foreign Office from the British Consul in Flushing, Mr Gilliat-Smith, via the British Ambassador at The Hague: "It appears that the information about her capture was brought in by a fisherman by the name of Schroevers of the *V46*. This is the boat which had previously been suspected of taking supplies to German submarines, but no concrete evidence has been obtainable up to now. It is a fact, however, that she often puts to sea when no other boats are out, and comes back after thirty-six or thirty-eight hours with no fish on board."

Communications between London and Berlin were conducted via the US Ambassadors in each country. On 28 June Foreign Secretary Sir Edward Grey sent to Ambassador Page:

No. 1218/16. Immediate: The Secretary of State for Foreign Affairs presents his compliments to the United States Ambassador and has the honour to state that he would be much obliged if the United States Ambassador at Berlin could be requested by telegraph to ascertain the names of the British subjects who were on board the steamship *Brussels* when she

105

was recently captured by German warships and taken to Zeebrugge.

Sir E. Grey understands that there were six British stewardesses on board, and he trusts that they will be repatriated at an early date.

The reply came on 1 July:

> The American Ambassador presents his compliments to his Majesty's Secretary of State for Foreign Affairs and in reply to the Note Sir Edward Grey was good enough to address to him on 28 June (No 1218/16) concerning the British subjects who were on board the steamship *Brussels* when that vessel was captured by German warships has the honour to state that he is now in receipt of a telegraphic communication from the Ambassador at Berlin to the effect that the officers and crew of the Harwich steamer *Brussels* are safe and well and are now interned at Ruhleben.
>
> The Master of the vessel desires that his wife may be informed and it is requested that parcels may be sent from England to these prisoners.
>
> It appears that the five [sic] stewardesses were separated from the crew at Cologne and Mr Gerard is inquiring of the German Government as to their present whereabouts and urging their prompt repatriation.

The *Brussels'* crew were taken secretly up to Bruges in motor-cars and later imprisoned in various places – the stewardesses in Holzminden, some in Brandenburg and some in Bruges itself, for the duration of the war, but special treatment was reserved for Fryatt and Hartnell. They were taken to Ruhleben. It will not be amiss to say a little about the place.

At the outbreak of war in August 1914 there had been about 30,000 people with German citizenship on British soil. With the utmost rapidity they had been rounded up and interned. When Berlin learned of this, they issued an ultimatum to the effect if these Germans were not released from internment by 15 November 1914 the same treatment would be given to the 5,000 British subjects living in Germany. No response came and the round-up of enemy aliens began. These included the crews of several merchant ships trapped in harbour at Bremen and Hamburg, plus that of a South African warship which had been paying a goodwill visit to Germany. But where to house all these people?

At Ruhleben racecourse, in Spandau, a suburb of Berlin, the stable complex became the residence of 365 male internees. Each stall accommodated six prisoners. Each had a cold water tap, but there was no heating at all and they were open to the weather. The inmates received no blankets or bedding, nor lockers in which to keep their personal belongings. The only lighting came from a single electric bulb in the connecting corridor.

However, when the US Ambassador James W. Gerrard visited Ruhleben during the winter of 1914–15 and saw these conditions, which had been made many times worse by the extremely wet autumn turning the racecourse into a twenty-acre field of well-churned mud, he interceded on behalf of the prisoners. From then on the Germans adhered strictly to the Geneva Conventions. They delivered bedding and plentiful supplies of timber for the prisoners to make into doors and windows and they promptly forwarded Red Cross consignments of food and supplies. Soon Ruhleben had acquired a new face.

With the pressing needs of the advancing German army demanding all available soldiers to be at the front, some long-retired officers, some of them in their seventies or eighties, were recalled to act as guards. These elderly men, seeing that the British were not likely to cause them any trouble, adopted a policy of *laissez faire* and within a short time the interned community evolved into a remarkable little cell of civilization. It had its own internal postal system, educational facilities (two dozen Cambridge graduates were interned there), newspapers, theatre and shops. Prisoners were freely allowed into the town, after giving their parole of course, where they were often to be seen drinking coffee in company with a guard or two and freely conversing in English. The camp even held its own comic election on the 3 August 1915. The winner was one Reuben Castang, who had stood for the Suffragette Party, promising that, as the Red Cross had been so efficient in delivering tinned food for them, he would import 10,000 tinned girls for the benefit of the prisoners!

Captain Charles Fryatt arrived there on 2 July 1916, but for him Ruhleben was not to be such a happy place. He was subjected to over three weeks of severe interrogation at the end of which he was taken back to Bruges and ushered before a court, charged as follows: "Although he was not a member of a combat force, he made an attempt, on 28 March 1915, to ram the German submarine *U-33* near the Maas Lightship." At half-past four o'clock in the afternoon of 27 July 1916 he was pronounced guilty and sentenced to be shot.

The British Government had not even been aware that there was going to be a trial until about ten days before. It had been assumed that Fryatt, along with all the others, would be simply held as a prisoner of war. Fryatt's impending trial by Naval Court Martial for ramming the *U-33* was only learned of in London from an article which appeared in the Amsterdam *Telegraaf*. Once more the telegraph wires hummed in Whitehall as Grey requested the Americans to obtain confirmation of the story and to take all possible steps to ensure that Fryatt was properly represented. The Note went on to inform His Excellency confidentially that "in committing the act impugned, Captain Fryatt acted legitimately in self-defence for the purpose of evading capture or destruction."

The British Government attempted unsuccessfully to negotiate a postponement of the trial and it was thanks only to US Ambassador James W. Gerrard's efforts that Fryatt was indeed legally represented at all, by a Major Neumann, a retired German army officer on the Reserve, civil attorney and *justizrat*. Little, if anything, is known of the proceedings, but only two and a half hours after he was convicted the sentence was carried out in the Jardin de l'Aurore, adjoining an army barracks in the Rue Longue in the south-eastern suburbs of Bruges.

At five o'clock M. van Hoestenberghe, a sheriff of Bruges, and a colleague had been summoned to the Kommandantur and first ordered verbally, and then, when they protested about this lack of courtesy, in writing, to be at the Jardin de l'Aurore for an execution at seven o'clock that evening. They were shocked at the way Commandant von Büttlar, the German officer in charge, hurried forward the execution. They were ordered to have a coffin ready and a grave dug in the cemetery. When they reached the place of execution they found von Büttlar pacing up and down impatiently, with a cigar clamped in his teeth and his dog at his heels. When he saw them he exclaimed with a sigh of relief, "At last! Here are the sheriffs!" A man of middle height, dressed in plain clothes, was standing near the firing party which had arrived accompanied by a band playing a cheerful bouncy march. The sheriffs were not to know until some days later that this man was, in fact, Captain Fryatt. He took no notice when they saluted him and his attitude throughout was one of complete indifference.

Judge Schoen read the sentence, but the sheriffs did not understand it properly. They had already witnessed several similar trials and, as far as they were concerned, the prisoner was simply another Belgian convicted of espionage. Fryatt was tied to a post and his eyes blindfolded. Köhne, a naval chaplain who had sat with him since he was sentenced, spoke a few quiet words to him. As the volley was fired, van Hoestenberghe shut his eyes. When he opened them again, Fryatt had slumped forward in his bonds, dead. He needed no *coup de grâce*. Half an hour later a telegram arrived from Berlin ordering the sentence to be postponed.

They buried him in the communal cemetery. His grave was the fourth in a line of thirteen persons executed by the Germans. Later, it was seen to bear a black cross with an inscription in white, "Here lies Captain Fryat. [sic] Master of s.s.Brussels of glorious memory. R.I.P." At the base of the cross was a little garden planted with flowers.

Chaplain Köhne sat down to write to Mrs Fryatt,

Dear Madam,

No doubt you have meanwhile heard of the death of your husband on 27 July by judgment of a duly instituted Court Martial.

As I spent his last moments with him, in order to prepare him for the fateful journey, he naturally spoke to me of you and his children; he begged me to convey to you and them his last goodbye and tell you how he died. This I do willingly as follows:

I met your husband calm and collected in his room. I told him that he had to prepare for his doom and appear before his heavenly judge. He knew what he had done, and thought by doing so, to do something for his country. He had to bear the penalty for his deed, which, accordingly to the laws of war, could not be passed over by us. He acknowledged it with a nod and said he took it all upon himself. We then prayed together out of the Book of Common Prayer, read the 23rd Psalm and the Lord's Prayer; he promised me to be brave to the end.

Overshadowed by beautiful trees he spoke again much of you and of his children. He told me their names and expressed the hope that they, especially the elder ones, would stand by their mother and help her in her great bereavement. To all, and above to yourself, he sends his best love. As his last hour had come, we spoke again of God, before whom he was about to appear, and hoped to be forgiven for his wrongdoings. He then asked me where his body would rest; I told him it would be committed to the Belgian authorities and buried in the Bruges cemetery. He begged me, if possible, to send you a photo of his grave, which I shall be pleased to do, if allowed. After a last prayer, which we said together, he met his death calmly, and his body was handed over to the Belgian authorities.

Now, I beg to send you and your children a word of consolation. May you bear this terrible blow, and tell yourself, as your husband did, that it is the consequence of a deed punishable by the laws of war. He thought he had a right to act as he did for the sake of his country, and has suffered death for it. Let us hope that God, to whom he has resigned, has received him in His mercy.

May the Almighty and Merciful help you and your children. (signed) Köhne. Naval Chaplain. Bruges 3. VIII. 16.

And a letter was sent to Mrs Fryatt by command of King George V:

Buckingham Palace, August 3.

Madam,

In the sorrow which has so cruelly stricken you the King joins with his people in offering you his heartfelt sympathy.

Since the outbreak of war, his Majesty has followed with admiration the splendid services of the Mercantile Marine.

The action of Captain Fryatt in defending his ship against the attack of an enemy submarine was a noble instance of the resource and self-reliance so characteristic of that profession.

It is therefore with feelings of the deepest indignation that the King learned of your husband's fate, and in conveying to you the expression of his condolence I am commanded to assure you of the abhorrence with which his Majesty regards this outrage.

Yours very faithfully,
Stamfordham

In the House of Commons, when Prime Minister Asquith rose to speak on the afternoon of Monday 31 July, there was a spontaneous outburst of passionate cheering. He denounced the murder as an atrocious crime against the law of nations and the usages of war. Coming as it did contemporaneously with the lawless cruelties to the population of Lille and other occupied areas of France, it showed that the German High Command had, under the stress of military defeat, renewed their policy of terrorism. Amid more loud cheers, he emphatically reiterated the resolve of the British Government that such crimes should not, if they could help it, go unpunished, and when the time arrived they were determined to bring to justice the criminals, whoever they might be and whatever their station. In a clear reference to the Kaiser himself, Asquith said that the man who authorized the system whereby such crimes were committed might well be the most guilty person of all.

Sir Edward Carson asked whether the time had come to ensure that, at the end of the war, the German people would not be admitted within the comity of nations until these crimes had been expiated. The Prime Minister replied that he was willing to consider any such proposal.

Throughout Great Britain feelings ran high, and nowhere higher than at the Baltic Shipping Exchange in the City of London. There was already a movement to close all British ports throughout the Empire to German ships for a period of years after the war, and this was strengthened by the news of Fryatt's death. Strong sentiments were being crystallized there, said *The Times*, particularly among the younger members, that Fryatt should not have died in vain. The British Workers' League organized a mass rally in Trafalgar Square in protest against German barbarity, and a resolution urging Government action was passed at a meeting of the London County Council.

The Amsterdam *Telegraaf* stormed that the German sword was

stained already with the innocent blood of women and children and now of Captain Fryatt. The only way to make the Germans feel was to apply their own methods, it said, and they must be made to realize that means existed for avenging such deeds as the *Lusitania*, Nurse Cavell and Captain Fryatt.

"What kind of trial is likely to have taken place under the military governorship of one with a reputation such as that of General von Bissing?" asked *The Times* rhetorically. It said that there was nothing more certain than that this latest example of cowardly ruthlessness would steel the resolve of the British troops on the Western Front. And from as far away as Australia came a wire to the Colonial Office in London that the Governor-General had withdrawn the four shillings weekly allowance to interned enemy merchant navy officers as a direct reprisal following the Fryatt execution.

The German press had anticipated that the world would be aghast. Anxious to put its case to the widest possible audience, just as it had done following the *Baralong* uproar, the Berlin news service sprayed bulletins around the globe. One reached the *Chicago Daily News*. The German Navy Department says that Fryatt was shot as a *franc-tireur*, it said, and it believed that the USA would agree with that view. Submarine crews must be protected against such attacks as these, it maintained, and the fact that the British Government had sanctioned such warfare did not alter the German view, but only strengthened it.

The callous *Weser Zeitung* too foresaw another outcry over the death of Fryatt, but Germany could pass it over with a cold smile, it condoned, for there was no shadow of doubt as to the justice of the sentence. There was not even any ground for the least feeling of human compassion. In this case, the captain of the merchantman, from vanity and lust for gain, deliberately transgressed what he knew to be the international laws of naval warfare and endeavoured to destroy a whole German crew with their ship, while he must have known that his life and the lives of his crew were immune against German attack.

The *Kölnische Volkszeitung* crowed, "This is the first time that the German Navy have had an opportunity to show what it thinks of British merchant captains who seek to destroy German submarines. It is language that will be understood in London, because it is not expressed in diplomatic notes, but in powder and shot."

Under the headline "A Chapter on Piracy" the *Cologne Gazette* blasted, "The British Government's prescriptions for the conduct of merchantmen in this war recommended just what is called in England piracy. War is no game. It is bloody and earnest. They know this very well in England. If the English press rants and rages it leaves us cold. We have, above all things, to create the necessary respect for our submarines, for the life and security of our brave blue-jackets stand for us incomparably higher than the forfeited life of a nefarious Englishman, who knew he had a war vessel before him and yet ventured to attack it in a perfidious way."

With the coming of the Armistice, and as the delegates struggled in Versailles to hammer out the shape of a new world order in the spring of 1919, the Fryatt debate reopened. A Commission of Inquiry into the Treatment of Prisoners, under a Professor Schücking, sitting in the Imperial Military Court in Berlin, heard the report of a Dr Rocholt, for the Legal Department, on the case of Kapitänleutnant Gansser, of the submarine *U-33*, who had charged Fryatt with endeavouring to ram his vessel on 28 March 1916. Rocholt said that it had originally been intended simply to commit Fryatt to Ruhleben, but he was retained by order of the *Admiralstab* of the Marine Corps. The sentence of death had been confirmed by Admiral von Schröder, the president of the court-martial. The verdict of the Commission was that the killing of Fryatt had involved no violation of international law.

Immediately there were protests. John C. van der Veer, London Editor of the Amsterdam *Telegraaf*, wrote on 7 April 1919, "The verdict should not be treated as a matter of passing interest. It was clearly based on German Prize Law, which is not the international law, but differs materially from it, in that it does not recognize the principle of self-defence on the part of belligerent merchant vessels, whether they are armed or not, as was pointed out by the German expert Dr. Hans Wehberg in his valuable book *Das Seekriegsrecht*. Dr. Wehberg asks in his book, 'Should large merchant vessels of great value, without more ado, allow themselves to be taken by smaller vessels simply because the latter answer the description of warships?' He declares that the act of resistance on the part of a merchant vessel, whether armed or not, makes no difference to the fate of its crew when captured; they can only be taken as prisoners of war. Hence, Captain Fryatt was perfectly justified in doing what was alleged against him. His execution was illegal."

A gentleman signing himself Captain Perseus, writing in the *Berliner Tageblatt*, also decried the Commission's decision. He thought that "the old obstinate Prussian militarism" must have influenced the Commission, and it was the duty of every honourable man to protest against the judgment as in the interests neither of humanity nor of the German people. It would have an adverse effect on the attitude of the Allies, prejudice the peace negotiations then currently in progress and woefully retard the restoration of friendly relations.

Two members of the Commission itself, Herr Bernstein and Dr Cohn, then considered that they had the right to publish their own views on the matter, which were those of dissent, in the socialist newspaper *Vorwärts*. They did not challenge the honesty of their colleagues on the Commission they said, but could not agree with their verdict. Fryatt had a clear right to defend his ship by active measures, they contended. If the order of the British Admiralty, produced in Court, were a real document, Captain Fryatt was only carrying out the orders of his superiors, and was therefore guiltless, even if the order itself were illegal. He had not been allowed a proper defence; as a civilian prisoner he should not have come under the jurisdiction of a court-martial and he had been treated with gross inhumanity. The sentence against him, they concluded, had been one of "unpardonable judicial murder".

Meantime, the Fryatt family and their many supporters, even in the Government, were pressing for the Captain's body to be returned home. With permission granted and arrangements made, First Mate Bill Hartnell and the Captain's brother William went to Bruges to identify the body. In the stillness of the cemetery, they watched the diggers go to work with the exhumation of coffin number 29. When the cheap rickety lid was lifted, they gazed on the face of their brother and friend. It was an awful moment. The Captain still wore his uniform (this makes for yet another twist in the story – van Hoestenberghe had said he was in plain clothes), with his cap on his chest and his boots by his side. The lid was replaced and the whole coffin lifted out to be lowered into a larger new one.

The Dover-based destroyer HMS *Orpheus* slipped her moorings at 4.00 am on Sunday 6 July 1919 and picked up speed to twenty-two knots to sail on a dead calm sea for Antwerp. She secured to the quay there at 11.35 am. Her stay was brief. One extra petty officer and six able seamen had been taken on board in Dover to form the funeral escort party and by 5.20 that afternoon they had taken Fryatt's body on board and were being piloted back down the Schelde towards the open sea. They dropped the pilot at Flushing and put in to Ostend to anchor for the night. Then, next day, escorted by HMS *Teazer* and HMS *Taurus*, all wearing flags at half-mast, *Orpheus* brought Captain Fryatt's body into Dover. Commander Birkett eased her into the Admiralty Basin and secured to No. 24 buoy at four o'clock in the afternoon of 7 July. The coffin was on the quarter-deck, guarded by four blue-jackets with fixed bayonets.

Thousands of people lined the harbour in respectful silence and every flag in the town was at half-mast. Waiting on the pier were Rear-Admiral Dampier, commanding the Dover Station, with Major-General Sir Colin Mackenzie, commanding the Dover Garrison, and a host of other dignitaries. The wreaths, including one of lilac and roses from King Albert and Queen Elizabeth of Belgium and another from the town of Antwerp, were brought to the pier first. The coffin was then transferred from the destroyer to the tug *Adder* and was brought to the pier steps, whence eight blue-jackets carried it to a bier covered by the White Ensign while officers saluted and civilians stood with bared heads.

Dover paid as deep and sincere tribute to the remains of Captain Fryatt as it had to those of Nurse Cavell. Soldiers from the Garrison lined the route to the station. All snapped to attention and saluted as the coffin passed. In Snargate Street, at the grand shaft entrance to the Castle, the guard turned out and presented arms. The procession was met at the Indian Mutiny Monument by the Mayor and Town Council. With the band playing Chopin's Marche Funebre and the Royal Marines presenting arms, it proceeded up the hill into the station. A special coach, internally arranged as a chapel, the same one which had taken Nurse Cavell's body to London, waited at the platform. The coffin, again on the shoulders of blue-jackets, was lifted from the gun-carriage and gently laid in the purple-draped coach with the wreaths placed on and around it, while the guard stood with arms reversed.

It stood there overnight, under an armed guard, to be attached to the 7.35 train to Charing Cross in the morning. At Chatham the coach was attached to a special train which carried a naval detachment and band. Groups of schoolchildren gathered to pay tribute and were standing on the platforms of many of the stations through which the train passed on its way to London. Flags on village churches flew at half-mast. The train drew into a specially reserved platform at Charing Cross at eleven o'clock. Outside the station a dense crowd had assembled to pay homage to the now-famous dead sailor. The naval escort left the train and stood to attention while blue-jackets removed the wreaths and placed them in an open carriage. Then the coffin was lifted and reverently laid onto the gun-carriage, and a wreath from the Captain's family placed on the Union flag which draped it. All this was done in a silence which was only broken by a sharp word of command, and the escort, with arms reversed, set off at a slow march.

With the naval band playing a solemn funeral march and blue-jackets pulling the gun-carriage, the procession made its way into the Strand followed by a large number of official mourners, who were led by Bill Hartnell and Mr and Mrs William Fryatt. Large crowds, some spreading into the road, had gathered in the Strand and Trafalgar Square, where Nelson himself gazed stony-eyed down from his column. And so into Northumberland Avenue and down onto the Embankment where trams came to a standstill and ships' sirens wailed from the river as the escort came into view. All the way to St Paul's Cathedral men removed their hats and women gazed in silence as the coffin passed. All that could be heard were the sad strains of the music and the steady even-paced foot-treads of the sailors.

The cathedral was packed to capacity. Music by Purcell, Handel and Bach soared into the high roof, played by the orchestra of the Great Eastern Railway Company as the crowded gathering awaited the arrival of the procession. It was met at the west door by the Bishop of London and his attendants. Blue-jackets bore the coffin to the catafalque under the dome, where it rested surrounded by six large lighted candles during the service.

The service opened with the sailors' hymn, "Eternal Father, strong to save". Those who were there said that they had never heard it sung with such emotion. So too was the closing hymn, "Abide with me". Then the procession retraced its way to the west door to the sound of the Last Post played by buglers of the Royal Marines. More crowds lined the pavements through the City to Liverpool Street Station. The booking-hall, where a Fryatt Memorial Tablet already graced the wall, was bedecked with flags and floral tributes. One, an enormous creation of an anchor in lilies and orchids, came from the Navy League of Canada and was inscribed, "To the immortal memory of Captain Fryatt, who gave his life to the cause of human freedom". Silently, the coffin was placed in the Dovercourt train, which steamed out of the station at ten minutes to two.

Even though it was July, the day was bleak with a leaden sky and a chilly wind. The funeral train sped through the flat green Essex countryside, passing knots of schoolchildren who had gathered on station platforms along the line, just as they had right across Kent. Long before it arrived at Dovercourt, at 3.35 pm, a big crowd had assembled at the station and all the way along the road to the churchyard. From the station the procession climbed the winding hill into Dovercourt, and then turned onto the seafront, so that in going to his grave the dead sailor passed once again the North Sea that he knew so well. Blinds were drawn and shops were closed as he was borne past cottage gardens bright with summer flowers, between green hedges and under the ancient trees at the churchyard gate. There, as the coffin entered, the last strains of the Funeral March died away and the bell, which for forty minutes had tolled solemnly, fell silent. In the churchyard a space around the grave was kept by Girl Guides and Boy Scouts. The coffin was lowered into the flower-trimmed grave by a party of seamen. And once more the familiar rolling notes of "Eternal Father, strong to save" swelled out. The Bishop of Chelmsford led the service. He spoke briefly, saying that the Germans had touched the depths of national ignominy by murdering Charles Fryatt. Then came the Benediction and buglers sounded the Last Post.

A correspondent of *The Times* found some beautifully moving words to finalize the day: "Now he was in a quiet place, where sailor men have lived and loved and died since there were ships. A place welded by time and tradition to the sea and holding the bones of not a few of those who knew the ocean in their day and helped to keep it free."

As for the *Brussels*, the GER were paid £51,000 by their insurance underwriters for her loss and the Germans made good use of her. They renamed her *Brugge* and converted her into a submarine depot ship. She was in Zeebrugge Harbour at the time of the famous St George's Day raid by HMS *Vindictive* and other ships in 1918. And here again historical versions differ. According to the Harwich Society's *Highlight* magazine, she was "internally mined at the entrance to Zeebrugge Harbour to protect the submarine base". But *The Sphere* magazine of 11 May 1918, as well as Barrie Pitt's comprehensive book *Zeebrugge*, depict her as tied up alongside the inner wall of the Mole, next to the seaplane shed. (Had she in fact been used as a depot ship for seaplanes rather than submarines?) *The Sphere* said that she was torpedoed during the famous raid, but did not say by whom.

After the war she passed back into British hands and was sold at auction for £3,100, the money being used towards the building of the Fryatt Memorial Hospital at Harwich, which opened in 1922. The hulk was raised and towed to Leith where, after being repaired, she was converted into a cattle boat and renamed *Lady Brussels*. Her last voyage was from Liverpool to Dublin on 19 April 1929 and she was broken up at Port Glasgow shortly afterwards.

Postscript.

No clear picture of the Fryatt trial proceedings, or the rationale behind the Court's decision, has ever emerged. Indeed, some of the scant official comment seems dubious to say the least. For example, according to many organs of the press much importance seems to have been put on Fryatt's gold watch from the Admiralty. And the Dutch *Telegraaf* had of course already stated that it seemed to be the sole reason for his arrest. Apparently, it was the inscription carried by the watch, commending Fryatt for having rammed the submarine over a year before, which was held to be the conclusive proof of his guilt.

Yet how was this known to the Germans? The watch could not have been produced as evidence at the trial, because Fryatt had left both of his watches at home with his wife for safe-keeping. And, in any event, neither bore any such inscription. There again, one journalist, whose 'facts' are often questionable to say the least, said that it was not a watch but a medal which the Germans found on Fryatt, and it was this that was so inscribed.

"If only he had admitted that he was acting on Admiralty orders in trying to ram the U-boat as a means of escape," wrote a contributor to the Harwich Society's *Highlight* magazine eighty-odd years later, "the case would have had a different outcome, because the German code of warfare gave protection to an enemy in such circumstances." As it was, he did not so admit, with the result that the prosecution successfully labelled him as a *franc-tireur*, an activity for which the Germans had long professed to have a particular distaste. All he would say was, "I have done nothing wrong". However, the London *Evening News* reported on Friday, 28 July 1916, the day after the execution, under the banner "Another Hun Crime against Humanity" that Fryatt had, in fact, admitted that he had been following the instructions of the British Admiralty.

Notwithstanding the obfuscation befogging the story, the outcome was nevertheless strange. Whether it was a watch or a medal, if something of the sort *had* been produced at the trial, as was suggested by several sources, and if it *did* bear such an inscription despite the denials of this, surely that would have been the main piece of evidence in securing Fryatt's acquittal if the *Highlight* contributor's statement is correct.

Possibly, the feelings that imbued the thoughts of many at the time, and have done so since, were nearer the truth than any other, i.e. that Fryatt was convicted before he was even tried. That he was given no opportunity to appeal, but was dispatched out of this world with what was surely indecent haste, gives good reason for such an opinion.

Some poorly informed writers have clearly either obtained their material from unreliable sources or their own research has been skimped. At best, they can only be regarded as fanciful. In Finland, a country that had been sympathetic to the German cause, an article appeared in the press in July 1919 in which the story of the *Brussels* was hopelessly confused with that of the *King Stephen*. It had Fryatt ignoring the pleas for help from the crew of a crashed Zeppelin, who then swam to board his ship which was later captured by a submarine.

Even as late as 1991 fresh arguments were being advanced which indicated a vivid imagination on the part of the writer. Dutch journalist Han Andriesson, writing in the naval magazine *Marineblad* laid the blame for Fryatt's death on the head of Winston Churchill, First Lord of the Admiralty in 1915, who had instigated the advice to merchant captains to steer at top speed towards an attacking U-boat. The object of this, as we have seen, was not necessarily to ram it as Andriesson needed to imply so as to set his argument, but to make it dive and resurface astern of the ship. But he pushed his case over the threshold of fantasy when he claimed that Churchill had ordered, "Any master who surrenders his ship will be prosecuted". Therefore, according to Andriesson's imaginative reasoning, British merchant captains had a simple choice; either to become a *franc-tireur* with the risk of being executed by the Germans, or to be tried by their own countrymen for cowardice in the sight of the enemy.

Winston Churchill was to take the blame for many unfortunate occurrences in both World Wars. Some were indeed justifiable. Churchill is not the only wartime leader in history to have made an order which was later seen to be regrettable. But as regards Andriesson's clumsy attempt to inculpate him for Fryatt's death, he had not, of course, issued any such order.

8

MAX VALENTINER STRIKES TWICE

    •

At £206,390 and 7,951 tons, the Egypt-class liner *Persia* was the most expensive and largest ship yet built for P & O when Laird & Co. sent her 499-foot hull down their Greenock slipway into the Clyde in 1900. It was a time of high Empire and on the 'India run' her decks soon became accustomed to the feel of the feet of Princes, Nawabs, Maharajahs, Government ministers, diplomats, military officers, civil servants, engineers, well-to-do planters, surveyors and the wives and the children of all these, worldly wise beyond their years, to-ing and fro-ing between England and the Indian sub-continent for boarding school and holidays.

The threads of Empire required continual maintenance, whether in time of peace or war, and the sailing routine was disturbed as little as possible. Accordingly the *Persia* sailed from Tilbury Docks on 18 December 1915, bound for Bombay, with another typical load of passengers. At fifteen years old she was already obsolescent. Rudyard Kipling had once sailed in her and wrote on his return, "The single screw goes Wop Wop Wop at sixty times the minute and she thumps along at thirteen miles an hour." All told, as she moved slowly down the Thames Estuary towards the open sea, her crew and passengers numbered 501.

Her first port of call was to be Marseilles, from where she sailed on Boxing Day, all on board having celebrated Christmas with the sumptuous fare prepared by the galley staff. At the other end of the Mediterranean, the German submarine *U-38* was 'showing the flag' in Beirut for Christmas, and her Captain, Max Valentiner, and his sailors were being duly fêted by local dignitaries sympathetic to the Kaiser's cause.

Next stop for the *Persia* was Valetta Harbour, Malta, to disembark and pick up passengers and take on coal. She sailed from Malta at 10 pm on 27 December. It turned out to be the last time that the *Persia* would weigh an anchor anywhere.

For the passengers it was pleasant to feel the Mediterranean sunshine and to spend happy evenings dancing to the ship's orchestra, after leaving behind the dreary winter greyness of London as the liner steadily throbbed her way eastwards, south of Crete, through the calm water. All the same, there was a war on. It was prudent to be vigilant. Not too far away to the north the Dardanelles campaign was being fought; things were coming to the boil in Mesopotamia and the enemy submarines of the Cattaro flotilla were known to be able to slip past the Otranto Barrage and out of the Adriatic to hunt along the shipping lanes to and from the Suez canal. The eastern Mediterranean was certainly a dangerous place. And, quite without warning, when the *Persia* was about 70 miles SSE of Capa Mátala on the southern coast of Crete, she was struck by a torpedo. It was 1310 Greenwich Mean Time on 30 December 1915.

Second Officer Geoffrey Wood had gone on watch on the bridge at noon to find that the Captain, William H. Selby-Hall, had taken charge of navigation. For the first hour of the watch, therefore, there had been little for Wood to do except check on the look-outs. There was an able-seaman in the crow's nest and another on the fo'c's'le. On the bridge there was an AB and a Lascar on either wing, while two ABs and a Marine manned the defensive gun on the poop right aft. But, for all these pairs of eyes, it was Wood himself who spotted the bubbling streak of a torpedo speeding towards them, four points on the port bow. Instinctively, without waiting for orders, he reached for the whistle and blew five blasts. Everybody on board knew, or should have known, that five whistle blasts was the signal for "Boat Stations!" because Captain Selby-Hall had carried out a general Boat Drill only the previous day.

Able Seaman Albert Scrivener was having a quiet smoke and enjoying the sunshine, discreetly out of sight on the forward well-deck, while he waited to take his turn at the wheel at two o'clock. He saw no submarine or torpedo. All he knew was that there was an explosion and then he heard Wood's five blasts on the whistle. The liner shook from stem to stern and immediately took on a ten degree list to port. Scrivener rushed to shake his mates in the watch below, who were all turned in and asleep. "We're torpedoed!" he shouted at the slumbering forms. Then, after making sure that they were all tumbling out, he raced to his boat station, which was No. 4 Boat. It had already been lowered and sent away, so he went to No. 2. There was nobody there except the Baggage-master. Together, they climbed up the davits, slipped the gripes and slid down the falls, but this left the lifeboat dangling just above the water. Two stewards appeared at the rail above them. These men lowered the boat the last six feet or so, by which time the big ship's hurricane deck was completely awash. They had just enough time to unhook the tackles and cut the painter before the *Persia* rolled over on her side and took her final plunge. As she did so one of her giant funnels missed the stern of the lifeboat by no more than four feet as it crashed down amid a choking cloud of exhaust smoke, smuts and steam. Somehow, the two stewards had managed to get into the lifeboat, as had the Chief Officer, whose face was black with soot. They rowed round among the mass of floating debris, looking for bobbing heads and plucking them from the water. Eventually, No. 2 Boat was to hold twenty-seven survivors.

Leonard Dowling, a young steward, was just starting his own lunch after serving passengers in the saloon. To be more precise, he had just polished off a couple of anchovies on toast for hors d'oeuvres when there was a loud roar and the tinkling crash of falling glass. Then the saloon became full of smoke. Lunch forgotten in an instant, he hurried to his cabin which was only a few steps away, to fetch his lifebelt. Returning, he found there was no panic, but people were hurrying in an orderly fashion up the companionway to the deck. Dowling made his way up with them. The *Persia* had been hit between her two funnels and was taking on a pronounced list to port. This meant that, although she carried enough lifeboats and life-jackets to cater for almost double the number of people on board, it would be impossible to launch any of the boats on the starboard side, which was where Dowling's Boat Station was, as the portside list would cause them to swing inboard if it were attempted. In addition, she was still making considerable headway, even though her engines had been blown to smithereens. Until she lost momentum, it would be unwise to try to launch any of the boats. Dowling was pondering the situation when Captain Selby-Hall came along the deck calling, "All women and children down the port side!" Dowling had already come to the conclusion that that would offer the best means of saving his life and made his way quickly to the port side and began throwing deck-chairs, tables and anything else that would float to serve as a raft into the sea.

It had been a mere four minutes or so since the torpedo struck, but the port rail was already almost under water and the list was so heavy that it was impossible to climb up across the deck to the starboard side. He could see that in a few seconds he would be trapped between the cabins behind him and the boat deck above. There was no more time for hesitation. He walked up the rail and into the water. Still the *Persia* was underway. Several thousand tons of ship travelling through the water at eleven knots will 'freewheel' for a considerable time unless she is able to 'go astern' to counter her forward impetus. The *Persia*, of course, was quite unable to do this with her wrecked engines. Consequently, Dowling found himself in the water and in danger of being run down by the lifeboats which were being towed along beside the moving ship. It took three attempts before he was able to snatch hold of the grab lines of one of the boats and haul himself inboard to join Second Mate Geoffrey Wood and a few Lascars, whom he presumed were its crew. He was just in time to have an even narrower escape from one of the liner's huge funnels than Scrivener experienced. It was looming, huge and terrifying, immediately above him. All Dowling could do to save the boat being swamped was to brace his feet against the hot metal side of the giant soot-encrusted ship's chimney and heave backwards with all his might to shove himself, Wood, the Lascars and the heavy lifeboat away from under it.

After the *Persia* had finally disappeared and they had caught their breaths they rowed around looking for survivors and pulled seven Second Class ladies and two children out of the water.

Having gone to the port side as ordered by Captain Selby-Hall, about forty ladies from First Class were caught in a death trap. Patiently, they had waited for the boats to come alongside. But they had waited in vain. The boats never came and they were trapped at the bottom of the slope of the listing deck as the *Persia* went under. She had gone down like a brick, hastened no doubt by the 540 tons of cement, 100 tons of railway seats and 1,577 tons of mail in her holds. A total of 334 out of 501 people had lost their lives.

A French passenger, Monsieur de Teuquin, recounted his experiences in the *Echo de Paris* issue of 17 February 1916.

Of the twenty-five or thirty people who had been round me on the upturned hull of a lifeboat, not one was alive. I caught hold of a beam, then a barrel; I was vomiting water and coal dust; the great ship had disappeared. I was holding onto the barrel with my left hand; with my right I was fending off the chairs, the tables and all the wreckage which was eddying around and which held the risk of wounding me if it had been thrown against me. At that moment, I saw some heads out of the water, screaming for help with terror in their eyes – then disappearing. At last a lifeboat approached me. I made the final effort to get aboard it. I am good at gymnastics; then I fell into the boat exhausted. I was saved!

I shall never forget – and above all, a voice which came from I know not where, a far-off voice of a woman, or a child or a young man who was shouting 'Mother! Mother!' I then raised myself up to look for the voice, to hold out a hand or an oar to it, to save it – but I saw nothing. A-ah! that voice – the shout 'Mother! Mother!' How heartrending it was. These wretched people, once in the lifeboats, remained for thirty-two hours without anything to eat, without clothing, soaked, so squeezed they could not sit down and for the first hour coughing up all the coal-dust and salt water they had swallowed. My young Swiss friend told me that when he came up to the surface for the third time he banged his head violently against a floating table. He thought maybe he was under a lifeboat, or even the *Persia* herself.

One woman had an eye completely blackened and her cheek torn open by claw scratches. She had saved her panic-stricken dog by holding it tight against her breast, but the poor animal died on the warship from having swallowed too much sea water. The French girl who was going to rejoin her husband in Egypt had a bad wound on her head and a cut over one of her eyebrows. She was floating on the water, half conscious, when she was picked up. 'I said a little prayer,' she told me, 'and then I resigned myself to death.'

Leonard Dowling searched around in his lifeboat to see what he could find in the way of water and provisions. There was half a cask of fresh water and a box of ship's biscuits. It was hardly enough to sustain them all for more than a couple of days. Nevertheless, Wood had taken command and issued a beaker of water to everybody.

Laboriously, they hoisted the boat's sail with unpractised hands. By now the other three boats had drifted some distance away, so far that they appeared merely as black shapes. During the afternoon one or two steamers passed by in the distance, but a lifeboat is a very small object on a wide open sea, especially when the water is sparkling in bright sunshine, and none of them saw it. It had been a hot exhausting day, but in those latitudes the temperature can drop rapidly as darkness falls. They took down the sail and all crawled under it for warmth and to try to get some sleep, leaving Wood and Dowling to take turns on watch in the stern.

The next night was rather cloudy and visibility was not good. Dowling was on watch. He had never been blessed with first-class eyesight, but he was sure that he could see a light in the distance. Not a very bright light, and very small, but a light nonetheless. He blinked and screwed his eyes. Yes. Quietly he touched the elbow of the dozing Wood and silently pointed, so as not to raise the hopes of the others. But some of them had already seen it and within seconds, the sail was heaving as everybody struggled to get out from under it and they were rowing furiously towards the light, shouting "We're British!" at the tops of their voices, quite unmindful of the fact that the light may have been just as easily a foe as a friend.

Suddenly a searchlight snapped on, fixing them in its pale yellow beam, and a deep voice came the darkness from behind it. "Thank God you sang out like that. We saw you, but, not knowing who you were, had our forward gun trained on you and were about to blow you out of the water." It was a Chief Petty Officer aboard the Flower Class corvette HMS *Mallow*. Strong hands helped them aboard, a stiff tot of Navy rum was dispensed all round, hammocks were given up (officers' cabins for the ladies), and soon they were all fast asleep. They had quite forgotten to wish each other a Happy New Year.

Max Valentiner, captain of *U-38*, was fearlessly outspoken, ruthless and no stranger to controversy. Born in Tondern, Schleswig-Holstein, on 15 December 1883, he had enrolled as a cadet in the *Kaiserliche Marine* in 1902 and was accepted into the submarine service on 30 March 1908. At the outbreak of war he was serving as a training officer at the U-boat School at Kiel. On one occasion, having been received by none other than the Kaiser, and in company with Wilhelm's brother *Großadmiral* Prince Henry of Prussia, the question of the performance of *U-3*, an elderly boat with which he was having difficulty, came into the conversation. Most officers of his rank would have displayed a diplomatic reticence in such exalted company. Not Valentiner. How could the *Admiralstab* expect him to produce good results with a boat of such vintage? "*Königliche Hoheit*, the *U-3* is an old horse," he told Queen Victoria's grandsons with vigour, thumping the desk with his fist so hard that the inkstand danced, "and it doesn't matter how many sugar lumps you give an old horse, it won't gallop any faster!"

On 13 August 1915, in mid-patrol with *U-38* in the Western Approaches, he had met up with Wegener in *U-27*, (who was only days away from being blasted by the *Baralong*), and it was decided between them that Valentiner would carry out the planned rescue operation of some German naval officer POW fugitives. He had lain just off a North Wales beach, mainly on the bottom, for two days trying to rendezvous with them. They had escaped from the camp at Dyffryn (where the embittered Iwan Crompton of *U-41* was eventually held). His patrol diary reads:

14 August	
2305 Irish Sea. Wind SE batteries.	Surfaced. Charged
No seaway.	Proceeded towards Great
Clear sky. Good visibility.	Ormes Head. Navigated by coastal lights. Ran with half-flooded tanks. From a depth of 10–20m ran on electric motors towards coast.
15 August.	
0100 Great Ormes Head.	Plumbed 10m. Nothing in sight. Distance from beach 300m.
Overcast. Dark night.	Proceeded seawards at
0400	dawn. Batteries fully charged. Difficult at half-flooded depth owing to much traffic. Decided to put boat on bottom outside of the steamer track.

0512	Plumbed 26 m. Boat on bottom with 20m chain out. With 1/2 ton of negative buoyancy boat is berthed well on sandy bottom.
2200 Liverpool Bight. Wind NW2 Some cloud, sea NW 3. Dark night. Limited visibility.	Surfaced proceeded half-speed to Great Ormes Head. Approached to 8m depth of water. Position about 900m W of Great Ormes Head. 200m off beach. Nothing extraordinary in sight.
16 August. 0320 Gt Ormes Head. Wind NW3	Went on northerly course towards bottom berthing position.
0505 Sea NW3	Boat on bottom 26m.
1015	Surfaced. Due to bad visibility headed submerged at 20m towards Isle of Man to recharge batteries there. Decided to try again to solve task at Gt Ormes Head during the night.
1550 Wind NW4. Sea NW4. batteries.	Surfaced. Charged.
Overcast and misty.	Weather worsening. Decided to discard plan to try again. Headed W
1728	Submerged due to a destroyer.

Having failed to make any contact with his escaped fellow-countrymen, Valentiner resumed his patrol. Later, it turned out that they had been waiting, cold, wet and shivering, on another beach just 500 yards away, obscured from his view by a rocky promontory.

On his way to join the Cattaro flotilla in the Adriatic Valentiner had sunk the Italian liner *Ancona*, with the loss of 220 lives. The fact that Germany was not even at war with Italy at that time exacerbated what was already a matter of outrage. And *U-38* had been wearing an Austrian flag when she sank the liner, with the result that an angry Austria-Hungary was saddled with the responsibility for the illegal attack. It was not the first or the last time that he would pull such a trick, although the Austrians refused to act as scapegoats for any of his future misdemeanours. Ironically, on the very same day that Valentiner had sailed from Cattaro on his present patrol, far away in London, the Chairman of P & O, Lord Inchcape, was addressing the Company's Annual General Meeting. "P & O mail steamers," he told his shareholders, "are sailing to the ends of the earth with unfailing regularity and complete immunity from enemy ships." Only days later they were proved to be hollow words; by then Valentiner had sunk the *Persia*. It was the start of a four-day orgy of destruction, in which he was to sink another five Allied ships totalling 44,000 tons. In fact, he barely had to move from the scene of the *Persia*'s sinking before a 4,823-ton freighter with a black funnel with two red collars hove into view in his periscope that same evening, plodding down the Malta–Suez track at ten knots. She was the Clan Lines's *Clan Macfarlane*, humping a general cargo from Birkenhead to Bombay.

Nobody on board the *Clan Macfarlane* had seen either a submarine or a torpedo when there was a mighty explosion. Her master, Captain James Whyte Swanston, ordered his crew to abandon ship at once and rushed to collect his confidential papers and throw them overboard. It was a fine, clear night, with a calm sea, and all six lifeboats were lowered without any problems. Then a submarine appeared and began to shell the abandoned ship from point-blank range. The British crew of eleven Europeans and sixty-three Lascars, sitting in their boats, watched as at least six shells burst in her. It was obvious that she would not stay afloat very long. They did not see her actually sink owing to the darkness, but in the light of dawn there was nothing to be seen of her. In the meantime the boats were all made fast, in line astern, to Captain Swanston's boat. All of them had serviceable sails and at daybreak Swanston decided to head northward, to try to make landfall on Crete. At four o'clock the following afternoon, New Year's Eve, they thought they sighted land ahead, but the wind had dropped and the

129

exasperating smudge on the horizon had not drawn any closer by nightfall. In fact, it had disappeared altogether. Had it been just a low shelf of cloud after all? Swanston decided to separate the boats and resort to the oars. They rowed steadily until ten o'clock the next morning, when they were able to hoist sail again to take advantage of a light breeze, and all join up together again astern of the Captain's boat.

Land appeared again in the distance as the light cleared on the morning of 2 January. This time there was no doubt about it. It was the western tip of the island of Crete. Their hearts rose as they sailed towards it. But Swanston could see that it would be impossible to beach the boats, because by now the wind and sea had risen to such an extent that all they could do was to shorten sail and run westwards along the coast, about four miles offshore and wait for conditions to improve. At about mid-morning the Third Officer's tow rope parted, thus casting off his boat, together with that of the Second Engineer, from the main body. The Captain cast off and went in search of these two, leaving the Mate, Fred Hawley, at the head of the line. Wisely, Hawley decided to lay to for the rest of the night, as the weather had become extremely bad and they were obliged to bale continually. How different the conditions had suddenly become, when only seventy-two hours before they had been enjoying a calm cruise in the Mediterranean sunshine. During that night Swanston's boat re-appeared, although he had not been successful in finding the others. And, sadly, the Lascars now began to succumb to the effects of exposure and by dawn on the 3 January eight of them had died. Later that day one of the boats had to be abandoned (the reason is unclear) and the occupants transferred to Swanston's and Hawley's boats. Now there were only three of them.

Almost immediately after this had been done the Captain's boat lost its rudder. He cast off and moved to the back of the line. All this time the wind had been howling and the sea had risen so much that, owing to the strain on the other two boats and the danger of them being swamped, the Captain lay to and set a reefjib, using an oar to keep her head-on to the sea and stop her from broaching. Hawley also lay to through the night, with his sea anchor down. All three boats were shipping a lot of water each time the waves crashed over them and everybody was exhausted from endless baling. At dawn on 4 January Swanston's boat was nowhere to be seen. They caught occasional glimpses of it again, around noon, whenever the gaps between the racing hillocks of water permitted them to see it. It was rushing at a considerable pace to the westward. They tried to catch up with it, but were unable to do so in such fearful conditions. Finally, they lost sight of it altogether at dusk that evening. James Whyte Swanston was never seen again.

Hawley, now in command, decided to abandon No. 4 Boat the next morning and took the Second Officer, Fifth Engineer and some Lascars into his own boat. He lost his own rudder in the process and was forced to use an oar to steer. In such weather this is an extremely taxing exercise. They saw the smoke of a steamer that day, 5 January, but it was too far away and passed by without seeing them. Now there were only two of them.

The forenoon of 6 January was a sad time. They lost the second cook, one of the Lascar firemen and an apprentice. All had died from exposure. It seems that Hawley had lost all hope of making landfall on Crete, or perhaps the wind had shifted and, to make for easier sailing, he now set a course ESE towards Alexandria, which would be a voyage of about 250 miles. At least it would take them across the main shipping lanes where there was more chance of rescue. It came as a welcome relief that at last the weather began to moderate, but, all the same, the mess-boy died at six o'clock the next morning, having suffered for so long from the cold and wet. However, their ordeal was almost over. They had reached the shipping lanes and after a couple of hours sighted a steamer about three miles off. And she saw them! No more than half an hour later the bedraggled party of survivors from the *Clan Macfarlane* sat in their boat alongside the steamship *Crown of Aragon* waiting to be helped aboard. Given dry clothes, hot drinks and the chance of a good sleep, they all relaxed as their rescuers' ship continued on its passage to Malta, but before she tied up in Valetta Harbour at half past four on 10 January two more of the Lascar crew were to die. They had been in their lifeboats for seven and a half days, and endured some of the roughest weather that the Mediterranean could produce. The Clan Line had lost one of their most respected Captains in Swanston, as well as Third Officer T.M. Whyte, Third Engineer A. Ballingall, Carpenter H. Downie and Steward W.S. Macintyre, besides forty-five members of the Lascar crew. That there had been any survivors at all after such an ordeal was largely thanks to the superb seamanship skill of Chief Officer Fred Hawley.

Another 4,623 tons could be added to the war record of a German submarine captain by the name of Max Valentiner.

Meanwhile, those of the survivors from the *Persia* who had booked for Aden or Bombay were accommodated courtesy of the Royal Navy and enjoyed service hospitality aboard the obsolete battle-ship HMS *Hannibal* which served as a base at Alexandria, while arrangements were made for their onward passage. The next India-bound P & O steamer due to call at Port Said was to be the *Medina*, which arrived on time the very next day.

There were emotional scenes of jubilation mixed with tearful sorrow at Bombay's Ballard Pier as a noisy excited crowd of Europeans, Parsis and Hindus, chattering in a variety of tongues, gathered to meet the *Medina* as she landed her *Persia* survivors at four o'clock in the morning of 19 January 1916. The *Advocate of India* reporter interviewed an American passenger, a Mr C.H. Grant, who was on his way to take up an appointment as the agent for the Premium Oil Co. in Calcutta. When the explosion occurred, Mr Grant had been chatting over lunch with another American, Robert McNeeley, who had recently been appointed to take up a consular position in Aden. Grant had been one of the few people on the high-riding starboard side as the ship sank. He had hung on to the rail as long as possible, but had eventually been dragged into the sea by the suction and counted himself fortunate not to drown, because his left foot had become entangled in a rope as he tried to swim towards a boat. McNeeley was never seen again and was listed among those drowned. Mr Grant paid tribute to the magnifi-cent way in which both the officers and crew of the *Persia* had behaved and the general absence of panic among the passengers.

A Parsi gentleman from Bombay, Mr G.M. Cooper, said he had been five hours in the water before being picked up, but it was far from being his only experience of a similar emergency. Only 133 days before, he had been aboard the *Arabic* as she entered U-boat Alley.

His Highness the Maharajah of Kapurthala had been travelling with his Spanish wife and a considerable entourage, some of whom had been lost. Their Highnesses had been fortunate to be saved, but were mourning the loss of jewellery worth 75,000 rupees which was now on the bottom of the Mediterranean.

HMS *Mallow* had wirelessed the survivors' names to the

Admiralty and they had been published in all the main British newspapers. Relaxing in the luxurious surroundings of the Regent's Palace Hotel, Alexandria, Leonard Dowling wrote a long 'stiff upper lip' letter home to his mother in Saltdean, Brighton. "Isn't it all too awful?" he said.

But *Mallow*'s list of survivors had been incorrect. She had not seen or heard the desperate cries for help from another lifeboat which was wallowing in the water some way off in the darkness as she was rescuing the main body of survivors. This boat had been badly damaged in the explosion. Barely afloat, it had a big split in the bows, besides a hole in its bottom. And there were nineteen people in it, including the forty-nine-year-old Colonel Lord John Douglas-Scott-Montagu, 2nd Baron Montagu of Beaulieu, the famous motoring enthusiast and Chief Inspector of Motor Vehicles for the Army in India.

Montagu had been travelling to India, accompanied by his thirty-five year old private secretary, Eleanor Velasco Thornton, with whom he had been conducting an extra-marital affair for fifteen years. This situation seems to have been accepted stoically by his wife Lady Cecil, although it was kept as a secret as far as possible outside family circles. Eleanor planned to leave the ship at Port Said and return home. They, too, were lunching when the torpedo struck. The cutlery, chinaware and plates of food were all jolted from the tables by the impact, and the room was instantly full of the acrid smell of guncotton and TNT. Great fractures appeared in the deck, some two feet wide, through which issued a choking cloud of steam and fine hot ash, filling the saloon. Montagu stumbled to his state-room as quickly as he could to fetch the life-jackets which his cousin Admiral Mark Kerr had recommended him to purchase from Gieves, the well-known naval tailors, in preference to 'ship's issue' jackets, then hurried his mistress along briskly to their lifeboat station, which was the portside No. 6 Boat on the promenade deck. By the time they got there the port rail was already awash. There would not be time to launch any more boats before the ship went down, that was plain. Montagu clambered up the wet and sloping deck, trying to make for the starboard rail, dragging Eleanor with him. But a racing wall of water suddenly engulfed the pair of them, sweeping him off his feet and the girl from his grasp. He never saw her again.

Eventually he found himself in a lifeboat, albeit a badly damaged one, in company with several other people. During the first night eight men died of exhaustion and exposure. His own right leg was skinned raw from the knee down, his left leg was badly bruised, he had two cuts on his head and his left ear was torn. A steamer passed by at about 2000 hours. They fired flares, but she did not stop. By the next night they had drifted some distance from the others. They had seen *Mallow*'s searchlight, but were too far away in the darkness to make her see or hear them. It must have been a heart-breaking experience to sit in that half-swamped boat, with everybody shouting in vain at the tops of their voices to try to catch the attention of the crew of the corvette as they carried out their floodlit rescue work.

The warship departed and their hearts sank. Montagu sat himself up on a dead body so as to gain height in order to make a better lookout for other ships. The night wore on and his head started to nod with fatigue. But wait! Was that twinkling thing a star or a masthead light? It was a ship, the Blue Funnel Line's *Ning Chow*, 7,000 tons, homeward bound from Yokohama. Her Officer of the Watch, Donald McClean, thought he could see something in the murky light. It looked like a small boat. He turned the ship to investigate. They had been saved. "As I felt the bowline tauten around my shoulders," Montagu wrote later, "I looked down on the egg-shell to which we had clung and realized that a miracle had saved us. Even as I looked, the cockleshell grated against the ship's side and broke in two."

He took Eleanor's death very badly, blaming himself for not keeping a tighter hold of her against the force of that charging torrent of sea-water. It is doubtful, though, if any man could have done more. Still grieving two and a half years later, he wrote in desperate hope to the British Consular authorities in Greece, Cyprus, Egypt and Crete, inquiring if anything had ever been heard of her. Could she, somehow, by another miracle have been saved after all? No, the letters came back one by one. They were all nega-tive. Alas, he had to accept it. The Mediterranean had become the tomb of the woman who, it was strongly rumoured, had been the original model for the 'Spirit of Ecstasy' statuette which has graced the bonnet of Rolls-Royce motor-cars since 1900.

Max Valentiner was to finish the War as Germany's third most successful U-boat ace, with 300,000 tons to his 'credit' from seven-teen patrols. Fifteen cases of alleged breaches of the Laws of War, some even being described as "inhuman", were to be raised against him in the British list of criminal cases selected for trial. But he was never brought to trial for any of them.

In the Second World War Valentiner was recalled to the *U-Boot-Waffe* in January 1940 and served as a training officer until the end of March 1945. He died aged sixty-five in Jutland, Denmark, on 19 June 1949.

9

THE HOSPITAL SHIPS

The 1907 Hague Convention adapted the principles of the Geneva Convention to lay down a code of International Law in the context of Maritime War. Great Britain, Germany, USA, France, Russia, Japan and Italy were, *inter alia*, the signatories to it.

Articles 1, 2 and 3 laid down that Hospital Ships shall be immune from attack or capture provided that they have been placed under the orders of one of the belligerents . . . and on condition that the latter has notified their name to his adversary before they are so employed. Articles 4 and 5 stated that these ships should be painted white and clearly marked with a band of green or red about five feet wide along their length. They should also fly a Red Cross flag alongside their own national flag. (In addition, it is customary for hospital ships to have their white sides brightly illuminated at night, often with rows of red and green lights along their length. There could be absolutely no mistaking a hospital ship.) They would be required to provide relief and assistance to the wounded, sick and shipwrecked of the belligerents without distinction of nationality and their Governments must give an undertaking not to use such vessels for any military purpose. The belligerents would have the right to stop and search them, however, and even detain them if need be. Article 11: Sick or wounded sailors or soldiers on board, or other persons officially attached to fleets or armies, whatever their nationality, shall be respected and tended by their captors. Article 16: After every engagement, the two belligerents shall, so far as military interests permit, take steps to look for the wounded, sick and shipwrecked, and to protect them, as well as the dead, against pillage and improper treatment. They shall see that the burial, whether on land or at sea shall be preceded by a careful examination of the corpse.

During the course of the First World War seventy-seven ships were commissioned into the Royal Navy for use as hospital transports. Mainly there were converted passenger liners, including some of the largest and most well-known names of the day. The famous Cunarders *Aquitania* and *Mauretania* both served stints in this capacity. In 1915, on one voyage home from the Dardanelles to Southampton, *Aquitania* had nearly 5,000 patients on board, which required several special ambulance trains to disperse them from the docks to various hospitals around the country.

Despite the protections provided by the Convention, the hospital ships faced much danger. Several of them were to become the centre of controversy during the war as a result of them being either sunk or damaged, sometimes with loss of life. One fortunate early escapee was the Royal Mail Steam Packet Company's beautiful schooner-rigged liner *Asturias*, 12,000 tons, when she was attacked on 1 February 1915 by the soon-to-be-famous *U-20* off Havre. Kapitänleutnant Droescher's torpedo failed to find its target, despite her bright lights and large red crosses. However, as will be seen, it was not the only time that a U-boat was to line the *Asturias* up in its sights.

Another early hospital ship incident came on 17 November 1915. The ex-London & North-West Railway Company steamer *Anglia*, 1,862 tons, was nearing Folkestone from Boulogne at 1100 with 200 cot cases and 100 walking wounded on board. It was a fine day and it had been just another run-of-the-mill crossing. With *Anglia* passing through the specially reserved buoyed entrance channel for hospital ships, Captain Manning had just climbed to the bridge in preparation for entering harbour. Suddenly, near No. 8 buoy, there was an enormous explosion which threw Manning to the deck below. Realizing that his ship had been mined or torpedoed, he raced back up to the telegraph to ring down to Stop Engines, but everything was damaged and out of action. The engines were still going ahead and the engine-room crew had swarmed up onto the upper deck, driven by the torrent of water entering the stokehold. Manning then ran to the wireless cabin to order an SOS to be transmitted, but the flimsy apparatus was in fragments. By now the hospital ship was down by the nose so far that her starboard screw was clear of the water, still turning, and she was steaming in circles, out of control. The lifeboats had managed to get away, but her forward way was forcing the water into her all the more rapidly. Acting quickly, the captain of the destroyer HMS *Ure*, Lieutenant-Commander H.B.L. Scrivener, took his ship right over *Anglia*'s submerged bows and thus was able to take off many men to safety. It was a magnificent piece of courageous seamanship. Then, tragically, the collier *Luisatania*, having seen the plight of the sinking hospital ship, moved towards her to assist. She had just reached one of the lifeboats and the first man was halfway up the rope ladder when there was another explosion. She too had struck a mine and began to sink.

Having seen all his boats away, and without even a life-jacket, Manning slipped into the sea and began to swim away from the ship to avoid being sucked down. Exhausted, he floated on his back to catch his breath awhile and gazed at the blue sky. The next thing he knew he was being tended in the doctor's cabin in the depot ship HMS *Hazard*. The loss of life in the *Anglia* was put at 150, which was surprisingly low, given that 200 of her 300 patients were cot cases and that it had all happened so suddenly. The tragedy was deepened by the fact that Manning had been unable to stop *Anglia*'s engines and her continuing forward thrust had hastened her sinking. Without doubt, but for this many of the nursing orderlies, who had chosen to stay with their patients, would have been saved.

One other thing was sure. The Germans must have quite deliberately mined the course of a hospital ship. No other type of vessel was allowed to travel down that reserved path, which was marked with specially lit buoys.

Towards the end of November 1916 two attacks on hospital ships within the space of three days outraged the British. The White Star Line's *Britannic*, a four-funnelled 48,000-ton big sister of the ill-fated *Titanic*, was one of the biggest ships afloat anywhere in the world. Originally to be called the *Gigantic*, she was surpassed in size only by the Hamburg-Amerika Line's *Vaterland*, which was then interned in New York harbour. Having been requisitioned by the Admiralty on 13 November 1915 and converted into a hospital ship, *Britannic* had accommodation for 3,069 patients, fifty-two medical officers, 101 nurses, 336 orderlies and 675 crew. She had only been completed by Messrs Harland and Wolff in Belfast about a year before and had never yet been employed on the luxury passenger service for which she was intended. Her owners had become obsessed with safety after their disastrous experience with the *Titanic*. With greatly extended water-tight bulkheads and re-inforced rivetting, the *Britannic* was double-hulled up to three and a half feet above the middle deck, i.e. well above the water-line. Her forty-eight extra-large lifeboats were arranged in tiers across the deck rather than along the ship's length. The idea was for the occupants to take their places in them before the boats were launched by way of huge davits, taking them well clear of the ship on both sides, even if she were listing.

Britannic sailed for the Aegean from Southampton at noon on Sunday 12 November 1916. It was her sixth voyage as a hospital ship on the 'Dardanelles Service'. So far, apart from an outbreak of suspected food-poisoning among the staff six weeks before in the Greek islands, her war career had been uneventful. As this was an outward-bound voyage, naturally she carried no patients. Five days later she made her usual stop at Naples for coal and steamed on towards her destination, Mudros, on the island of Lemnos. Tuesday, 21 November looked like being a beautiful calm day as *Britannic* made her way northwards through the channel which runs between the island of Zea [Kea] and the south-eastern point of Attica on the Greek mainland. Soon the distant peaks of Mount Ochi would be appearing over the horizon fine on the port bow. The opportunity to savour the idyllic scenery would be but a short one for the crew and medical staff. When they reached Mudros they would find yet another sad and bloody cargo of thousands of sick and wounded men to be taken back to England from the carnage of the Turkish campaign.

Just after 8 o'clock there was a fearful explosion as the *Britannic* was struck, for'ard, by either a torpedo or a mine. Astonishingly quickly*, given her safety-minded construction, she began to settle by the bows. Her Master, Captain Charles Bartlett, had been a White Star man since 1874 and had held a Master's Certificate for thirteen years. There was not much that Bartlett did not know about ships and the sea. He tried to steer for Zea, so that he could beach her, but she was going down too rapidly and she sank four miles west of Port St Nikolo. In fifty-five minutes one of the largest ships in the world had vanished. There had been just 351 days between her sea-trials and her sinking. In keeping with maritime tradition, Bartlett was the last to leave the ship and join the rest of the people who had taken to the boats. Among them were two

139

survivors of the crew of the *Titanic*, one of whom, Violet Jessup, had also been on board the *Olympic* when it collided with HMS *Hawke*. They were fortunate that two British convoy escort destroyers, HMS *Foxhound* and HMS *Scourge*, were not far from the scene. These ships, together with the light cruiser HMS *Foresight*, which was based at Port St Nikolo, and the French tug *Goliath* hurried to the spot and took the lifeboats in tow, some to Zea and others to Piraeus, where the injured among them were cared for in the Greek and Russian hospitals.

The Admiralty announced that there were 1,106 survivors, twenty-eight of whom were injured, and about thirty lives lost. Most of the deaths occurred when two of her lifeboats were launched prematurely, while the ship was still underway, and were sucked into and mangled by her giant propellers. Immediately the accusations and counter-claims began to fly back and forth between the belligerents.

German Wireless resorted to its customary stance that British hospital ships were being used to carry illicit bodies of troops to and from war zones under the protection of their red crosses. It had been making similar accusations, periodically, ever since the attempted torpedoing of the *Asturias* in 1915. It claimed that German agents in Portsmouth had seen two "deeply loaded hospital ships" leaving there daily for France and regularly returning there empty. Obviously, the agents concluded, these ships must have been carrying war material and ammunition. These events had also been observed by German prisoners-of-war interned on the Isle of Wight. On 21 November 1915 German Wireless, describing what it said was "the biggest fraud the British Navy had practised", said that seventy British transports "heavily laden and painted like hospital ships", had been seen by their agents in Spain to pass by Gibraltar into the Mediterranean. These too were carrying war materials, cunningly concealed in boxes marked 'soft soap'. The British Admiralty made a strong denial of these accusations. There were only forty-two hospital ships working in the Mediterranean, retorted Their Lordships, and when

---

* It has been suggested that the reason for the rapid sinking may have been the fact that the watch was in the course of changing. Many members of the crew would having been moving around the ship and this meant that many of her water-tight doors would have been open simultaneously.

empty they were always fully ballasted for safety and comfort. Moreover, the hospital ship *Mauretania* had been inspected at Naples by the American, Danish and Swiss consuls, who had jointly signed a declaration that they had found no evidence that the vessel was being used for anything other than a hospital ship.

Such allegations of misuse were entirely false, growled the British Admiralty. All British hospital ships had had their names registered with the belligerents as required by the Geneva and Hague Conventions. A large number of wounded soldiers being brought back from France were 'walking wounded' and of course would be plainly visible on deck. As for any accusations surrounding the provision of lifebelts, this was nothing but a sensible safety precaution against ordinary marine dangers. Indeed, universal provision of lifebelts was a regulatory requirement of the Board of Trade.

German Wireless then argued on another tack: "According to reports so far to hand, the ship was on its way from England to Salonika. For a journey in this direction the large number of persons on board is extraordinarily striking, which justifies the forcible suspicion of the misuse of the hospital ship for purposes of transport. Inasmuch as the ship carried the distinguishing marks of a hospital ship, there can naturally be no question of a German submarine in connexion with the sinking." Back came the instantaneous reply from the British Admiralty: "In view of the remark in the German Wireless that 'the large number of persons on board [the *Britannic*] is extraordinarily striking' . . . the number has now been accurately determined and is as follows:-

Crew	625
Medical Officers	25
Nurses	76
Sergeants, orderlies, dispensers, operating and laboratory attendants, skiagraphists and clerical staff.	399
Total	1,125."

"It is of interest to note," remarked *The Times* dryly, having done its homework in support of the Admiralty statement, "that according to the *Handbuch für die Deutsche Handelsmarine* for 1914, which is issued by the German Ministry of the Interior, the total complement of the German SS *Imperator*, which is approximately the same size as the *Britannic*, is 1,184 officers and men."

The question 'Mine or Torpedo?' was never finally settled satisfactorily. After the War the log of a U-boat captain, Siess, stated that he had sailed from Cuxhaven on 1 April in *U-73*, (one of a slow, clumsy class of boat known derisively in the German Navy as the 'Children of Sorrow') laden with thirty-four mines, bound for the Mediterranean, where he was to be attached to the Adriatic flotilla. He had rounded the north of Scotland to emerge into the Atlantic. En route he sank the sailing smack *Inverlyon* (which herself had accounted for *UB-4* in 1915 when serving as a Q-ship – see the chapter *King Stephen* and the Zeppelin) and was the probable layer of the mine which two months later would sink the cruiser HMS *Hampshire* off the Orkneys with Lord Kitchener on board. He had laid a field of mines off Lisbon, but had been prevented from doing so off Gibraltar by the vigilance of the defence patrols and a full moon. The last of his 'pineapples' were laid off Malta. Later, by then based at Cattaro, on the coast of Montenegro, he had made forays around the Aegean, the intention being to destroy British support ships bound to and from the Turkish theatre. It was on one of these, sometime before the sinking of the *Britannic*, that he had sown a field of mines in the Zea Channel.

On the other hand, it was known that the Zea Channel had been cleared by Allied minesweepers only the day before the sinking. Could it be that they had missed one or two?

Just three days after the *Britannic* went down another hospital ship followed her, barely sixty miles to the east of where the corpse of the giant liner now lay at the bottom of the sea. The Union-Castle Line's 6,318-ton four-masted *Braemar Castle* was getting on in years, having been built on the Clyde by Barclay Curle and Company in 1898. She had been a familiar figure on the South Africa run before the outbreak of war, when she was requisitioned for work as a hospital ship. On 24 November 1916 she was picking her way between the Aegean Islands, bound for Malta from Salonika with another load of broken men. There was very little recorded in connection with her loss about noon that day, either by mine or torpedo, in the channel which runs between the islands of Tinos and Mykonos, perhaps because of the fact that everybody on board was saved, with the exception of one sailor who was drowned and buried with naval honours. Allied destroyers came quickly onto the scene and conveyed the wounded to Syra.

On 31 January 1917 a German Note was presented in Washington. It constituted a hypocritical excuse for opening up the war on to a widely unrestricted basis and served to give notice that Germany was about to defy International Law with arrogant blatancy:

> Every day by which the war is shortened preserves on both sides the lives of thousands of brave fighters and is a blessing to tortured mankind. The Imperial Government would not be able to answer before its own conscience, before the German people, and before history, if it left any means whatever untried to hasten the end of the war. . . . *It must therefore abandon the limitations which it has imposed upon itself in the employment of its fighting weapons.* The Imperial Government hopes that the United States will appreciate the new state of affairs from the high standpoint of impartiality, and will also on their part help to prevent further misery and sacrifice. [author's italics].

The Note went on to define an area which thereafter should be considered dangerous for all sea traffic. It extended from Cape Finisterre out into the Atlantic to 20° West (about 400 miles from the coast of Ireland), then followed a line north, and then north-eastwards, bisecting the Orkneys and Faroes across to the limit of Norwegian territorial waters and then south through the eastern part of the North Sea to the neutral Dutch coast. Almost the whole of the Mediterranean was included, save for a corridor extending down the eastern seaboard of Spain, embracing the Balearics, and a narrow channel which hugged the coast of North Africa then turned north to Piraeus, to give access to Greece. Thus, no vessel of any nation could approach or leave the British Isles or France without the risk of attack, although it was conceded that two American ships were to be allowed to steam weekly between New York and Falmouth, provided that they were painted with vertical red and white stripes, arrived on a Sunday and departed on a Wednesday. Likewise a Dutch ship might ply between Flushing and Southwold during the hours of daylight, painted in colours to be decided by the Germans.

Yet more accusations were made that the British were conveying

143

troops and war materials under the protection of the Red Cross hospital ships. Therefore, hospital ships would not be tolerated within an area between lines drawn Flamborough Head – Terschelling and Land's End – Ushant. "If in this sea zone after the expiry of the stated time any enemy hospital ship is encountered," said the German announcement, "it will be considered as a vessel of war and it will be attacked without further ceremony." In the Mediterranean, a rider to the Note stated on 29 March, hospital ships were advised to give six weeks' notice of their arrival and departure, put in at the Greek port of Kalamata to register their presence and then steam for Gibraltar at a speed to be arranged.

It was highly likely, indeed it was certain, that no self-respecting enemy sea-power would accept such towering impudence from Berlin. Three days later the moment came when President Wilson finally took positive and concrete action. The United States broke off diplomatic relations with Germany. In a speech to Congress Wilson said, "I cannot bring myself to believe that they will destroy American ships and take American lives in wilful prosecution of the ruthless naval programme they have announced. If American ships and lives should be sacrificed by their naval commanders in heedless contravention of the just and reasonable understanding of international law and of the obvious dictates of humanity, I shall take the liberty of coming again before Congress to ask that authority be given me to use any means that may be necessary for the protection of our seamen and our people in the prosecution of their peaceful legitimate errands on the high seas. I can do nothing less."

There was little time to ponder on whether or not the Germans were bluffing. On the same day that the Note was delivered in Washington, 31 January, *U-45* held up an American tanker, *Westego*, and demanded oil. On 3 February an American sailor sitting in a lifeboat was killed by shellfire from the unidentified U-boat that had already sunk his ship, the *Eavestone*. The 3,000-ton American freighter *Housatonic*, with wheat from Newport News for England, went down off the Scillies on the same day at the hands of the chivalrous captain of *U-53*, Korvetten-kapitän Hans Rose. The German towed the crew of the sunken steamer in their lifeboats almost to Penzance before being forced to cast them off by the approach of a Royal Navy patrol. Notwithstanding Rose's humanitarian behaviour, however, Berlin had earned for Germany the heightened revulsion of the whole non-

Teutonic world by the prospect of *schrechlichkeit* [terror] warfare on a scale which went even beyond such incidents as the murders of Nurse Cavell and Captain Fryatt and the horrified outrage which followed them. War between the USA and Germany was now, surely, inevitable.

In 1976 an underwater exploration team headed by Jacques Cousteau located the wreck of the *Britannic*. She lies on her side in only 350 feet of water. With a length of 852.5 feet, her bows would have hit the bottom well before her stern disappeared from view, as had happened with the *Lusitania*.

The vendetta against hospital ships commenced in earnest in the spring of 1917. Both the *Britannic* and the *Braemar Castle* had possibly, if not probably, struck mines, but there was no doubt whatever about the 12,000-ton *Asturias*. She had been lucky to evade attack back in 1915 off Havre, but on 20 March 1917 she was torpedoed by a U-boat. *Asturias* had left Malta six days previously and had safely landed her 900 sick and wounded at Avonmouth. Now on her way to Southampton, she was steaming at fourteen and a half knots, fully lit and bearing all the distinctive markings of a hospital ship as required by the Hague Convention. It was a fine night, although the sea was a little choppy. She was off Start Point on the south Devon coast when a torpedo caught her, aft, at about midnight. It penetrated her hull near the rudder and went through as far as the engine-room, putting out all her electric lights. She settled down quickly and sank off Bolt Head, but the water was very shallow and she was later refloated and towed into Plymouth, where she was used as an ammunition hulk for the rest of the war. Forty-three of her RAMC staff and crew were killed, and thirty-nine injured were among the remaining 300–400, many of them shivering in thin night-clothing, who took to the boats and landed safely, where they were cared for by local residents.

The usual German accusations of misuse of hospital ships as military transports continued to flow from Berlin. This was vigorously denied by the British Government, who reminded them yet again that belligerents had the right to stop and inspect hospital ships in the case of suspicion, but it was a remedy which the Germans had never utilized.

This time Berlin did admit responsibility for the sinking via a report in the German Wireless Press listing U-boat achievements, adding the jaundiced observation that, "Even in spite of our warnings, wounded and sick have been sent into this sea zone and exposed to the dangers of being sunk. It would, moreover, be remarkable that the English in the case of the *Asturias* should have abstained from their customary practice of using hospital ships for the transport of troops and munitions; we are constantly receiving proofs that our enemies, as formerly, misuse hospital ships for the purposes of war."

Ten days later, off the Isle of Wight, the 8,000-ton *Gloucester Castle* was torpedoed. She had about 450 patients on board. A destroyer, HMS *Beagle,* and the patrol boat *P-19* stood by with the liner *Karnak* to take the people off, although rescue operations were hampered by gale-force conditions. Many of the wounded were stretcher cases, but the only lives lost were those of three members of the crew – Henry White, William Williams and Alexander Lamb. The torpedoing was admitted in a Berlin Official Wireless *communiqué* on 11 April. As for the *Gloucester Castle* herself, she was towed into shallow water before foundering and was later refloated and repaired.

17 April 1917 was a black day for the hospital ships. At half-past seven in the evening, HMHS *Lanfranc,* 6,287 tons, escorted by the destroyer HMS *Badger* and the patrol boat *P-37,* was about forty-two miles out from Le Havre with 234 British and 167 German wounded on board. Her crew numbered 123 and there were fifty-two medical staff. Suddenly there was the roar of an explosion, right for'ard, as she was hit by a torpedo. Thirteen British wounded, one RAMC staff member, five of the ship's crew and fifteen wounded Germans were all killed by the explosion. There had been no warning and none of the lookouts had seen the torpedo coming. A survivor of the crew said later that "The first intimation we had was the force of the explosion". He went on:

> When the war is over and the Germans repeat their excuses for sinking hospital ships by alleging that they are carrying on the work of transport, some of their countrymen will be able to give them the lie direct. As it happened, we had about 160 to 170 German wounded on board, men who had been captured in the recent advance of the British Army. They included about forty officers, some of whom were of a high rank, and they must know that the ships were genuinely engaged in hospital work. Of course, as soon as we realised what had happened to the ship,

our first thoughts were for our own wounded. Our fellows were as calm as anyone could possibly be in the circumstances, and what little panic there was was largely due to the anxiety of the Germans to save their own skins. The funny part of it, although it did not strike us as funny at the time, was that the Germans honestly believed that their own submarines could save them, and in fact, when other vessels came to our assistance, they thought they must be German ships. Although they were on a British ship, they believed that the British had been 'wiped off the sea', and that the Fatherland 'really ruled the waves'. Some of the Germans shouted at the top of their voices to the other vessel, thinking apparently that the German tongue would hasten their countrymen to the rescue, but when they found out their mistake, they altered their tone completely. Many of them herded together in one part of the stricken ship, and never shall I forget their long and repeated cries, in which the words 'mercy' and 'kamerad' were very prominent.

Some of the more venturesome Germans jumped into the sea and tried to attract the attention of what they thought were German ships. One of the firemen who rushed up on deck said that the Germans had no thought for others. They were much too afraid for their own skins, and it was only with great difficulty that they were kept from rushing the lifeboats. Fortunately, the crew acted in a prompt and gallant manner. They knew what was expected of them in such an emergency. Their first thought was for the wounded. There were 234 British Tommies, the majority of them cot cases. The task of getting these men on their stretchers up to the boat deck and then transferring them to the lifeboats can be better imagined than described, but the crew and ship's officers worked unceasingly; time and again they went below to get the wounded men, and they had the satisfaction of saving nearly all. The German wounded were dealt with in the same manner. After all, they were probably victims of the German military machine, and we could not stand by and see them perish, even as the result of the foul deed of their own countrymen.

The force of the torpedo smashed one or two of the lifeboats, but the crew were able to swing out the majority of them. One, which was loaded with Germans, fell headlong into the water and some of the occupants must have drowned. Many of our

147

own wounded were lifted, cot and all, into the boats most of which were able to get away. The captain and the few who remained behind with him on the stricken ship were rescued by a vessel which hurried to the scene in answer to our distress call.

The lifeboats drifted about for a long time, but eventually they were picked up and the occupants landed at various places along the south coast. At one dockside YMCA hut the manageress, a Miss Waldegrave, gave a moving description of the landing of some of the *Lanfranc* survivors.

We had a most stirring and exciting day. We got down to the hut in the morning to find that part of the crew and some of the wounded soldiers rescued from a torpedoed hospital ship had been brought into the dock. They were sent in to us to wait for the ambulances. The ship, HM Hospital ship *Lanfranc*, was struck at eight o'clock the previous evening. Some French fishing smacks dashed to the rescue and brought them in in the morning. Many of the men were only half-dressed and all were cold and hungry. We made a great horseshoe of our tables round the stove and got them all a hot breakfast.

Three of them were so badly wounded that they had to be laid on tables. It was awful to see men with bandages torn off their wounded limbs, and the stories they told bring home to one most forcibly what a shipwreck of wounded soldiers must be like. Some of the crew seemed all right, but I suppose after a while the shock began to tell and they looked too dreadful for words. They were all so nice and so brave, for some were clearly in a great deal of pain. Of course, before we had anything like served them all, some dockers came in for their meal. It was a trying time – men waiting in the kitchen, others dressing their wounds in our retiring room; dirty plates, cups and jugs everywhere; lifebelts strewn on the floor, blankets on the tables and litter everywhere. One of those rescued was the officers' mess boy, a mere child of fifteen. We were told that there were 242 British soldiers, only two of which were walking cases, and 130 Germans, thirty-five of whom were officers. Two RAMC men were lost and it was feared some of the crew. Some of the less badly wounded Germans had stampeded and jumped into a boat, partly filled with their own wounded. This they swamped

148

and the only person saved in it was an English boy, brought in to us with a crushed hand and leg. He was caught in a chain down the ship's side, but it held him until he could be removed.

After the dockers had left and we had all got straight and tidy, some of the wounded men went to the piano and began to sing – they were wonderful! It made us feel queer to hear them sing 'Pack up your Troubles in your Old Kit-bag &c'. After a while I went to them and said that I felt they ought to give thanks for being safe, and would they join in a hymn? Every man came to the piano, except one who was too bad to move. They sang most wonderfully 'O God our help in ages past'. Then I said a short prayer, but before I could move away one of them said, 'Might we have "For those in peril on the sea" for our mates, as we do not know where they might be?' I have never heard anything like it. Many broke down. In the middle the cars came to take them away. They finished the hymn and then said Goodbye. They gripped our hands until it was painful. Many of them ran back two or three times and said, 'Thank you, thank you. We shall never forget this morning.' We shall certainly never forget them and the stories they told. One of those rescued had neither arms nor legs; another who had lost both hands and feet had managed to get up on deck unaided!

The 1,885-ton *Donegal*, a Midland Railway Company ferry on the Heysham–Belfast run before the war, now serving as an ambulance-transport, was bound for England from France with 639 wounded on board, which included thirty-three stretcher cases. She was escorted by the destroyers HMS *Jackal* and HMS *Liffey*, but had had her distinctive hospital ship markings removed. The Secretary of the Admiralty explained the reasons why this had been done: "Owing to the German practice of sinking hospital ships at sight, and to the fact that distinctive markings and lighting of such vessels render them more conspicuous targets for German submarines, it has become no longer possible to distinguish our hospital ships in the customary manner. One of these two ships therefore, although carrying wounded, was not in any way out-wardly distinguishable as a hospital ship. The hospital ship markings of the other had not yet been removed. Both were provided with an escort for protection."

Such tactics served little good, however. In fact, they played straight into the hands of the Germans, as was proved barely an hour and a half after the *Lanfranc* had been torpedoed when the *Donegal* suffered the same fate about nineteen miles south of the Dean Light Vessel. The torpedo blew her stern away, causing part of her deck to collapse. Within an hour she had sunk and twenty-nine of the wounded and ten of her crew had lost their lives. *The Times* gave an account of the sinking:

> The *Donegal* left a French port at about 2.30 on Tuesday, and just before eight o'clock at night she was attacked without the slightest warning. The torpedo struck her on the port side, and in just over half an hour the vessel went down stern first. Her rudder had been blown completely away. Fortunately the spirit and pluck of the British seamen stood them in good stead. The ship's officers set a splendid example to the men, and the crew acted with extreme gallantry. The wounded soldiers, who were all British, were not seriously incapacitated. The majority were walking cases, and this greatly facilitated the rescue. The troops maintained a calmness which gave them great credit, and whenever possible they did what they could to assist their less fortunate comrades. 'There was an entire absence of panic,' said one of the firemen, 'and I shall never forget the way in which our men worked for the wounded soldiers. Everyone did his utmost to get the troops into a place of comparative safety. It was not until the whole of them were placed into the lifeboats that the remainder of the crew left the ship.' One of the ship's lifeboats was blown to pieces by the torpedo but the others were safely launched.

The British Admiralty report on the sinkings of the two hospital ships included the statement, "We were fortunate in being able to save the lives of ten German officers and 108 men from the vessels which were sunk." The French newspaper *Gaulois* was quick to pick up on this. "Yesterday the British declared themselves happy at saving German sailors. That is civilization, that is humanity", it said, adding scornfully, "Some days earlier we read that a German submarine had sunk a hospital ship without even attempting to come to the help of the wounded it carried. That is '*kultur*' – that is barbarity."

Reuter cabled from Paris that the French had decided to play a clever card. As the Germans had decided to torpedo hospital ships without warning, it reported, in these circumstances the French Government had made it known that they had adopted the practice of embarking German prisoners in such vessels.

In the Reichstag General Friedrich demanded that reprisals be made if German prisoners were carried aboard British or French hospital ships and exposed to the danger of being torpedoed, and appropriate Notes along these lines were sent to both British and French Governments via the mediation of Switzerland. The *Rheinisch–Westfälische Zeitung* warmly endorsed this action. It repeated the now familiar accusations that the British frequently abused the Red Cross, and asked, "Who could count the shells shipped to France aboard British hospital ships?" It went on to remind its readers that "the German Admiralty guaranteed British hospital ships a fairway in which they could move with complete security, and also warned them against traversing forbidden waters. The English disregarded the warning and unfortunately German wounded had to pay with their lives for the British Admiralty's presumption." The newspaper said that it believed that German wounded were intentionally placed on the torpedoed ships and that England, as a great part of her Press had demanded for months, carried Germans on board as a means of deterring Germany from sinking British ships. Should that be so, the sharpest reprisals would be appropriate.

The *Dover Castle* was the fifth and final hospital ship to come under attack in the 1917 springtime spate of spite against them. On 26 May the 8,271-ton ex-Union Castle liner was steaming westward in a calm sea, bound for Gibraltar from Malta with 700 patients and staff and a crew of 141 in company with another hospital ship, the *Karapara*. She was still painted white and carried all the usual hospital ship markings. The ships were escorted by the destroyers HMS *Cameleon* and HMS *Nemesis*. Just before 7 o'clock in the evening they were fifty miles north of Cape Bon when the *Dover Castle* was torpedoed by *UC-67*, commanded by Kapitänleutnant Karl Neumann. The German had been stalking them all afternoon, waiting patiently until the big ship turned on the leg of a zig-zag which would bring her into a perfect angle of juxtaposition for a shot. Six stokers were killed, but all the patients were safely transferred to *Cameleon*, while *Nemesis* laid down a smoke-screen for the *Karapara* to make her escape towards Cape

Bon. The screen was largely ineffective because of a following wind which lifted it away from the surface of the sea, but nevertheless the *Karapara* was unscathed and was rejoined later by *Cameleon* with a total of 950 men on board. Despite being holed, *Dover Castle* remained afloat, but stopped, for an hour and a half, after which time Neumann put another torpedo into her. It hit under the bridge on the starboard side and within three minutes she had disappeared.

But the curtains were far from falling over the affair of the *Dover Castle*. On 4 June 1921 Karl Neumann, Merchant, retired Commander, of Breslau, born 22 December 1887 in Katowice, appeared before the German Supreme Court in Leipzig charged with War Crimes, being the sinking of the hospital ship without warning and with excessive brutality, namely that the accused "in the Tyrrhenian Sea on 26 May 1917 intentionally killed six men after full consideration".

During October 1918, when Germany was in the grip of revolution, starvation and despair, and the final throes of the Great War were being enacted, the Kaiser had fled from Berlin, first of all to Spa, in Belgium, where were situated the General Headquarters of the German Army. At Spa Wilhelm and his Generals had received, considered and replied to the proposed terms of an Armistice made by American President Woodrow Wilson on behalf of the Allies. One of the many points laboriously negotiated was that Germany would bring up for trial, experimentally, a selected number of those who appeared on the Allies' list of war criminals.

The trials were to be experimental in the sense that the Allies wished to assess the willingness of Germany to deal adequately with those who had transgressed the accepted 'civilized' codes of war conduct as had been agreed between nations at Geneva and The Hague. Dozens of witnesses (there were twenty-one against Neumann alone) had appeared before Sir Charles Biron, Chief Magistrate of the Metropolis, at London's Bow Street Court to make sworn depositions for transmission to Germany.

The Special Correspondent of *The Times* wrote, "Leipzig, where the momentous trials are taking place, is one of the most serene of the cities which sprang up in the prosperous days of the Empire. It is a handsome city of open places, red tiled roofs and columned façades such as were beloved by the makers of modern Germany. It is upon one of its stateliest and perhaps the most august of its buildings, the German Supreme Court, that the eyes of the outside world in the next few days will be fixed. The colossal figure of Truth, dominating the outside and cupola of this imposing building, will be as much upon trial as the puny human figures called to the bar beneath her to answer charges which have roused the indignation of most of Christendom."

The Berlin press had taken to pre-judging the cases to be heard, particularly those papers of the right wing. All the old accusations of misuse of Hospital Ships were brought out to air. Public feelings were roused. Leipzig Citizens' Council appealed to people to stay away from the Great Hall unless they had some connection with the trials. It was inconsistent with German dignity, it said, that people should gather there simply out of morbid curiosity.

The trials took place on the first floor, in a long room with galleries and a dais at one end. It was ornately decorated in grey and gold with abundant floral designs. One of the English legal observers, who all appeared in full black morning dress, thought it was more like a *salon* than a courtroom. It reminded him of the theatre at Monte Carlo. On the dais was a semi-circular table and a row of imposing chairs for the Judges and Prosecutors. The accused and his lawyers were provided with a sort of choir stall at one side and the audience sat in rows of chairs set out as if for a concert. Unlike a concert, however, the audience were hard-pressed to hear a word of the proceedings, because the acoustics were abysmally poor. The Court opened at 9 am each day, which the English party thought somewhat late. The seven judges entered, clad in maroon robes with velvet collars, as was the *Reichsanwalt*, the Public Prosecutor. All those present rose whilst the President read out the Oath. That having been done, they resumed their seats, leaving the accused standing alone to face the Bench. The Judges donned their ceremonial caps of office and the proceedings commenced.

Neumann, the former captain of *UC-67*, (which had been ignominiously surrendered at Harwich on 21 November 1918 along with the bulk of the surviving German submarine fleet) was the fourth on Britain's list. He freely admitted sinking the *Dover Castle* knowing that she was a Hospital Ship, but pleaded that in doing so he had merely complied with the explicit instructions of the German Admiralty, which had issued an order on 29 March 1917 and which had been given to him before he sailed from Cattaro: "As from

Facsimile of the certificate Neumann gave to Captain Williamson of the SS *Elm Moor*.

8 April Hospital Ships generally are no longer to be permitted in the blockaded area of the Mediterranean, including the route to Greece. A few special Hospital Ships, which have been notified by name at least six weeks previously, may use the channel up to the port of Kalamata. Advise submarines that as from 8 April every Hospital Ship on the routes named is to be attacked forthwith, excepting such as have been expressly notified from here, in which cases speed, times of arrival and departure will be exactly stated."

The *Dover Castle* had been escorted by two warships, making it impossible for any warning to be given before firing torpedoes, and which also put her outside the protection of International Law. Despite this, Neumann had waited for an hour and a half before firing his second torpedo, thus allowing time for all the sick and wounded to be transferred to the escort destroyers. There was no case that he had acted as a criminal accomplice of the *Admiralstab*, because the views of Berlin that the British were misusing Hospital Ships were well-known throughout the German Navy and, as far as Neumann was concerned, their instructions of 29 March constituted justifiable and legitimate reprisal.

In further support of his defence, it was pointed out that the accused had allowed an English captain, Captain Williamson of the SS *Elm Moor*, which had been sunk by *UC-67* on 23 May and who was held as a prisoner on board, to observe his approach to the *Dover Castle*. Later, when going ashore as a prisoner of war at Cattaro, Williamson realized that he had lost his papers when his ship was sunk, and, not relishing the prospect of trying to cross war-ravaged Europe without them, he had asked Neumann for a certificate, which was readily provided. It gave complete details of the German's full name and rank. These were hardly the actions of a man who knew that he had acted in any way illegally. Neumann was acquitted.

Three 'army' cases had preceded that of the *Dover Castle*. They had all resulted in sentences being handed down which, in Allied eyes, were trifling. Now that Neumann had got off scot free, it was the last straw. Indignation and uproar pervaded the British Press. "Ten months imprisonment, six months, two months, acquittal," snorted *The Times* in disgust on 6 June, "That is the history of the four experimental trials of Leipzig, organised to test Germany's disposition to punish adequately those who, in the words of the President of the Tribunal himself, had shamed the reputation of the German armies in the eyes of the outside world. . . . One almost expected the Defending Counsel, Dr Huhlemann, to rush forward and shake the President by the hand."

Following the sinking of the *Dover Castle*, the Germans seem to have concentrated their efforts on attacks on oil-tankers and the hospital ships were left in comparative peace. Underlining this state of affairs was the fact that, in August 1917, the German Government agreed that a dozen Spanish officers be appointed as invigilators in British hospital ships on the Mediterranean run. They would inspect and travel on these ships, boarding and disembarking from them at Gibraltar, having reported that their use was in conformity with the Hague Convention. Moreover, it was agreed by Berlin that the North Atlantic and North Sea were 'free' to hospital ships. And they seemed to have kept their word, because there were no further hospital ship casualties of note. None, that is, until New Year 1918.

On the night of 4 January the 7,267-ton hospital ship *Rewa* was heading up the Bristol Channel in clear weather at about eight knots, bound for Avonmouth from Malta. She had 279 patients and 286 medical staff and crew. The Spanish officer-observers had left her at Gibraltar, having testified as to her *bona fide* purpose. She was brilliantly lit and painted white, with all the other hospital ship markings. (Apparently, the British had resumed this practice.) At about a quarter past eleven she was passing Hartland Point on the north Devon coast when she was suddenly hit by a torpedo, midships, which killed outright three Lascar seamen in her crew. Only minutes before, her master, Captain I.F. Drake, had warned that, although they were nearly home, vigilance should be maintained until they docked. Quartermaster William Moyse had stood his watch from 2000 to 2200 when he was relieved at the wheel by his colleague Jacob Fisher. Moyse stayed on the bridge for a few minutes, however, to chat to his friend. He then went on to the saloon deck to check that all the *Rewa*'s 'convention' lights were showing brightly and confirmed this to the Third Officer, Mr Evans. Seven months later, when his new ship called at Marseilles, Moyse swore a statement before the British Consul-General:

> When I struck the bell for 11 pm, I noticed a light about two points on the port bow about three miles distant. The light

seemed to be of a flashing nature, and I thought it might be the stern light of a sailing vessel on the starboard tack. I reported this to Mr Evans, Third Officer, who was Officer of the Watch and who was on the flying bridge at the time. And he went on to the lower bridge.

Almost as Mr Evans came onto the main bridge another light appeared, quite close to the first but not so bright. The first light then became quite steady. Both lights appeared horizontally and were very low in the water. Had I been on the lookout for a flashing buoy, I would have considered this to have been it.

When the helm was ported, I am of the opinion that if the lights had belonged to a sailing vessel or steamer I should have seen the sails above the haze on the water, and had it been a steamer we should have seen something of her also.

The captain was called by the Third Officer and the order was given for the helm to be ported, and I heard the order 'steady' given. On this order being given, I should say that the course had been altered two points. At this time the lights in question were still to be seen and appeared about 4 points on the bow. I did not see them disappear. The explosion took place about three or four minutes after the vessel had been steadied.

The captain blew five blasts on the whistle which is the order for boat stations. The order was given by the captain to stand by the boats and to get lifebelts on. I went to my boat which was on the port side. The boat was lowered on to the saloon deck and we were the first boat away on the port side. All the boats were kept together and red flares were burned until we were picked up by a trawler. We proceeded to Swansea and were landed at that port at about 10 a.m. on 5 January. After I was relieved by Quartermaster Fisher, the steaming navigation and 'convention' lights never failed and were alight when the vessel was struck. The Mine Protection gear had been put out during the afternoon and was in working order at the time of the explosion. The vessel sank on an even keel. There was no panic and everybody went to their boat stations.

Previous to signing on in the SS *Rewa*, I was boatswain on the SS *Whateley Hall*. I have been to sea all my life.

It took until two o'clock in the morning for the *Rewa* to sink, which gave ample time for the crew to get the cot patients into the lifeboats and for themselves to be picked up by offshore fishing smacks. All were landed safely at Swansea, the only casualties having been the three Lascars.

There followed the expected protests from the British Government, especially in view of the fact that the attack had taken place in waters supposedly guaranteed safe. In reply to this the Germans suggested that the cause of the sinking must have been a mine. This was highly improbable, countered the British Foreign Secretary, Arthur Balfour, because only that very day a naval patrol had been attacked by a U-boat in that same vicinity.

Later it was revealed that the sinking of the *Rewa* had been another dastardly act performed by the callous Werner, captain of *U-55*, who was described by Maurice Prendergast, editor of *Jane's Fighting Ships* from 1916–1921, as "one of the most cruel and cowardly of those men who defamed their nation, dishonoured their flag and disgraced the uniform they wore". Nine months earlier this man had already committed two of the most hideous of all war crimes at sea.

10

TORRINGTON AND *TORO*

On 8 April 1917 the Totem Steam Navigation Company's SS *Torrington*, 5,597 tons, was plodding home to Barry Roads from Savona, Italy, to fetch another cargo of Welsh steam coal for the Italian State Railways. At about half past eleven in the morning she was 150 miles south-west of the Scilly Isles when a sailor called out from aloft that he could see lifeboats in the distance. The ship's master, Captain Anthony Starkey, altered course slightly so as to close the boats and render any help they may have required. As he did so, he noticed the wake of a torpedo streaking towards him. He swung his helm to avoid it, but it was too late; the torpedo struck the *Torrington* in No. 3 hold, just forward of the bridge, causing considerable damage. Nos 2 and 3 holds started to fill rapidly and the freighter went down by the head, bringing her rudder and propeller clear of the water. Without any means of propulsion, she lost headway and stopped.

After a short while a submarine surfaced fine on the starboard bow and began to attack the collier with shellfire. The *Torrington* was not in a sinking condition at that point, but she was helpless and immobile. Nobody, so far, had been hurt. Unable to use his defensive gun owing to the fact that the *Torrington*'s superstructure obstructed the target, Starkey hauled down his flag and ordered his two lifeboats away. The portside boat contained half of the crew under the command of the Mate, and Starkey himself took control of the starboard boat with the remainder of the men. Before pulling away from the ship Starkey took his boat towards the Mate's and gave him a few words of advice on what to do if he was taken prisoner. When they had gone about a quarter of a mile from the *Torrington* a shell burst immediately above them. The submarine,

U-55, approached Captain Starkey's boat and ordered all the occupants of it to go on board her. Starkey was ordered below, leaving all his starboard boat men on the upper casing of the submarine. The German captain interrogated him in a most hostile and insulting way.

When asked his name, the British captain replied, "Starkey". This brought the German into a rage. "You lie!" he shouted, brandishing an out-of-date copy of Lloyd's Register which showed the name of Starkey's predecessor.

"Have you a ship's gun?" he next demanded.

"Yes."

"Where are your gunners?"

"On deck."

"I don't see anyone in uniform."

"You did not give anyone a chance to change into their best clothes before you fired that torpedo."

"It does not matter. You are a bloody pirate and will be shot. As for the others, let them swim."

With that the German left and, moments later, an electric bell sounded and the U-boat dived, remaining submerged for about twenty minutes. When she re-surfaced, some German sailors arrived back in one of the lifeboats with loot from the *Torrington* and provisions taken from the other lifeboat. Later Starkey saw provisions being consumed in the submarine which included bottles of spirits and tins of meat of identical brand to that which had been carried in the port lifeboat and which he remembered well as he had noted earlier how they differed from those in his own starboard boat. As regards the fate of the twenty men who had been on the deck of the submarine when she dived, the only conclusion that could be drawn was that they had been washed into the sea. Certainly they were never seen again. There was no other ship in sight at the time, nor was an alarm sounded for any emergency. No attempt was made to bring the men on the upper deck inside the submarine before she submerged. There can only have been one reason for her to dive and that was to drown them. Nor were any of the remainder of their shipmates in the other lifeboat ever seen again. The sea was dead calm and the boat was in excellent condition, except that the Germans had taken most of the food from it. Therefore, it is highly unlikely that any of the more common maritime misfortunes could have befallen them. Neither the men nor their boat were ever reported as being seen or picked up by another passing ship, or having made land. There is every reason to suspect that they had been 'disposed of' while the U-boat was submerged, probably at the same time as the Germans took the food.

Starkey, the only known survivor from the *Torrington*'s crew of thirty-five, remained on board the *U-55* as a prisoner, along with four others whom the submarine had already captured. They were Captain Draper of the British ship *Umooti*, Captain Ashfield of the *Petridge* and two Royal Navy gunners.

Six days after the attack on the *Torrington*, another British ship, the 3,000-ton *Toro*, met *U-55* and was dealt with in exactly the same way 200 miles west-south-west of Ushant. She had been on her way to Hull, in ballast from Alexandria. Her captain and gunner were brought below, leaving their shipmates on the upper deck while the boat dived for about twenty minutes. On returning to the surface, and receiving back on board the boat's crew with 4,000 looted eggs from the *Toro*, the U-boat captain asked Starkey if he would like to see a ship sink. He was taken to the conning-tower and from there observed the incident. However, after about an hour, the submarine moved off without waiting for the *Toro* to sink.

About 17 or 18 April Werner attacked and sank a small Danish sailing ship with his deck-gun. She had been bound for a French port with a cargo of rum. Again the German followed his routine of diving for twenty minutes whilst a boarding-party went aboard the victim for loot. They returned with a portable gramophone and records in English and Danish, several brand new cloth caps with a London maker's name in them and the ship's compass. He saw no prisoners from her, but Starkey did see the sail from her lifeboat in the submarine. He guessed that Werner had taken this as proof of the sinking. Eventually the captains were landed in Germany and repatriated after the war.

There was a special sitting at Bow Street Court on Tuesday 31 August 1921, before Sir Chartres Biron, to hear the evidence of Captain Starkey so that his deposition could be placed before the tribunal in Leipzig, although the accused, the captain of *U-55* who had been identified as the vile Werner, had not yet been arrested. Mr Vernon Gattie appeared on behalf of the British authorities while Dr Bunger represented the German Government.

The written statement of a German ex-soldier witness named Shimm, from Frankfurt am Main, stated that while held as a prisoner of the French in about May 1915 he had been working in the docks at Marseilles. He swore that he and several other prisoners had seen the *Torrington* lying alongside Mole No. 8, displaying distinctive hospital ship markings. Her name had been clearly visible and she was being loaded with guns and ammunition, which he assumed were for the British Army on the Salonika front.

Starkey, by that time master of the SS *Brandon* of Cardiff, had been on a voyage to Mexico and when he put in to São Vicente in the Cape Verde Islands he found a message for him asking him to make a sworn statement to HM Consul there for onward transmission to London and Leipzig. He said that one of the *U-55*'s sailors, Obermatrosen Küper from Bremen, who, by co-incidence, had worked aboard the *Torrington* before the war, had told him that he was lucky to have escaped with his life. On another occasion the wireless operator had asked him, "Do you think your men got home, Captain?"

"I should think so. The weather was not too bad."

"Believe me, Captain, your men never got home. There are too many here now, or I would tell you something else." Later he told Starkey that his men had all drowned.

One submariner, a German-Pole who manned the machine gun, had remarked that it was not war, it was murder. Starkey heard this man whisper *"Dank Gott"* when Werner fired a torpedo which missed. It was clear from these and other conversations that Starkey had with the crew, as well as their statements made later under interrogation, that they regarded Werner's actions as inhuman and that the cases of the *Torrington* and *Toro* were by no means isolated atrocities. Two hospital ships had been sunk by him, the *Rewa* and, on 10 March 1918, the *Guildford Castle*. Other sinkings without warning were the steamers *Clearfield* and *Artist* in October 1916 and January 1917 respectively and the trawler *Trevone* on 30 January 1917. The crew also claimed that they had been operating under Werner in the Black Sea, where they had sunk a ship called the *Paddington* outside Odessa harbour. It was not clear whether this had been in *U-55* or an earlier boat, but in any case it was common in the German submarine service for the whole crew to follow their captain when he changed boats.

After the Armistice *U-55* was surrendered at Harwich on

27 November 1918 as part of a batch of twenty-seven German submarines. They showed no identification numbers, which made things difficult for the young officer, Lieutenant Cope, RNVR who had been assigned to their interrogation. First of all Cope needed to establish which of the boats was *U-55*, and, with a heavy workload on his plate, his time was limited. Under questioning, Engine Room Artificer Albert Tiefenbach said he had served in her since 28 May 1917. He admitted that they had sunk the *Rewa*, but he had been personally unaware that she was a hospital ship. He also said that he had heard that prisoners were left on deck to drown when the boat dived, but as an engine-room man he had not been a witness to this. But he did know that the crew had elected a deputation to approach Werner to ask him to abstain from committing further atrocities, to which the captain had replied, "We are at war."

When Leading Seaman Augustus Faller was questioned, he said that he had been in *U-55* since June 1916. Werner had on at least two occasions dived while prisoners were on deck. Faller was convinced that this had been done intentionally and not because of the approach of a British ship. He said that Werner's actions were inhuman. Seaman Ferdinand Weber confirmed many sinkings, including that of the *Torrington*. He appeared to be vehemently anti-Kaiser and said that the whole German population had been fooled by those in power. Leading Seaman Walter Sprengel said that he had joined *U-55* in June 1917 and, as far as he knew, Werner had 'fled' sometime during the autumn of 1918.

On his return to England, Starkey was called to the hearing at Bow Street Court, where he was cross-examined by Dr Bunger.

Bunger: "How do you explain the fact that the captain allowed you to live when you were such an important witness?"

Starkey: "I do not know. I cannot explain it. I don't think Captain Werner realised that I knew what happened." He went on to explain that all the time he was on board *U-55* he said little and was careful to pretend that he was ignorant of the crimes that had taken place.

Bunger: "Several German witnesses have mentioned that a destroyer was approaching at the time the *Torrington* was sunk. What do you say to that?"

Starkey: "I did not see any destroyer. If one had been near, surely Captain Werner would have stayed dived, but he re-surfaced. And if there had been a destroyer, it would have picked up the men in the other lifeboat, but they were never seen again."

The despicable Werner was never caught and brought to book. His crimes, if not the most violent and blood-thirsty, had surely been the cruellest, coldest and most callous in all the long catalogue of horrendous acts committed by submarine captains in either of the World Wars. In his absence, the Court ordered that all his assets in Germany be confiscated.

11

KIESEWETTER AND THE *GLENART CASTLE*

The German attacks on British hospital ships all followed a similar pattern. The attackers invariably failed to exercise their right to stop and inspect the ships before sinking them, but then insisted either that the ship had been sunk by a mine or that their victim was being used as a machine of war and was therefore fair game. This accusation was then, of course, strenuously denied by the British, who pointed out *ad nauseum* throughout the entire war that, had the Germans' right to stop and inspect been invoked, it would have provided an easy solution to what became a very sore point between the belligerents and which led to a number of cases being presented as War Crimes.

However, the tale of Wilhelm Kiesewetter's encounter with the hospital ship *Glenart Castle* is a little different. It contains enough twists to save it from being just another version on the same theme, of which there were several. And it was not the first time that she had fallen prey to the perils of war.

The war was only a few days old when she was homeward bound from Cape Town on 15 August 1914, still sailing under her Union Line name of *Galician*, and not yet taken over as a hospital ship. She was waylaid by the German armed merchant cruiser *Kaiser Wilhelm der Grosse*, which ordered her to turn round and proceed southward. All that day and the following night the German watched her closely. All those on board were apprehensive of their fate, but in the morning their captor signalled, "On account of your women and children I will not sink your ship. You are released. Bon voyage." Alas, such chivalry was to become rarer and rarer as the war progressed.

At 11.40 pm on 1 March 1917 she had been steaming from Le

Havre to Southampton when she was struck either by a mine or torpedo, (it has never been proved conclusively either way), when about eight miles NW of the Owers Light Vessel. Fortunately, all the patients and medical staff were taken off safely by various trawlers which were standing by and she was taken in tow by the Admiralty tug *Magnet* and towed into Southampton. She was well down by the stern and, despite pumping by two other tugs, *Grappler* and *Sprite*, by the time they reached the docks at 9.45 next morning only about a foot of *Glenart Castle*'s after-part was visible above water.

Almost exactly a year to the day later, at 2 am on 26 February 1918 to be precise, she was on her way from Newport (Mon) to Brest to fetch another cargo of wounded soldiers back to Blighty. But as she sailed down the Bristol Channel in cold moonlight, ablaze with hospital ship lights of red white and green, unseen eyes were watching her – the eyes of one Kapitänleutnant Wilhelm Kiesewetter, who sat in the conning-tower of a dark sinister shape, fifty yards long, in the sea just north of Lundy Island. It was *UC-56*.

Kiesewetter had commanded the little 417-ton coastal minelaying U-boat since the previous April, working chiefly in the English Channel and Irish Sea, but so far he had little to show by way of victims. Now he had a 6,500-ton steamer in sight. Judging by the way she rode in the water, it seemed to Kiesewetter that she was heavily loaded. Later, he said that he could see two lights on her upper deck, two or three lights at her stern and a red light on her starboard [sic] quarter and that she was showing no other lights. He studied her progress for an hour and a half, finally concluding that she was either a cruiser or armed merchant cruiser and pre-pared to dive for his attack. Below, in the cramped space of the little U-boat, skilled hands deftly worked levers, switches and control wheels, the diesel engine clutch was thrown and power was switched to electric. "Main engines, full power!" rapped out Kiesewetter. Instrument needles swung hard across dials as a powerful surge of amperes was drawn from the batteries. Vents opened and tons of sea-water rushed into ballast tanks to send *UC-56* sliding out of sight. By 0400 *UC-56* was ahead of her target. Kiesewetter, peering attentively into his periscope waiting for the best angle of bearing on the target, suddenly called, "*Feuer ein!*" and a 50-centimetre torpedo sped towards the *Glenart Castle* from a range of 650 yards. It struck her on the starboard side with a loud explosion and Kiesewetter dived deeper to avoid detection by any watchful escort ships that might have come bustling onto the scene. As he did so he said he was just able to observe a second explosion on the ship before his periscope submerged.

Aboard the *Glenart Castle* Fourth Officer George Scarlett was about to take the Morning Watch, 0400–0800, when there was an enormous explosion and all the electric lights went out. He reported:

> I went straight up onto the bridge and received orders from the Captain to go and get my boat away at once. I went down to my boat, No. 5 lifeboat, the third boat on the starboard side. I then saw that the ship had been struck just abaft amidships on the starboard side under No. 7 boat, which was wrecked. My boat's crew were standing by and I ordered the boat to be cast adrift at once and had lowered it about four or five feet when the Chief Officer came and shouted 'Every man for himself!' The ship then took a heavy list to starboard, the water swept the boat up against the davit heads and smashed it to pieces before we could do anything to cut it adrift. I saw the other boats' crews on the starboard side trying to get their boats away, but none were cleared away in time.
>
> Two or three men jumped overboard. I was waiting for them to get clear of the ship's side but the next minute I was swept overboard as the ship went down. I managed to get hold of a raft and crawled onto it. There was another raft close by with three men on it. I saw nothing of anyone else from the ship, but could hear cries from the water for some time afterwards. I saw two schooners during the day, but neither of them saw my raft. I was picked up at about 1530 the next afternoon by USS *Parker*.
>
> All boats were carried swung out, the otters [a type of paravane] were over and running at the time *Glenart Castle* was torpedoed. The sky was clear. Wind Force 3. Sea state 3.

Greaser Alf Bale was also about to go on watch. He had just reached the top of the engine-room ladder when the torpedo struck. His boat station was the portside forward lifeboat. He hurried along the alleyway into the after well-deck and then up to the boat-deck. They had just got their boat into the water when the Chief Officer shouted, "Every man for himself!" Alf slid down the falls into the boat with two crewmates, but before they could cast off the ship sank and they were all thrown into the sea.

When Alf spluttered to the surface, he saw an upturned boat with three men clinging to it. He swam towards it and hauled himself up onto its keel. After a little while he saw a schooner coming towards them and they all shouted at the tops of their voices. But he quickly realized that he had been mistaken. In the slowly brightening dawn, he could see distinctly that she was no schooner. She was no more than 100 yards away. She had a long low silhouette, dark metallic and gleaming wet, with a conning tower. He turned to the man next to him on the gently heaving keel of the lifeboat and said, "We can expect nothing from him, it's the submarine." They too were picked up by USS *Parker* that afternoon.

Lance-Corporal Beveridge, 42855, of the Royal Army Medical Corps was one of the *Glenart Castle*'s forty-six medical orderlies. He was fast asleep at the time, but was thrown out of his bunk by the force of the explosion. He clambered to his feet, grabbed a lifebelt and ran up on deck to find that all the lifeboats had either left or had been smashed against the ship's side and the davits by the heavy sea that had got up. The ship was well down in the water, so much so that Beveridge had only to climb down a ladder and start swimming. He saw the submarine quite plainly and the two men in its conning-tower as it passed only twenty-five yards or so from the piece of wreckage he was using for a raft. Another crewman, T. Casey from Newport, had also been fast asleep in his bunk. He rushed on deck, clad only in his pyjamas, and made it into the third lifeboat to be launched, along with eight nurses. Luckily he was uninjured, but then came a chilly six hours in the open boat before they managed to hail a French schooner, the *Faon*, which took them into Swansea. He said, "We had a hard pull and a bad time in the boat, because most of us were entirely without clothing except what we had been sleeping in. We were thankful, I can tell you, to see that Frenchman hove into sight."

The 1,036-ton USS *Parker* (DD-48) had been on patrol off Cuba and the eastern seaboard of the USA more or less continuously ever since her builders, William Cramp & Sons, had sent her down the Philadelphia slipways in 1913 until she was transferred to escort the first troop convoy bringing the 'doughboys' in the build-up to fight 'over there' early in 1917. Since then she had been based at Queenstown and employed on escort duty in the Western Approaches.

She arrived to assist with the rescue of the *Glenart Castle* survivors about fifteen hours after the sinking. By this time the wind had got up and there was a heavy sea running. Rescue ships were always exposed to the danger of enemy submarines still lurking in the vicinity of their kill and the American captain, understandably, was loath to stop and lower a boat. With much bravery, two of *Parker*'s sailors jumped into the lumpy sea and swam fifty odd yards to the nearest raft, on which four men were riding, including the hospital ship's Navigating Officer, who was in a state of semi-consciousness. They brought them back to the destroyer, one at a time, swimming with great difficulty through the choppiness. All this time *Parker* was underway, so as not to present her 300-foot length as a sitting target for another torpedo.

168 crew and staff were aboard the *Glenart Castle*, all of whom, of course, had been granted special protection by the Hague Convention. Of these, twenty-two survivors were landed at Swansea, all from the *Faon*, seven at Pembroke Dock and nine at Milford Haven. Among those lost had been her Master, Captain Bernard Burt, who had last been seen alone on his bridge after artermaster to get away to the boats.

The British lost no time in setting up a Court of Inquiry. Within hours of the sinking, the Court's President, Lieutenant-Commander F. Buckeridge, RNVR, and his colleagues Lieutenants Jenman and Munk were listening to the statements of survivors and witnesses in Milford Haven.

John Hill, Second Hand of the fishing trawler *Swansea Castle* stated, "We were coming into Lundy Island. When we sighted Lundy, I called the skipper and he told me to keep her in N by E and said that if I saw any lights I was to call him, or when I got the light of the North Lundy light bearing E by N. I was also to call him if I saw any trawlers. As we were steaming along I had a look round with the glasses and away in the starboard rigging I saw the Hospital Ship with green lights all around her – around the saloon. She had her red side lights showing and her masthead light, and also another red light which I suppose was the Red

Cross light. We were steaming north and she was going W by N. As we were steaming along I did not know whether to alter course, but her speed took her across our head clear of us – she crossed our bow. When she got right ahead all her lights were out. When the lights went out, I turned with the glasses in my hand to see that she went clear of us and I saw the vessel in the moonlight. Every light on board had suddenly disappeared. Of course, that made me think that something was wrong and I remarked to my mate at the wheel that it was funny. Therefore, after I spoke to him, I picked up my glasses and looked around the horizon in order to see whether I could discover anything at all. As I came around with my glasses to about the NE, I saw something on the water with no lights, so also did my mate. As I looked at it my mate said, 'What's that, Jack?' I said I didn't know, but it looked like a Noah's Ark. After speaking to him I put the glasses down. We said a few more words, but when we looked again the object had disappeared.

"Such a thing as a submarine had not entered my mind, but as soon as the object disappeared my mate said to me instantly, 'A submarine, Jack – call the Skipper'. I shouted down to the Skipper, 'Submarine, Skipper!' As soon as he got his eyes open he said, 'Over her!' and I left the wheel and ran aft to call all hands to man the gun. 'Submarine!' I sang out. Everyone was at his post very quickly and the gun was trained right round at once. Before I left the bridge the Skipper said, 'Keep her ENE!' By going ENE it was impossible for us to go past that object without seeing it. As soon as I had warned everyone, I returned to the Skipper. I looked at the compass and said to him that she was on the port bow. After I had altered course, I said, 'It's a poor lookout Skipper, she will not give us another chance'.

We proceeded afterwards to Lundy. The Hospital Ship was sunk about eight to ten miles W by S of North Lundy Light."

"Can you tell us anything more?"

"Well, I thought it was a mystery when the lights of the hospital ship went out."

"When it got daylight did you see anything?"

"We went back to Lundy and tried to signal to HMT No. 1855 *Favorita*."

"Did you see the hospital ship afterwards?"

"No, the hospital ship was clean out of sight."

"Did you look for her?"

"No, the Skipper said we had done our bit for the country."

"You did not hear the explosion?'

"Nothing whatever. We thought the hospital ship got away. The remark was passed that she was going too fast."

"How far was the hospital ship away when she crossed your bows?"

"About a mile and a quarter – it would be no further."

The *Swansea Castle*'s skipper, Joseph Rust was then called. He told the Court: "My Second Hand said he saw this hospital ship on the port bow and then suddenly her lights went out. He said there was a dark object on her starboard bow bearing NE I said, 'Keep NE, run over it – general quarters!' The men were there in 30 seconds and a projectile was in the gun. By the time I talked to him the object had disappeared. I went round to the NW and back again to the NE to see if we could observe anything. I then started on a zig-zag course. I asked the Second Hand several questions about the hospital ship. I was a bit dubious about her lights going out. I thought she had seen the submarine and wishing to avoid it had put them out. I walked round the verandah to see if I could discover anything, but I saw nothing. I ran into Lundy and signalled to the *Dynevor Castle* with my torch. I tried to draw her attention as I thought her wireless would have enabled her to contact the Naval Base to report a submarine in the vicinity."

"Did you make contact with her?"

"No, Sir."

Lieutenant Charles Brewer, commanding officer of the trawler HMS *Okino* reported to the Vice-Admiral at Milford Haven that when he had observed the *Glenart Castle* at 0130 north of Lundy Island on the night of the sinking she had been displaying all the hospital ship lights and markings. He estimated her speed to have been eleven knots. The weather was clear, with wind Force Four and visibility was good. *Okino* had been escorting a steamer, the *St. Leonards*, from Milford Haven to Barry Roads, which made a welcome change from the dreary convoy escort work which had become her lot – two days out to about 12°W and two days back. But, strangely, Brewer's log makes no mention of sighting a hospital ship on 26 February 1918. In fact, other than to record that the wind had risen through the night to Force Five the next morning and the sea state was rough, the page is blank. The evidence of this officer was not likely to be of very much assistance to the British.

British Naval Intelligence was able to compile a part-history of the German UC boats from captured logs and patrol reports, Kiesewetter's movements in *UC-56* for the month prior to the sinking being entirely missing. His next recorded position was on 28 February 1918, two days after it, in 50°20'N–00°40'E which puts him in the mouth of the Somme off the French coast, and which ties in with his return to Zeebrugge.

He was next ordered on patrol in the Bay of Biscay to hunt for enemy traffic in and out of the French Atlantic ports. *UC-56* sailed from Zeebrugge on 12 May, but almost immediately Kiesewetter began to have problems. They were only three days out when it was noticed that a water-cooling pump had been torn away, putting the starboard heavy oil engine (for surface work) out of order. His engineers managed to rectify the problem and he was able to claim the first victim of the patrol the next day by torpedoing and sinking the steamer *J.C.McCullough* off Ushant. But his bad luck with *UC-56*'s machinery was to worsen. On the same afternoon her port electrical motor (which propelled the boat when dived) broke down and, although this was repaired by midnight, by 0300 its partner on the starboard side had incurred similar damage. Then a crankshaft bearing melted, which was found to be as a result of clogging oil. There was no means of repairing this with the facilities on board. This meant that one of her heavy oil engines was put out of action altogether.

On 21 May No. 4 outlet valve cylinder cracked, and the forward bearing of the starboard dynamo overheated. The port electrical motor had been performing erratically for days and on 22 May it finally gave up the ghost on account of melting connections of the armature coils. This meant that *UC-56* could no longer charge her batteries. A return journey to base was impossible, therefore, as this had rendered her incapable of running under water for more than a short time. In the First World War Germany held no French Atlantic ports. Kiesewetter had no alternative but to put into the nearest neutral haven.

The German Consul in Madrid sent to Berlin on 26 May: No. 677 "24 May at 6 a.m. there arrived at Santander the *UC-56*, Kapitänleutnant of the Reserves Kiesewetter, with damage to her electrical machinery. For the moment my presence there is not

172

necessary." And on 2 June: No. 732 "Reply to No. 706 of 29 May. I have already protested against the internment of *UC-56* and today received the customary reply that the Spanish Government regards the internment as justified and upholds it. Negotiations are still taking place concerning the necessary repairs. Ratibor."

Evidently, the repairs were eventually carried out, but of course *UC–56* was to play no further part in the war, which in any case had only a few more months to run before the Armistice, nor were the other four German U-boats with whom she found herself interned in the north-eastern Spanish port. She was surrendered at Rochefort on 27 March 1919.

In the meantime British Intelligence had connected the sinking of the *Glenart Castle* with *UC-56*. A talkative captured German sub-mariner, Wenninger of *UB-55*, had been heard to say that Kiesewetter had sunk a hospital ship off Hartland Point on 26 February 1918 and *UC-56*'s presence in Spain was practically public knowledge. The crews of four of the five internees were to be repatriated to Germany in the Dutch steamer *Frisia*. (*U-48* had been scuttled by its crew, who were being detained in Spain.) The *Frisia* was to call at Falmouth en route.

Accordingly, Kiesewetter was arrested at Falmouth on 6 May 1919 as an alleged war criminal. His luggage was searched, and among it the following items were found:

[1] Correspondence with the German Naval Attaché, Madrid, including copies of statements made by Kiesewetter regarding the sinking of the *Glenart Castle*.

[2] Copies of correspondence between the camp commandant at Alcola, Spain, where the internees had been held, and a Spanish General regarding the steps to be taken against *UC-56* crew members Petty Officer Engine-Room Artificer Engelhardt and Leading Seaman Keck, who were said to be plotting revenge on Kiesewetter for his alleged ill-treatment and withholding pay from his men. (Could this have meant that the machinery problems which beset the submarine were, in fact, a matter of sabotage? Engelhardt, for one, would have had ample opportunity to have been involved in such chicanery had he chosen to do so.)

[3] A letter from the French Embassy in Madrid, guaranteeing Kiesewetter safe conduct back to Germany. This was the first that the British authorities had known of it. Nothing about it had been communicated to them by their French counterparts.

The German did not deny sinking the *Glenart Castle*. Quite the contrary. On his arrest, Kiesewetter was interviewed and made a full statement to Lieutenant E.J Moseley, RNVR:

It was a heavily laden ship. I fired a torpedo from a distance of 600 metres which struck the ship on the starboard side. I then dived from a depth of 10 metres to a depth of 20 metres and just as the periscope was submerging I observed a second explosion on the ship. I remained at 20 metres and moved slowly to the south at four knots until 0730 when I surfaced and steered back towards the north. At about 0800 or 0830, I picked up a wireless message that the hospital ship *Glenart Castle* had been sunk. No other U-boats were working in the vicinity at the time and date mentioned. I continued patrolling in the Irish Sea but did not attack any further shipping, arriving at my base in Zeebrugge six days later.

On reporting, my chief, Bartenbach, asked, 'Did you torpedo a ship off Lundy Island on 26 February?' I answered, 'Yes.' 'Then you have torpedoed a hospital ship, the *Glenart Castle*, and you must proceed to Berlin to make a full report.'

I accordingly reported at the Admiralty Berlin and explained what I had done, viz, that [1] as the ship carried a red light on the starboard bow [sic], [2] was heavily laden and [3] did not carry the regulation lights for a hospital ship, I could not imagine that she was a hospital ship.

Lieutenant Moseley also interviewed other *UC-56* crew members. First Officer Gerhard Tetzlaff had joined the submarine after the incident and could only say what he had heard from others. Engineer Alfred Schmidt was on board at the time. He knew that a ship had been torpedoed but had not heard that she was a hospital ship until they arrived back in Zeebrugge, when Kiesewetter informed him he had been summoned to Berlin. Steersman Christoph Ubben and one or two others all said much the same as Schmidt.

The embarrassing discovery of the French guarantee of safe conduct threw the British into confusion. Which should take priority, their justification in arresting an alleged war criminal or his written guarantee of safe conduct? And should the *Frisia* be held up while they debated the matter? Most definitely she should be held up, contested Commander Cochrane of Naval Intelligence in his memorandum to colleagues TC4543/MI.5/G dated 13 May 1919.

But the Crown's legal advisers were unsure. After a fortnight they decided that Kiesewetter must be allowed to leave. And Foreign Secretary Arthur Balfour thought so too, making the naive comment that Section 228 of the impending Treaty of Versailles contemplated provision for Germany to surrender Kiesewetter on demand from the British, but firstly the safe conduct must be observed. Meanwhile the Spanish, sensing a complicated international argument brewing, wanted nothing but to make sure that they were not involved. And, to emphasize this desire, Señor Aguilar, the Spanish Consul in London, called at the Foreign Office on 26 May to announce formally that his Government were anxious that Kiesewetter should not be returned to their shores. Another month of debate had slipped by before Lord Curzon, new Foreign Secretary in Lloyd George's Imperial Cabinet, cast the final decision. Kiesewetter must be free to leave.

The Director of Naval Intelligence was furious with the lawyers. "To use meticulous legal points to allow such a diabolical scoundrel to escape", he seethed on 28 June, "is really too much." But the lawyers had their way and the *Frisia* sailed from Falmouth with Kiesewetter on board. And so it transpired that on 26 July 1919, a Hauptmann Lossnitzer telegrammed London from the office of the *Deutsche Generalstabsoffizier* in Cologne to confirm that Kiesewetter had arrived there under nil escort at half past four.

Needless to say, that was the last that the British authorities ever heard of him. The susceptibility of Balfour's over-trusting attitude had been proved. The time-honoured code of the cricket field no longer had a place in the game of war, if indeed it had ever had such a place. It was, no doubt, a painful lesson for a fair-minded man to learn, but the fact remained that another one had escaped the net.

12

THE *LLANDOVERY CASTLE*

The final episode of spite against British hospital ships is probably the best known. It was the case of the 11,423-ton liner *Llandovery Castle*. It was described by Prendergast as "the culminating outrage on these Red Cross ships, hitherto respected by all belligerent nations, until Germany prostituted her submarines to crime."

HMCHS *Llandovery Castle*, having been chartered by the Canadian Government for service as a hospital ship, was returning to England to collect more wounded Canadians for repatriation, having just delivered 644 military patients to Halifax, Nova Scotia, including twenty-seven stretcher cases, thirty-seven mental and fourteen with tuberculosis. She had already made the round trip four times in the previous three months without major mishap. With no patients to tend, the west–east crossings usually gave her hard-pressed medical staff of fourteen nursing sisters and eighty Canadian Army Medical Corps personnel time to relax a little. Most of them had volunteered for service at the outbreak of war in August 1914 and had arrived in England with the First Canadian Division, since when they had seen active service in casualty clearing stations in the hellish carnage of Flanders, and had only recently been transferred to hospital ship duties to give them a comparative 'break'. But their 'holiday' came to a sudden end at 9.30 pm on Thursday 27 June 1918 when the *Llandovery Castle* was 116 miles west of the Fastnet and a torpedo exploded against her after hull. She had been making about fourteen knots and her forward thrust caused her to start filling very rapidly. Nobody on board had seen the wake of the torpedo as it approached. It was not until they heard the enormous roar and felt the violent shudder of the explosion that they knew anything was amiss. Almost immediately all the ship's lights went out. Her master, Captain E.A. Sylvester, rang down to the engine-room to "Stop" and then "Full Astern", but there was no response on the telegraph. Good discipline and regular emergency practice showed their worth as the crew groped their way along the darkened listing decks to their boat stations and waited quietly for orders. Sylvester leaned from his bridge, megaphone in hand, and bade them not to lower any boats until the ship had lost way. He sent the carpenter to inspect the damage. The man reported that No. 4 hold had been blown in and that in his opinion the ship could not remain afloat. In the wireless cabin the Marconi operator tried vainly to transmit a distress call, but there was no spark to his key. Sylvester then ordered the boats away and to abandon ship. Then he hurried to his cabin to fetch an electric torch and his pipe. By the time he returned all the lifeboats had got away, except for one which was still hanging vertically by one of its falls. Sylvester, together with Second Officer Chapman, Major Lyon of the CAMC and one of the stewards, somehow managed to launch it and a few people still on board joined them by sliding down a two-inch rope dangling from the ship's side.

Sergeant A. Knight of the CAMC took charge of Boat No. 5. It was launched safely, containing Knight himself, eight crew members and all fourteen nursing sisters, two of whom were still clad in their nightdresses. They had trouble in freeing the boat from the fall ropes. Knight tried to cut them with an axe, but was unsuccessful. And the *Llandovery Castle* was still moving forward slowly – not always an easy thing to detect from the deck of an unlit ship at night in the open ocean. The sea had become a little choppy, with the result that Boat No. 5 was continually hurled against the side of the ship. They tried to save the boat by holding her away from the ship with the oars, but all these soon broke. Then the worst thing of all happened. The fall ropes worked themselves free at the top and No. 5 began to drift towards the stern of the still moving ship. There was nothing anybody could do to stop it. As they drew near to the stern, a large section of the poop-deck broke away and sank. Seeing that the suction was dragging them towards almost certain death, Nursing Sister Margaret Marjorie 'Pearl' Fraser, from Moosejaw, Saskatchewan, who was the matron, and who had caringly given a drink of water to many a parched and wounded German soldier in her three years at the front, turned to Knight and asked, "Sergeant, do you think there is any hope for us?" Knowing that without oars they were completely powerless to arrest their drift, Knight could only reply, "No". A few seconds later No. 5 was sucked into the vortex of the sinking after-deck, tipped over sideways and everybody was jettisoned into the swirling water. All were wearing lifebelts, but none came to the surface except Knight, who went down and came up three times, finally managing to cling to a piece of wreckage until, barely conscious, Sylvester's boat picked him up. When the submarine approached, such was Knight's still dazed condition that he mistook it for a British rescue ship and instinctively grabbed a rope to haul himself aboard. Four German sailors asked him what he wanted, in English, and without waiting for an answer, promptly threw him back into the lifeboat. Later, Knight wrote of the amazing courage of the dedicated nurses, "Unflinchingly and calmly, as steady and collected as if on parade, without complaint or a single sign of emotion, our fourteen devoted nursing sisters faced the terrible ordeal of certain death – only a matter of minutes away – as our lifeboat neared that mad whirlpool of waters where all human power was helpless."

The fourteen nursing sisters were Matron Margaret Marjorie Fraser and Sisters Christine Campbell of Victoria, British Columbia; Carola Douglas of Swan River, Manitoba; Alexina Dussault of Montreal; Minnie Follette of Cumberland County, Nova Scotia; Margaret Fortescue of Montreal; Minnie Gallaher of Ottawa; Jessie McDiarmid of Ashton, Ontario; Mary McKenzie of Toronto; Rena McLean of Sourls, Prince Edward Island; MacBelle Sampson of Duntroon, Ontario; Gladys Sare of Montreal; Anna Stammers of New Brunswick and Jean Templeman of Ottawa.

The doomed ship sank after ten minutes, stern first. Her long bows stood erect from the surface of the sea and she seemed to hesitate for a moment before taking the final plunge to the bottom. As she did so, there was another rumbling crash from deep within her as one of her boilers exploded when the sea water reached it. She twisted sideways to starboard and her funnel came adrift and floated away. There had been just enough time for all her people not killed by the explosion to get away, some in the boats and others by jumping into the sea. And so she disappeared, leaving lifeboats, rafts, tangled coils of hawser, wooden gratings and all kinds of wreckage as well as people in life-jackets floating around on the long swell. Sylvester and his companions rowed their boat around picking up floundering people from the water. They had rescued eleven when a submarine appeared among them. Its conning tower was open and shadowy figures were to be seen moving about her upper casing in the darkness. It was *U-68*, commanded by Kapitänleutnant Patzig.

Orderly Private Hickman was in Boat No. 7. About an hour and a half after the *Llandovery Castle* had disappeared the U-boat drew alongside. Hickman was taken on board and made to write down the name of his ship. When he had done this, a German officer checked it from a book which he produced from a desk. Then Hickman was asked whether his ship had any American officers on board. He replied in the negative and was put into Sylvester's boat when that came alongside.

In English, Patzig had ordered Sylvester's boat to come alongside the submarine and, when there was no immediate compliance with this instruction, a pistol shot was fired as a warning, with the added threat that the big gun would be used if the occupants did not bring the boat alongside at once. Bluntly, the German accused Sylvester of carrying eight American flying officers, which was flatly denied. The master added, however, that he did have seven Canadian medical officers with him. This information was offered, no doubt, in an attempt to bring the encounter to a conclusion whereby the U-boat would go away and leave the lifeboats to make what they could of their predicament. But Patzig was far from satisfied with it. He demanded to see one of the Canadian officers. With that, Major Lyon was hauled on board from the lifeboat so roughly that he incurred a broken bone in his foot. After questioning, he was allowed to return to the lifeboat together with Sylvester. As they were leaving, Sylvester asked, "Where are our other boats?" Patzig did not answer, but his second-in-command, without speaking, motioned with his field-glasses over his left should towards the north-west. Another German officer discreetly advised Lyon that it would be better to "clear off at once".

The U-boat began to circle round the wreckage at speed, several times narrowly missing Sylvester's boat by the barest couple of feet. Finally she stopped beside it and took on board Second Officer Chapman and Fourth Officer Barton. It had occurred to Patzig that there had been another 'offence' committed by the *Llandovery Castle*. He had heard the second explosion as she sank, which could only indicate that she was being used for the illegal transport of ammunition. Calmly, Chapman explained that what Patzig had heard was the boiler exploding and that this was a common occurrence in sinking ships, whereupon the two officers were allowed to return to their lifeboat. Again the submarine took off on its criss-crossing of the spot, again coming so close that they were convinced that she was trying to ram them. Eventually she moved off to a short distance and stopped.

"From that position," stated Sylvester's official report, "she opened fire at an unseen target, firing about twelve shells." What was the unseen target? It cannot be proved conclusively, but it is not beyond reasonable doubt to assume that it was one, or some, of the other lifeboats. At only a short distance a small unlit boat can be perfectly invisible at night in the middle of a choppy ocean, and there were no other vessels in the vicinity, the *Llandovery Castle* having sunk.

Sylvester reasoned that, as none of the other lifeboats were in sight and that no wireless distress call had gone out, the best plan was to make for the Irish coast, 116 miles distant. He hoisted the sail to assist their rowing with the intention of removing themselves from the spot as far and as quickly as possible. After some thirty-six hours, just after nine o'clock on the morning of 29 June, the sail was spotted by the British destroyer *Lysander*. In this war of deceit and cunning there was always the possibility that the little boat was merely a decoy, and, by stopping, the destroyer would become a sitting target for a lurking U-boat. Nevertheless, *Lysander*'s captain, Commander F.W.D. Twigg, took that chance and he did stop. But he did not tarry. His log reads: "9.7 Sighted sailing vessel, 9.15 Picked up survivors, 9.25 Proceeded at 18 knots". They left the lifeboat to bob on the ocean, empty and alone, to meet whatever fate, and by half-past four that afternoon they were back in Queenstown alongside the oiler. On that same day, nine miles away, the corvette HMS *Snowdrop*, Commander G.P. Sherton, found a drifting, undamaged and empty lifeboat of the *Llandovery Castle*. It was evident that the boat had been occupied, because the sail was still set. It was established later that *Snowdrop* had found the same boat that had been abandoned by *Lysander*. The little corvette, together with the American destroyer USS *Kimberley*, spent the next two days thoroughly searching the area, zig-zagging with their guns' crews closed up, ready to deal with any intrusive U-boats. *Snowdrop* alone logged more than 350 miles on 1 July. But they found absolutely nothing else to connect itself with the sunken hospital ship. Finally, the American officers were entertained to lunch on the British ship, by way of a thank you, and they went their separate ways.

As for the survivors, it was midsummer, the weather had not been too unkind and they had had plenty of biscuits and water in the boat. They had even enjoyed the luxury of Sylvester's pipe, which he had gone back to collect from his cabin before taking to the boats, and which he had generously passed around his fellow castaways from time to time so that they might taste the tobacco. At that time the twenty-four occupants of the lifeboat were the only known survivors from the *Llandovery Castle*. Their names were listed in *The Times* of 2 July 1918:

Captain E.A. Sylvester, Second Officer L. Chapman, Fourth Officer D.C. Barton, H.M. Evans [purser], Record [lamp trimmer], Davies [painter], Scott [ordinary seaman], Hunt [able seaman], Murphy [able seaman], Schroeder [able seaman], Goodridge [able seaman], Ward [able seaman], Tredgian [fireman], McVey [fireman], Mounsey [trimmer], Heather [deck steward], Savage [assistant steward], Abrahams [ward attendant], and of the CAMC Major T. Lyon, Sergeant Knight and Orderlies Taylor, Hickman, Pilot and Cooper.

It was reported later that an unofficial cable had been received by the Director of Medical Service, Canadian Contingents, from an American Atlantic port stating that a twenty-fifth survivor, Captain G.L. Sills of the CAMC, had been landed there, having been picked up at sea by "a westbound ship". This was welcome news, of course, but exhaustive research has failed to trace that anything further was ever heard about it. And the Canadian Virtual War Memorial lists Lieutenant George Luther Sills, No 829, born in Tweed, Ontario, on 14 March 1888 as having lost his life on the day of the sinking. It would seem that the cable received by the Director of Medical Service was simply an unkind hoax.

Worldwide condemnation was heaped upon Berlin for what the Canadian Minister of Overseas Military Forces, Sir Edward Kemp, KCMG, called "a crime surpassing in savagery the already formidable array of murders of non-combatants by the Germans".

On learning of the British Seamen's Union decision to ostracize German shipping after the war, the President of the French Maritime League, M. Millerand, and his deputy M. Guernier, the delegate to Great Britain and the Dominions, sent a telegram to the British Navy League: "The French Maritime League would be grateful to the British Navy League if it would be good enough to transmit to the National Sailors' and Seamen's Union, of which Mr Havelock Wilson is President, its cordial congratulations on the noble sentiments inspiring the decision by which the seamen of Great Britain have bound themselves to refuse, after the war, for a certain number of years, varying in proportion to the crimes committed, all collaboration with the maritime transports of Germany."

Not since the sinking of the *Lusitania* had the indignation of Americans been roused to such a pitch. Writers found themselves hard-pressed to find fresh adjectives of adequate vituperation to express their sentiments. The *New York Times* seethed: "The Hague Convention gives belligerents the right to visit hospital ships. But these cold-blooded assassins refused to exercise that right; they strike and slay because it is in their hearts to glut their cruelty upon helpless non-combatants after trumping up a case of justification, which is only another infamy. The Allies in the presence of this crowning atrocity have a duty to perform. A German officer recently captured said, 'We are going to win, or we are going to Hell'. The Germans are not going to win, but if there is Hell for Germans in retribution, the Parliaments and Legislatures of the Allies should ensure that retribution. The British Seamen's Union has blasted the way, and it is for the statesmen of Allied countries to formulate and sanction the plan. To talk of reprisals is vain. Punishment should take a form of excommunication, isolation and deprivement until the guilty nation makes amends and qualifies for re-admission to civilisation."

In Liverpool, at a Seamen's Union meeting, 600 seamen and stewards passed a resolution requesting Havelock Wilson to add another five years to the boycott of Germany for "this most diabolical and cowardly murder of our brothers on the sea".

In Cardiff Havelock Wilson addressed a meeting of the Merchant Seamen's League. If anybody wanted to send Germany food and raw materials, he cried, then he must train conscientious objectors as sailors and firemen, because British seamen would never carry them.

The Dutch *Handelsblad*, commenting on the sinking, said, "Again a repulsive crime has been committed which is not only against international law, but is a deed which arouses horror because it conflicts with every idea of humanity."

In Canada itself, where there was a sense of mournful anger which swept right across the nation, the *Halifax Herald* conducted a vigorous editorial campaign against enemy aliens. It alleged that enemy aliens with no regular occupations had been associating suspiciously with seamen and soldiers in Halifax and watching marine movements. The local civic authorities responded positively to this by urging the rounding up and interning of all enemy aliens.

A national mass demonstration in Trafalgar Square on Saturday 13 July was attended, among many others, by representative parties from Beccles, Higham Ferrers, Chard, Wednesbury, Hartlepool, King's Lynn, Hornby, Wandsworth, Macclesfield, Lyme Regis, Dartmouth, New Romney, Ramsgate, Carlisle, Gillingham [Kent], Wrexham, Beaumaris and Harrogate. A resolution was passed demanding "the immediate internment of all aliens of enemy blood, whether naturalised or not, and the removal of such aliens from Government or public office". In Kent Broadstairs Urban District Council went even further. It demanded the immediate deportation of all enemy aliens as soon as peace was declared. It also called for the immediate winding up of German banks after the war and the closure of all enemy businesses. The full wording of the resolution was shown nightly on the local cinema screen by the Broadstairs Cinema Company.

A correspondent wrote to *The Times*: "It should be an indubitable condition of peace that for every hospital ship sunk and every hospital bombed there will be a period of time [I suggest six months] after the war during which no German ship can visit any Allied port. The Germans know well enough that they are going to lose the war, and will frame their frightfulness accordingly. Yours &c, J.E.G. Montmorency, Lincoln's Inn."

And Mr Harry Lauder, the famous Scottish singer and entertainer, speaking to a lunchtime meeting of the Brighton & Hove Rotary Club, said that every enemy alien should be put under lock and key.

Even the Vatican felt bound to comment, although its stance was somewhat surprising and certainly not in accord with most of the world. Discussing the British Government's *communiqué* announcing the sinking of the *Llandovery Castle*, the *Osservatore Romano* said on 5 July: "As we have no reason to doubt the exact truth of the above communication, we cannot do less than express the extreme horror which such a narration arouses in us. We are sure that Germany herself will be the first to feel this sentiment of horror, and, after having investigated the news, will not fail to take opportune measures in this regard."

"Probably the official organ of the Vatican is only newspaper in the world," remarked *The Times* acidly on 8 July, "which could suggest at this date that Germany is capable of feeling any sentiment of horror at any of the countless crimes committed by her sailors and soldiers."

The reaction from Germany was predictable. *Reuter* cabled from Amsterdam on 2 July that the following *communiqué* had been received from Berlin: "Like all similar assertions by the British Government, it is probably in this case also incorrect that a German U-boat is responsible for the ship's fate. It appears from later news that no one on board the steamer observed a U-boat or a torpedo. At all events the loss may be attributed to a British mine."

Three years later, on 16 July 1921 in Leipzig, the Second Criminal Senate of the Imperial Court of Justice heard the Case of the *Llandovery Castle*, command paper 1450, 1921. The President of the Division was Dr Schmidt, sitting with Judges Hagemann and Backs, Dr Schultz, Dr Vogt and Dr Sabarth. The Officials of the Public Prosecutor's Department were Dr Ebermeyer, the *Oberreichsanwalt*, and Dr Feisenberger the State Attorney.

The accused were

[1] Ludwig Dithmar of Cuxhaven, First Lieutenant and Adjutant of the Cuxhaven Command, born in Aix-la-Chapelle on 13 May 1892, and

[2] John Boldt of Altona, retired First Lieutenant, merchant, born in Danzig on 26 January 1895.

The Court heard that in 1916 the *Llandovery Castle* had been commissioned by the British Government for use as a hospital ship. Since that time she had never been put to her previous work as a transport. Her name had been communicated to the enemy Powers and she had subsequently been used correctly as a hospital ship, in compliance with the Tenth Hague Convention of 18 October 1907. One witness, Meyer, stated that he had seen the ship at Toulon and did not observe anything about her to indicate that she may have been used improperly for war purposes.

Another witness testified that he had been a prisoner of war in

England and, while waiting to be repatriated in December 1916, he had seen 120 khaki-clad men go aboard the *Llandovery Castle* in Tilbury Docks. This man was none other than the embittered but miraculously lucky-to-be-alive Oberleutnant Iwan Crompton, ex-gunnery officer of the doomed *U-41*, which had been blasted to the depths by the Q-ship *Baralong* six years before. It is easy to imagine how eagerly the British-hating Crompton would have presented his testimony. However, the Court was persuaded that the men that he saw were Medical Corps personnel, who did wear khaki tunics. (It is surprising that these men were not dressed more distinctively.)

An expert witness, Korvettenkapitän Saalwächter, told the Court that in his opinion it would not be possible to distinguish with certainty between the sounds of a ship's boiler exploding underwater and that of ammunition.

There then followed lengthy statements from survivor witnesses surrounding the actual number of lifeboats still afloat after the ship herself had gone down, and which ones they were. Second Officer Chapman had seen five boats lowered from the starboard side, but two of these had capsized, leaving three. This agreed with the evidence of Able Seaman Murphy. Steward Heather saw only three, one of which capsized, leaving two; Ward Attendant Abrahams saw two and Major Lyons, who had come from his home in western Canada to testify and for whose arrival the hearing had been suspended for a day, saw only one. Two boats got away from the port side, in one of which was Captain Sylvester, who had by the time of the hearing unfortunately died. At least one of the boats which got away had been the one containing the fourteen nursing sisters. Finally, it was established that, after the ship had sunk, there were still three boats afloat with people in them.

Chapman and ex-Fourth Officer Barton said that both they and Captain Sylvester had been ordered aboard the U-boat at different times and were closely questioned about some American Officers who were allegedly being carried. They were also challenged about the cause of the second explosion which the German captain suggested was that of munitions. They had firmly denied the presence of any American officers on board and had explained that second explosion had been caused by the bursting of the *Llandovery Castle*'s boilers. They were released back into their lifeboat and the U-boat went away. However, it soon returned, at

185

speed, heading straight for the captain's boat, which it missed only narrowly, made a full circle and returned on a second run. After that it went away.

A fortnight before the Leipzig hearing, at London's Bow Street Court, the ex-purser of the *Llandovery Castle*, Henry Evans, by then a forty-six-year-old Stanton Harcourt, Oxfordshire, poultry farmer, had testified that after swimming in the sea he had been pulled, exhausted, into the captain's boat. As the submarine had approached at speed the twenty-four people in the lifeboat feared that it was intent on ramming them. Two of its occupants had flashed electric torches over the stern of the boat when the U-boat was only a few yards off and he imagined that this may have distracted the helmsman momentarily, causing him to swerve instinctively, missing them by a margin of only a few inches. The intention to ram the lifeboat could not be proved conclusively, however, and the expert witness Saalwächter even held the view that, having considered the evidence, he felt that such a thing was not likely to have been the case. In any case, the two accused were not involved in the management of the submarine and therefore the question did not need to be answered.

The submarine went away again and a short time later they heard shellfire. Two shots landed in the sea on the far side of their lifeboat – well over. Then they heard another dozen shots. The U-boat was now visible to them in the half-light and, judging by the almost non-existent interval between the flash of the gun barrel and the splash of the exploding shells, the range of their target must have been very short. After the firing stopped, they saw no more of the Germans.

Witnesses from the U-boat's crew were the helmsman Popitz, the chief engineer Knoche, Ney, Käss and Tegtmeier. The first two named confirmed that they were on deck and took part in the interrogations of Lyons, Chapman and Barton, and that no proof was found that the *Llandovery Castle* was being used illegally. Patzig then ordered 'diving stations' and the deck crew went below, as is normal. This left only Patzig himself, the two accused as his Officers of the Watch and, by special order of the captain, Boatswain's Mate Meissner, who had since died. Some time later, from below, the witnesses all heard the 88mm stern gun begin firing. The submarine had not dived and was moving about on the surface the whole time. Popitz, lying on his bunk below, had asked another crew member what was going on and was told it was nothing and he was to stay below. If the submarine had become involved in a surface fight against any enemy ship, he would have been needed at his normal action station on the upper casing.

The suggestion of the defence that the submarine may have been firing at another enemy vessel which had come upon the scene was refuted, firstly because of Popitz's testimony that he was told to stay below and, secondly, if the U-boat had been firing at an enemy vessel, the normal and obvious course of action on Patzig's part would have been to dive as soon as he had finished firing in order to make his escape. But this he did not do. Nor was it likely that, being a very experienced submariner, he could have been firing mistakenly at some floating object, thinking it was an enemy vessel. The majority of the witnesses, notably including Popitz and Knoche, had gained the clear impression that the firing had been directed at the lifeboats, the exception to this being a few of the other German witnesses, who chose to keep silent and abstain from providing evidence at all. The Prosecution could only assume, therefore, that the firing must have been directed against the lifeboats of the *Llandovery Castle*.

As for the absent Patzig, his personal behaviour reeked of guilt. He had not only bidden his comrades to silence but had falsified the log of *U-86* to omit any reference whatsoever to the sinking of the *Llandovery Castle* and had altered the chart to show that he had taken a completely fictitious course, far distant from the scene. And he had called the crew together to assure them that for what had taken place the previous day he alone was responsible to God and his own conscience. It was a strange thing for a commander to do, unless driven to do so by his own feeling of guilt. If he had in fact fired on the lifeboat, there could be only one reason for it and that was to try to destroy all evidence of his torpedoing of the hospital ship. Germany's relationship with most of the rest of the world was at that time very fragile and Patzig may have realized, in the cold light of day, that in sinking the *Llandovery Castle* he had not helped the cause of his country in the least, and he had therefore tried to cover it up. "I have no doubt," said the State Attorney, "that Patzig knew and knows that his subordinates are being held responsible for these events. It would be his natural duty for him to appear to tell the truth. If Patzig believes that he, and not the accused officers, is guilty, he should come before the Court." Patzig's conduct, he concluded, was steeped in "colossal meanness and cowardice".

The Court then considered the question of the lifeboats. It had been firmly established and agreed that the three boats escaped when the ship sank – Captain Sylvester's boat and two others – and it was further agreed that, in the light of descriptions given of it, the boat found by *Snowdrop* was in fact the abandoned captain's boat and in any event it was definitely not Boat No. 3 which was the one which had been stopped by the U-boat. In other words, the other two boats and their occupants had disappeared without trace, despite diligent searching by the three warships.

The witnesses said little by way of evidence, presumably owing to their pact of silence with Patzig, other than to deny operating the deck guns and to say that whatever they had done had been done under the orders of their captain and that they were unaware that there had been anything in those orders which would render them liable to be punished.

The only people who could have fired on the lifeboats were the four men on the deck of the submarine – Patzig, who was absent from the Court, the two accused, Dithmar and Boldt, and Meissner, the Boatswain's Mate and gunlayer, who had since died. It had been established that some firing had taken place and that the order to fire must have come from Patzig, as commander of the boat. And it was reasonable to assume that Meissner, as gunlayer, would have actually fired the gun. This he would have been able to do unaided, which was confirmed by the expert witness. The two accused, as officers of the watch, would have performed the precautionary task of lookouts. In this they had knowingly assisted Patzig in his illegal act and were therefore accessories to it, although it had not been proved that they did so in agreement with his intentions.

The Military Penal Code laid down that if the execution of an order in the ordinary course of duty involved a punishable violation of the law then the superior officer was alone responsible. On the other hand, it also stated that the carrying out of such an order rendered the subordinate liable to punishment if he knew that it would involve contravention of the law. Subordinates were under no duty to question the legality of an order, but here was a situation where it was common knowledge among naval officers that it was illegal to fire on lifeboats. The Prosecution case was that the accused should have refused to be parties to the act of killing and stood to be punished.

For the Defence, it was stated that if the accused had so refused Patzig's orders, it was extremely likely that he would have enforced them, armed with his revolver. This argument was rejected as implausible. If Patzig had met with an attitude of blunt refusal to carry out his orders, he would have been unlikely to have shot his subordinates because to have done so would have meant that he would have been obliged to abandon his plans to conceal the sinking of the *Llandovery Castle*, because it would have been quite impossible for him to carry them out singlehanded.

The verdict of the Court was that a *severe sentence* should be passed on both of the accused and a term of *four years' imprisonment* was handed down to each of them. The time they had already spent under arrest was not to be taken into account owing to their uncooperative attitudes during the trial. Additionally, in accordance with Sections 34 and 36 of the Military Penal Code, Dithmar was dismissed from the service and Boldt, who had retired from the Navy and appeared before the Court with his Iron Cross pinned to his civilian coat, was deprived of the right to wear officer's uniform.

Patzig, as we know, did not attend the hearing, although warrants had been issued for his arrest. In his absence, the Court found him guilty of homicide. He had disappeared from his home in Danzig and his whereabouts were unknown. It was ordered that all his property in Germany was to be sequestrated. But Danzig, following the Treaty of Versailles, was no longer German territory.

There had developed an electrically charged atmosphere both in the Courtroom and among the sizeable crowd which had gathered outside. The British Mission retired to its private suite immediately after the sentences had been announced and afterwards left by a side door, heavily guarded by a squad of German police, thus avoiding any unpleasant or violent scenes.

If indeed it had been true that Captain Sills of the Canadian Army Medical Corps had been extremely fortunate in being rescued, his testimony as a witness would have been invaluable. He alone would have been able to verify what had befallen at least one of the other lifeboats. What was the name of the ship that picked him up and in what circumstances? His eye-witness evidence could have settled the question. The authorities would surely have been advised of his rescue, which equally surely would have made world headlines, and the fact that he was not called serves to underline the conclusion that there was no truth in the rescue story and he had, after all, perished in the Atlantic.

At home, the integrity of the Leipzig trials came under renewed embittered scrutiny in Parliament and the Press. In the House of Commons Mr Bottomley (Hackney South – Independent) began a series of pressing questions to the Attorney-General Sir Gordon Hewart (Leicester East – Liberal) which clearly revealed his anger at what was happening in Leipzig. Above all, Mr Bottomley wanted to transfer the trials to England and France, but he drew nothing but a non-committal blank. "Do I understand that France has withdrawn from this Leipzig farce altogether without any communication with the British Government? If so, why can't we do the same?" he persisted, but again a polished politician's evasion was his reward. Bottomley then put a direct question of the type which could only receive a straight yes or no in reply: "Are we going to send any further lists to Leipzig?" he demanded. But the Attorney-General, true to the politician's trade, was still quite unable to produce a one-word answer: "The Hon. Gentleman knows the answer to that question," he said. "It is in the negative."

The frustration on the Allied side was not requieted by the news that, after serving only four months of his four-year sentence, Boldt had absconded from custody. Apparently he had done so with the collusion of his jailers. The *Times* correspondent wired from Hamburg on 9 May 1922, "Three officials and two warders of the Hamburg prison from which the German war criminal Lieutenant Boldt was allowed to escape last November appeared yesterday before the Hamburg Court. They were charged with having by carelessness allowed Boldt to escape. They were all acquitted and the Court ordered them to be reimbursed from the State funds for any inconvenience they may have been occasioned by their trial." Little, it seemed, had changed. The Conservative Opposition in Westminster was determined not to let the matter drop. As late as Armistice Day (11 November) 1921, the Attorney-General was still under fire. When the persistent Sir J. Butcher asked, "In view of the atrocious crimes proved against those German criminals at the Leipzig Court, and the utterly inadequate sentences inflicted, will the Government use their utmost efforts to bring the remainder of these German prisoners before a Public

190

Tribunal?" the only reply the wretched Hewart could muster was that he needed notice of such a question.

The following summer, when Lord Cave addressed the 1922 Annual General Meeting of the highbrow lawyers club, the Grotius Society, he chose as his theme, "War Crimes and their Punishment". "It is food for indignation," he asserted, "that the Leipzig trials were little better than a farce, and that the Treaty of Versailles is almost inoperative as far as war criminals are concerned. After the sinking of the *Lusitania* and ten hospital ships and the destruction of lifeboats from the *Llandovery Castle*, the people were assured that the day of reckoning for Germany would come, and that her soldiers and sailors who had violated the long-established usages and customs of modern warfare would be brought to justice. Yet, up to the present, in only six of the sixteen selected cases put forward by the Allies have convictions been obtained. In the sight of all civilized people the acts complained of were criminal. They were certainly transgressions of the recognized laws of war as embodied in such documents as the Paris, Geneva and The Hague Conventions." But laws without sanctions were of little value, he pointed out, because unprincipled nations could always simply tear up treaties and coventions as mere scraps of paper. He criticized the woefully weak attempts of the Allied Governments to see that German war criminals were punished for barbarities which had horrified the world. In future wars it would be advisable for the terms of an Armistice to provide for the immediate surrendering into safe custody of all known offenders against the rules of war. Perhaps the day would come, he hoped, when an international court of justice would be founded with command of the force necessary to see that its orders were obeyed.

Lord Cave echoed the feelings of many on the side of the former Allies. The Treaty of Versailles, laboriously crafted as it was, had made special provisions for the arraignment of war criminals. Article 229 read, "Persons guilty of criminal acts against the nationals of one of the Allied and Associated Powers will be brought before the military tribunals of that Power. Persons guilty of criminal acts against the nationals of more than one of the Allied and Associated Powers will be brought before military tribunals composed of members of the military tribunals of the Powers concerned. In every case, the accused will be entitled to his own counsel. Article 230 read, "The German Government undertakes

191

to furnish all documents and information of every kind, the production of which may be considered necessary to ensure the full knowledge of the incriminating acts, the discovery of offenders and the just appreciation of responsibility."

Nothing of the kind was ever insisted upon.

13

THE VERDICTS

The punishments handed down at Leipzig for atrocities at sea during the First World War were infuriatingly light to the point of being farcical in the view of many, on the Allied side at least. But those proceedings had taken place in a comparatively chivalrous age. The naive trust which the Treaty of Versailles had placed in the courts of the defeated side to try, convict and sentence their own war criminals was typical of its time. But just as a family of rabbits playing in a woody glade will run for their boltholes in the bushes as soon as distant footsteps are heard but well before the approaching predator comes into view, so did many of those men with war crimes on their consciences vanish into well-prepared anonymity under the cover of the hellish confusion which existed at the end of both World Wars, well before the Allies had had time even to begin their investigations. This problem was highlighted by the shrinkage of Britain's original list of eighteen World War One U-boat captains whom, it was proposed, should be tried as war criminals, viz:

Kiesewetter (UC-56) – for sinking the *Glenart Castle.*
Patzig (U-86) – for sinking the *Llandovery Castle.*
Max Valentiner (U-38) – the *Glenby* 17 August 1915 and the *Persia* 30 December 1915 (it seems that the *Clan Macfarlane* was added later as an afterthought)
Werner (U-55) – the *Clearfield* October 1916; the *Artist* 27 January 1917; the *Trevone*, 31 January 1917; the *Torrington* 8 April 1917; the *Rewa* 4 January 1918 and the *Guildford Castle* 10 March 1918. (there was no mention of the *Toro*)
Jetz [sic] (U-96, U-90) – the *Apapa* 28 November 1917; the *Destro* 25 March 1918 and *Inkosi* 28 March 1918.

Adam (U-82) – the *Galway Castle* 12 September 1918.

Aust (U-?) the *Golden Hope* 9 June 1917.

Bothmer (U-66) the *Mariston* 15 July 1917.

Droescher (U-20) – the *Ikaria* and the *Tokomaru* 30 January 1915.

Gansser (U-33, U-156) the *Clan Macleod* 1 December 1915; the *Belle of France* 1 February 1916; the *W.C.M'Kay* January 1918 and the *Artesia* 8 February 1918.

Von Georg (U-57, U-101) – the *Refugio* 12 May 1917; the *Jersey City* 24 May 1917; the *Teal* 1 June 1917; the *Richard de Larrinaga* 8 October 1917; the *Glenford* 20 March 1918; the *Trinidad* 22 March 1918; the *John G. Walter* 24 March 1918 and the *Lough Fisher* 30 March 1918.

Glassenapp (U-?) the *Haileybury* 22 February 1918; the *Birchleaf* 23 February 1918; the *Landonia* 21 April 1918; the *Baron Herries* 22 April 1918 and the *Ethel* 26 April 1918.

Nostitz und **Jaenkendorf** (U-152) – the *Dvinsk* 18 June 1918.

Kolbe (U-152) – the *Clan Murray* 29 May 1917; the *Ellaston* 16 March 1918 and the *Elsie Birdett* April 1918.

Neumann (UC-67) – the *Dover Castle* 26 May 1917.

Rücker (U-103) – the *Victoria* ??1917. [sic]

Von Schrader (UB-64) – the *Dartmoor* 27 May 1917.

Wassner (UB-38 or UC-69) the *Addah* 15 June 1917.

This list had been subjected to much editing by the end of 1921 and had been shorn by half a dozen names. Some had been removed because of lack of solid evidence, others because the accused himself had vanished without trace. As for the remainder, it seems to have been simply utter despair with the proceedings in Leipzig, which had been reflected in the exchanges on the subject in Parliament between Attorney-General Hewart and the tenacious Mr Bottomley. On 30 December 1921 His Majesty's Procurator-General handed to the German Government a list of Cases 1–46, as required by Articles 228–230 of the Treaty of Versailles, which the British were presenting for hearing in Leipzig. The difficulties facing the Allied side in seeing proper justice done, obstructed as they were [a] by the limitations on their rights to control the proceedings, as agreed under the Treaty, and [b] by the fact that many prospective defendants had disappeared, can be readily understood from the list of Cases 1–46, of which the following is an extract.

Summary of Naval Cases.

Case No.	Name	Sinking	Lives Lost.
8	Kaiserwetter [sic]	*Glenart Castle*	135
10	Valentiner	P&O liner *Persia*	334
		Clan Macfarlane	55
16	Wassner	*Addah* – (firing on boats.)	9

The following are doubtful:-

9	Patzig	*Llandovery Castle* – whereabouts unknown.	
11	Werner	*Rewa, Torrington* etc – whereabouts unknown.	
12	Jess	*Apapa*	77
20	Rücker	*Victoria*	5
21	Gansser	*Belle France* (dived with survivors on deck)	19
22	Glassenap	*Landonia* – (refused to save lives)	22
27	Steinbrinck	*Sussex* – identity disputed. Germans say Püstkuchen, who is dead.	
45	Von Schröder	Captain Fryatt – *s.s. Brussels* see Note.	
	Admiral C.-in-C. Flanders		
46	Zapfel (Lapfel?) Public Prosecutor – Bruges.	"	"

Note: It does not appear that the British Government can furnish any evidence save as to the character of the *s.s. Brussels* or influence the proceedings of the Supreme Court in Leipzig if the German authorities have already made up their minds that no charges will lie. The trial will turn on a question of law and procedure in German Courts Martial and as the British Government will not have any right of audience all hostile criticism can and probably will be avoided as in the case of the hospital ship *Dover Castle*."

The eighteen cases had been reduced to a dozen, and of them eight were doubtful, as admitted even by their would-be prosecutors, and the footnote underlined the frustration felt by the Allies, particularly the British, in their desire to bring these alleged war criminals to trial. For all the bitter feelings on the losing side that the Versailles Treaty had humiliated them to an intolerable degree, the fact was that as far as retribution for war crimes was concerned, the Germans held most of the legalistic trump cards. For example, Heinrich Jess, captain of *U-96*, had illegally sunk the 7,800-ton passenger/freighter *Apapa*, allegedly, as she approached Liverpool from Lagos on 28 November 1917, while Erwin Wassner was accused of firing on survivors in lifeboats from the British cargo vessel SS *Addah*, 4,400 tons, thirty-five miles off the coast of Brittany on 15 June 1917. Both Germans denied that they had committed any crimes.

From the office of *Der Oberreichsanwalt* in Leipzig Dr Richter, the German Attorney-General, telegrammed his opposite number in London asking for evidence of proof and in particular the way in which Jess and Wassner were alleged to have been exceptionally cruel. On the face of it, that would seem to have been a perfectly reasonable request by a lawyer, but, in an astonishing admission of either bungling inefficiency or naivety or both, (it will be remembered that these particular officers had been especially selected by the British as subjects for trial), HM Attorney-General replied on 8 February 1921 that he was unable to supply any further information. So they were never tried.

At the time of the Armistice Valentiner was at sea. Rather than return to the dangerous revolutionary chaos that was currently the situation in any German dockyard, he put into Trondheim in Norway, to be interned there. Although the British named him as a war criminal, citing the sinkings of the *Persia* and the *Clan Macfarlane*, it is doubtful whether he would have been convicted, at least in respect of either of those two cases, if ever he had been brought to trial, given a reasonably competent defence counsel. And that is especially true in the light of the lenient judiciary attitude which persisted at Leipzig.

Firstly, the *Persia* was carrying a couple of dozen military officers and a few other ranks to India. That was enough to make her a legitimate target. Nor could it be denied, because there it was in black and white on her printed passenger list. Secondly, as

196

Archibald Hurd makes clear in *The Clan Line in the Great War 1914–18*, the lifeboats were all made fast astern of Captain Swanston's boat only *"after enquiries by the submarine commander."* It was a fine clear night, the sea was calm, the lifeboats were well provisioned, they all had serviceable sails and oars and they were just seventy miles from the coast of Crete not far off a well-used shipping lane. It could be argued that Valentiner had discharged all the responsibilities placed on him by the Hague Convention to ensure that the *Clan Macfarlane*'s crew were placed in a position of safety. It was only some hours after he had departed that the weather became inclement and the ordeal began in earnest.

Gansser, in *U-33*, the same officer in the same submarine that Captain Fryatt had brushed with in the *Brussels*, was a colleague of Valentiner's in the Cattaro flotilla, to which he had been transferred shortly after the Fryatt incident. On 1 February 1916 he torpedoed and sank the 3,876-ton cargo ship *Belle of France* about 125 miles NW of Alexandria. She had been bound for Algiers from Karachi with a load of grain. Her crew took to their boats, but one was capsized in the panic, throwing its nineteen occupants into the sea. The submarine surfaced and picked up these men, calling to the other boats to come and take them off. But then things started to go wrong. Four trawlers were sighted in the distance, and, being concerned that they may have been armed naval vessels, the German captain called his crew below and prepared to dive. Unfortunately, the nineteen British seamen were left on deck to drown. In his book *The Killing Time* Edwyn Gray suggests that this act may have been one more of "forgetful panic than cold-blooded murder". Gray says that the submarine was unidentified, but Gibson and Prendergast are quite definite that it was Gansser's *U-33*. But such an excuse as Gray propounds is very difficult to accept. Is it likely that Gansser could have quite properly remembered to call his own men below before diving and seconds later honestly "forgotten" that he had nineteen enemy seamen on his deck? Moreover, what were the four trawlers likely to have done? They probably witnessed both the sinking of the cargo ship and the rescue from the capsized lifeboat. Would they have opened fire on the submarine with those gesticulating men on its deck? More probably, they would have attempted to capture it.

Gansser was also responsible for sinking the 5,300-ton Russian hospital ship *Portugal* in the Black Sea on 30 March 1916. Ninety people were lost, including fifteen nurses. And the likelihood is that it was Gansser who shelled the Soukhoum Lighthouse on the Black Sea coast of Georgia and sank another Russian hospital ship, the little 859-ton *Vperyed*, on 9 July. In any event, Gansser was never convicted, nor even tried. It seems they never found him.

Klaus Rücker, captain of *U-34*, was another of the Cattaro flotilla, although he was occasionally based at Constantinople for work in the Black Sea. Earlier in the war he had been operating in the western Channel, stalking the heavily laden troopships that were lumbering out of Avonmouth bound for Gallipoli. Quite why he troubled to attack a couple of small Welsh fishing smacks, the 155-ton *Victoria* out of Milford Haven, and the Cardiff boat *Hirose* in St. George's Channel, 145 miles west by south of St. Anne's Head, on 1 June 1915, when there was much larger game to be had is somewhat baffling. The *Victoria* had on board her usual crew of nine, plus a schoolboy who had come with them for the trip. Skipper Steve Stephenson tried to run to safety, but he had no real chance of escape. The German began to pump shells into the trawler at a murderous rate. The first shot smashed her small boat and the second killed the schoolboy, James Jones. The fishermen hurriedly set about lashing some boards together to make a raft. Stephenson went for'ard to consult with the Engineer, Albert Cole, but just as he arrived in the doorway of the fo'c's'le another shell blew them both to pieces. Then deck-hand George Huddlestone was blasted in the arm and hand by shrapnel, which knocked him down the fo'c's'le ladder. The Mate, Dennis McCarthy, lay with both his legs blown off, while the legs of the trimmer Frank Slade, from Haverfordwest, were both broken. The survivors clambered aboard their hastily improvised raft but the cook, George Rudge from Milford Haven, fell into the sea and was drowned. The remainder were taken aboard the submarine, which was identified as *U-34*, and kept there throughout the night. They reported later that they had been treated kindly and had their wounds dressed by the U-boat's doctor, although while he was attending to them he took the opportunity to lecture them that it had not been Germany who had started the war. There were only four survivors from the *Victoria* – George Huddlestone, John Craig, the third hand, Clem Franklin the boatswain and the second engineer George Scriven from Great Yarmouth. They were landed at Milford

Haven the next night by the Cardiff steamer *Ballater**, together with the crew of the *Hirose*, who were all unharmed although the Germans had sunk their boat with bombs.

In May 1918, with the U-boat fleet on the doorstep of defeat, Rücker, now back in the Channel in command of the new *U-103*, met with disaster. Again he was hunting troopships, with special orders to concentrate on vessels bringing the American Expeditionary Force to France. The huge ex-White Star Liner *Olympic*, laden with thousands of 'doughboys', was coming up-Channel screened by four fussing US destroyers. Now Rücker had had much experience attacking escorted ships in the Mediterranean and he knew exactly how to position his boat for an attack of this type. First, get inside the screen. This he did. In fact he worked himself into such a position that the giant troopship was a point-blank target. But a terrible mistake with the submarine's trim on the part of its crew lead to the *U-103* breaking the surface close to the *Olympic*, quite unintentionally, and of course it was spotted instantly by her lookouts. Instantly, the big ship opened fire but the target was far too close for its guns to bear and the shells passed harmlessly overhead. There was only one thing to do from the troopship's viewpoint. Ram. Her helm went hard over and her gigantic bows sliced into *U-103*'s casing. Then the damaged boat bounced and banged its way all the way down the length of the ship to be cut clean open by the churning tip of a gigantic twenty-ton propeller blade. The doomed submarine pointed its bows to the sky and slid backwards to the bottom.

Miraculously, Rücker and sixteen of his crew were rescued by the destroyer USS *David*. It was a gesture of mercy in distinct contrast to that which he had shown the hapless crew of the little *Victoria*, almost exactly three years before. But he too, it seems, was nowhere to be found when it came to staging the Leipzig Trials.

The final number of submarine captains to suffer punishment from the original list of eighteen alleged German naval war

---

* It is unclear whether the men were put back onto their raft and then rescued by the *Ballater*, or whether the latter was held up by the submarine and ordered to take them on board.

criminals was precisely nil. Only Lieutenants Dittmar and Boldt, Patzig's subordinates, were to serve any kind of a sentence, albeit derisory, for their illegal activities. And one of them was allowed to escape. Those who claimed that the Leipzig Trials had been nothing but a farce certainly had a point.

BIBLIOGRAPHY

Bridgland, Tony, *Sea Killers in Disguise*, Pen & Sword Books – Leo
   Cooper, 1999
Gibson, R.H/Prendergast M., *The German Submarine War*,
   Constable, 1931
Giffard, Edward, *Deeds of Naval Daring*, John Murray, 1910
Gray, Edwyn A., *The Killing Time*, Seeley Service & Co Ltd,
   London, 1972
Hoehling, A.A., *The Great War at Sea*, Corgi, 1967
Humphreys, Roy, *The Dover Patrol 1914–18*, Sutton, 1998
Lyon, Hugh, *Warships*, Salamander, 1978
Maddocks, Melvin, *The Great Liners*, Time-Life Books, 1978
Massie, Robert K., *Dreadnought*, Jonathan Cape, 1991
Mullins, Claud, *The Leipzig Trials*, H.F. & G. Witherby, 1921
Whipple, A.B.C., *Fighting Sail*, Time Life Books Inc, 1978
Winton, John, *The Victoria Cross at Sea*, Michael Joseph, 1978

INDEX

G-132, 44
Gansser, K/L, 101, 113, 194–198
Garnock, Lieut., 54
Garrett, J.M., 36
Gattie, Vernon, 161
George V, King, 12, 110
Gerrard, James, US Ambassador, 107
Gilliat-Smith Mr, 105
Glenart Castle, HMHS, 165–174, 193, 195
Gloucester Castle, HMHS, 146
Godau, helmsman, 64, 65, 68
Goodbody, Manville, 88
Grant, C.H., 132
Greene, Graham, 45
Grey, Sir Edward, 38, 56, 105, 106, 108
Guildford Castle, HMHS, 162, 193
Gullflight, 13, 20, 21
Gunther, Captain, 20
Gwyer, Mrs, 8

Haack, Kommander, 44, 45, 56, 57
Hale, Miss, 86
Hall, Captain Reginald, 17
Hampshire, HMS, 142
Hannibal, HMS, 132
Hansen, K/L Klaus, 59–63
Hartnell, First Mate William, 103, 104, 106, 114, 116
Hawke, HMS, 140
Hawley, Chief Officer Fred, 130, 131
Hazard, HMS, 138
Hecla, 58
Henry, Prince of Prussia, 12, 126
Herbert, Lt-Comdr Godfrey, 30–34, 37, 52
Hewart, Attorney-General, 194
Hickman, Orderly, 179
Hicks, Captain Allanson, 61–63
Hightower, Charles, 36

Hill, John, 169
Hilton, Mrs, 83
Hines, Walter, 38
Hirose, 198, 199
Hissione, 61
Hoestenberghe, Sheriff van, 108
Holland, Larrimore, 37
Horton, Lt-Cmdr Max, 41
Housatonic, 144
Hubbard, Elbert, 6
Huddlestone, George, 198
Hudson, Mr E., 54
Huhlemann, Dr., 155

Inchcape, Lord, 129
Ingram, Wells, 22–23
Inverlyon, 76, 142
Ipswich, 99
Ivernia, 18

J. C. McCullough, 172
J.C. Le Cour, 52
Jackal, HMS, 149
Jackson, Isaac, 7
Jess, Heinrich, 195, 196
Jøhnke, Kommander, 46
Jones, James, 198
Julia, 8
Juno, HMS, 3, 8, 17, 18

Kaarsted, Tage, 56
Kaiser Wilhelm der Grosse, 55, 165
Kapurthala, Maharajah of, 132
Karapara, HMHS, 151
Keck, Leading Seaman, 173
Kemp, Sir Edward, 181
Kenworthy, Lt-Commander, 17
Kiesewetter, K/L Wilhelm, 165–167, 172–175, 193
Kimberley, USS, 180
King Stephen, 69–71, 74
Knight, Sergeant, 177, 178, 181
Knights, Able Seaman, 104
Knoche, Chief Engineer, 186, 187